R

LOOK, LISTEN AND LEARN!
Teacher's Book Three

PRACTICE BOOKS:

SIXTY STEPS TO PRÉCIS

POETRY AND PROSE APPRECIATION FOR OVERSEAS STUDENTS

ESSAY AND LETTER-WRITING

A FIRST BOOK IN COMPREHENSION, PRÉCIS AND COMPOSITION

QUESTION AND ANSWER: GRADED AURAL/ORAL EXERCISES

FOR AND AGAINST: ADVANCED ORAL PRACTICE

READING AND WRITING ENGLISH

THE CARTERS OF GREENWOOD *(CINELOOPS):*

TEACHER'S HANDBOOK
ELEMENTARY WORKBOOK
INTERMEDIATE WORKBOOK

NEW CONCEPT ENGLISH:

FIRST THINGS FIRST *(also in two volume edition)*
PRACTICE AND PROGRESS *(also in two volume edition)*
DEVELOPING SKILLS
FLUENCY IN ENGLISH

LONGMAN STRUCTURAL READERS, Stage 1:

DETECTIVES FROM SCOTLAND YARD
CAR THIEVES
MR PUNCH

LONGMAN STRUCTURAL READERS, Stage 2:

APRIL FOOLS' DAY
WORTH A FORTUNE
PROFESSOR BOFFIN'S UMBRELLA

LOOK, LISTEN AND LEARN! Sets One-Four

TEACHER'S BOOK THREE

Look, Listen and Learn!

An Integrated English
Course for Children

L. G. Alexander

Illustrated by Gil Potter

Longman

LONGMAN GROUP LIMITED
Longman House,
Burnt Mill,
Harlow,
England.

*Associated companies, branches and representatives
throughout the world*

*First published *1970*
*Second impression *1971*
*Third impression *1974*
*Fourth impression *1977*
*Fifth impression *1979*
Sixth impression 1985*
*Seventh impression*1986*

ISBN 0 582 51985 3

ACKNOWLEDGEMENTS

We would like to thank the following for permission to
reproduce the illustrations:

Archives Photographiques Caisse National des Monuments
Historiques, Paris, for Lesson 85; British Leyland for
Lesson 35, right; The Mansell Collection for Lesson 115;
Montagu Motor Museum, Beaulieu, for Lesson 35, left;
The National Aeronautics and Space Administration for
Lesson 105, centre; Paul Popper Limited for Lesson 105,
right; The Radio Times Hulton Picture Library for Lesson 65;
Topix for Lesson 105, left; United States Information Service
for Lesson 95.

*Produced by Longman Group (FE) Ltd
Printed in Hong Kong*

Contents

About this Course

Patterns

N.B. *Patterns shown in italics will be practised intensively in drill work. Teaching Units 1–8 are devoted to Revision.*

TEACHING UNITS

Yes, please. I'd love some.
(Is) there any (soup) left?
Yes|No, there's some|none left.
I'd like to have some (soup).

Mid-Year Tests

31 *Would you like to (win a prize)?*
I'd like|love to (win a prize).
I'd like (her) to (win a prize).
Tell (her) not to (lose her handbag).
I wouldn't like (her) to (lose her handbag).

32 *I've got nothing to (read)|(play) with.*
I want something to (read)|(play) with.
Have you got (a book) (for me) to (read)?
I want|I'd like (a book) to (read).
I haven't got anything to (read).
Have you got anything to (read)?
I've got (a book) to (read).
I don't know what to (read).

33 He was born in (1756).
What (would you like) to do?
(I)'d like|(I) want|hope|wish|need|(I) must remember|will try|began|learnt|forgot to (return by train).
That's just what (I'd like) to do.

34 *(I am) sure|certain|ready|afraid|glad|happy|pleased|sorry|allowed|surprised to . . .*

35 *(Father) (thinks|has told me) that (he) is|has|can|must|will . . .*
I know|I don't know what (father) (thinks|has told you).

36 *(Sandy)'s (sure) that (he will become a scientist).*
What's (Sandy) (sure of)?
I know what (Sandy)'s (sure of).
I know why (Sandy)'s (sure).

37 You wait here.
(Father) (thinks|is sure|has told me) (the food tastes awful).
Guess what (father) (thinks).

38 *I have to|I've got to|Do you (really) have to|Have you (really) got to|I'll have to|Did you have to|I had to (add these figures).*

39 *Don't|you mustn't|you're not allowed to (park here) because (it*

says 'No Parking').
Don't|You needn't|you don't have to|it isn't necessary to (take a taxi) because (a bus is coming).

40 *Yes, (he) should|ought to.*
No, (he) shouldn't|oughtn't to.
(I) should|ought to (clean my car), but (I) don't feel like it.
Should (he) . . .? Ought (he) to . . .?
What should (he)|ought (he) to do?

41 *Yes, but (I) needn't have.*
No, (I) didn't have to.
(I) needn't've (watered the garden) because (it rained).
(I) (watered it) for nothing.
(I) didn't have to (water the garden).
(It rained) so (I) didn't have to (water it).
Did he have to . . .? Yes, he had to, because . . .
Question Tags.

42 *Yes, (he) should have.*
(He) should have|ought to have . . . but (he) didn't feel like it| (he) forgot.
(What) did you have to (do)?
(What) should you have (done)?

43 *(He) mustn't (park here) and (he) isn't going to.*
(He) shouldn't|oughtn't to (park here), but (he's) going to.
(He) shouldn't have|oughtn't to have (parked here), but (he) did.
(He) shouldn't|shouldn't have (park(ed) here) because (it says 'No Parking'.)

44 Revision: *must|have to|have got to|mustn't|not allowed to|needn't| don't have to|it isn't necessary to|should|ought to . . . but| shouldn't|oughtn't to . . . but.*

45 Revision: *had to|it was necessary to|needn't have . . . (I) did it for nothing|didn't have to|it wasn't necessary to|should have|ought to have . . . but|shouldn't have| oughtn't to have . . . but.*

46 *(I) may|might (iron these trousers). I'm not sure.*
(I) may|might not.
Perhaps (she will) . . . Perhaps (she won't).

47 *(It) may be|can't be|must be (£5|22nd May|grey|English|*

size 30/square/tired/7 years old/a
butcher/reading).
Surely (it isn't)!

48 *How long/Since when (have you)*   194
been (correct)ing (exercise-
books)?
(I've) been (correct)ing (exercise-
books) since (yesterday) for (two
days) and (I'm) still
(correcting . . .)

49 *When/Just as/While (Sue) was*   198
(dry)ing (the dishes she dropped a
plate and broke it).
(Mother saw a nice hat) when/just
as/while (she) was (walk)ing
(through the Hat Department).
While (Sandy) was (play)ing (the
piano, Sue) was (play)ing (the
flute).

50 *(It) may have been/can't have*   202
been/must have been (£5/22nd May/
grey/English/size 30/square/tired/
7 years old/a butcher/reading).
Surely (it wasn't)!

51 *(It) may/must/can't (cost £5).*   206
(It) may have/must have/can't
have (cost £5).

52 *-self forms: (I didn't iron the*   210
dress) (myself).
Someone else (ironed it for me).
I had (it) (ironed).
I shall have/must have /it) (ironed).
Did (you) have (it) (ironed), or
did (you) (iron it) (yourself)?
Where/When did (you) have (it)
(ironed)?

53 *The man/woman/men/women who/*   214
that (is/are coming out of the
bank).
He's/she's/they're the man/woman/
men/women who(m) (I served).
Who(m) did you (meet yesterday)?

54 *Which (comic/comics) did you*   218
(read)?
This is/these are the (film(s)/
horse(s)/tree(s)) which/that I
(saw).

55 *Who . . .? The man/woman/*   222
people (coming out of the house).
(He's the boy I served yesterday).
Which . . .? (I read the comic on
the table).
(This is/these are the comic(s) I
read yesterday).

56 *(This is the boy/film) (about)*   226
whom/which (I told you).
(This is the boy/film) whom/
which (I told you) (about).
(This is the boy/film) (I told you)
about.

57 *(I) used to be (a waiter/rich) a*   230
long time ago, but (I'm) not any
more.
(I) used to (collect stamps) a long
time ago, but (I don't) any more.
No, but I used to be.
No, but I used to.
What/Where did you use to . . .?

58 *(I asked Sandy for a penny, but*   234
he) had already (spent his pocket-
money).
After/When (they) had (had
breakfast, they went to school).
(They went to school) after (they)
had (had breakfast).
(We) had (finished breakfast)
before (the postman arrived).
I hadn't (before), but I have now.

59 *If I (arrive home early) I shall*   238
(take you to the cinema).
I shall (take you to the cinema)
if I (arrive home early).
If (he) (arrives home early) (he)
will (take you to the cinema).
(He) will (take you to the cinema)
if (he) (arrives home early).
If I'm (hungry) I'll (eat my
dinner).
If he's (hungry) he'll (eat his
dinner).

60 *When I (come home from school)*   242
I shall (play a game of football).
I shall (play a game of football)
when I (come home from school).
When (he) (comes home from
school) (he) will (play a game of
football).
(He) will (play a game of football)
when (he) (comes home from
school).
When I'm (hungry) I'll (eat my
dinner).
When he's (hungry) he'll (eat
his dinner).

About this Course

**Basic Aims
and Methods**

The dominant themes of *Look, Listen and Learn!* Set Three can be summed up in two words: consolidation and expansion. After covering the basic groundwork in Sets One and Two, the pupils enter a period of transition in Set Three which will prepare them for wider English. It follows that they must consolidate what they know and anticipate what is to come. To this end, virtually the *entire* lexical content of Sets One and Two is reactivated in Set Three and a great many familiar patterns are revised. At the same time, some of the new features will be strikingly obvious. A change in the style of illustration will enhance the feeling of progression: the characters in the course, as well as the pupils themselves, are growing up. The new visual element reflects the change in subject-matter. There is a gradual but marked shift in the centres of interest. The dialogues become more adult in character and suited to the needs of pre-teenage children. Moreover, non-fiction pieces are now included and these will introduce the pupils to the kind of language used in specialised registers. They also mark the transition from *audio-visual* to *audio-lingual* presentation. While oral and written drills and exercises still have an important role to play, the pupils will be trained to use the language creatively through guided oral and written composition. This whole movement in the direction of *creative* usage will be further intensified in Set Four.

Teachers familiar with the techniques employed in Sets One and Two will have no difficulty in adjusting to the changing requirements of the course. The same basic form of audio-visual presentation is retained for the dialogues, but audio-lingual presentation techniques are adopted for the non-fiction pieces. Such changes are noted when they occur. Teachers who are using this course for the first time are strongly recommended to read the introductions to Teacher's Books 1 and 2.

Teachers are reminded that each lesson must have *pace* and *variety*. The whole range of activities laid down in each lesson should be tackled. This means that the time spent on individual exercises must be very brief. This applies in particular to the Graded Comprehension Questions which follow each dialogue and prose passage. Ten minutes should be the maximum time allotted to the complete exercise. Classroom lessons should be devoted entirely to aural/oral work and the accompanying written exercises in the Workbook should be set as homework.

**Material for the
Third Year's Work**

Set Three of **Look, Listen and Learn!** consists of the following:

PUPILS' BOOK THREE

TEACHER'S BOOK THREE

WORKBOOK 3a

WORKBOOK 3b

LONGMAN STRUCTURAL READERS, STAGE 2:
Professor Boffin's Umbrella

LINK READER 3: Marley Castle

LISTENING TAPE THREE (Optional)

Integration

The table on the next page indicates how the four skills are taught in relation to each other and how the materials in Set Three have been integrated. The table shows the point at which important features are introduced for the first time. Book titles are printed in heavy type.

Integration Table

Teaching Unit	Understanding	Speaking	Reading	Writing
1	**Pupils' Book Three** and **Teacher's Book Three.** Audio-visual-lingual presentation: Dialogues/Drills/Songs/Games. Lessons 1–16: Revision. Graded Comprehension Questions: the pupils will practise answering and asking questions based on the texts.		Prepared Reading (Dialogues). Unprepared Reading **(L.S.R. Stage 2: PROFESSOR BOFFIN'S UMBRELLA).** Extensive Reading: Class Library Scheme: LSR 2. Phonic Reading Drills.	**Workbook 3a.** Lessons 1–16: Revision Exercises. Spelling.
2				Dictation exercises based on written work will be given at regular intervals.
3	Stories for aural comprehension will be read at regular intervals.			
9				Guided Composition: the Simple Sentence. Multiple Choice Exercises.
13	Non-fiction pieces will appear at regular intervals. The Aural/Oral Procedure is modified for these texts. Presentation is purely audio-lingual. Oral Composition will be based on written notes.			
30			**Link Reader** 3: MARLEY CASTLE	Attainment Tests.
31				**Workbook 3b** Guided Composition: the Compound Sentence.
46				Guided Composition: the Complex Sentence.
60				Attainment Tests.

New Features Introduced in Set Three

The patterns to be taught in Set Three are broadly based on the *Handbook to Longman Structural Readers,* Stage Three. Patterns and vocabulary previously introduced are assumed to be known. However, it should be noted that Book 3 is designed to overlap Book 2. The first sixteen Lessons (approximately one month's work) are devoted entirely to revision exercises. From then on, patterns and lexical items derived from Books 1 and 2 are constantly re-introduced so that revision is a continuous process.

Non-fiction Texts

These first appear in Teaching Unit 13 and from then on at regular intervals (one in every five Teaching Units). The texts are presented as if they were part of a General Knowledge Television Programme which Sandy, Sue and their friends watch regularly at school. This device enables us to introduce the pupils to a large number of topics of general interest and, therefore, to specialised language registers. Though the structural content of these pieces is very carefully controlled (the passages are fully contextualised) the lexical range is, inevitably, fairly wide. These pieces differ from the dialogues in other important respects as well. They are laid out *across* the page and stress marks have not been added. Chorus and Group Repetition is no longer a part of the Aural/Oral Procedure and the meaning of each text is communicated audio-lingually through intensive reading.

The Readers

Two kinds of Readers are referred to under the heading *Material for the Third Year's Work:* Longman Structural Readers, Stage 2 *(Professor Boffin's Umbrella)* and Link Reader 3 *(Marley Castle).* The title, *Professor Boffin's Umbrella,* has been taken from Longman Structural Readers Library and will be read parallel to Lessons 1–60. This Reader makes use of patterns and vocabulary which have already been learnt in Pupils' Books 1 and 2. The Link Reader, on the other hand, makes use of new patterns which are introduced in Pupils' Book 3. It will be read parallel to Lessons 61–120. The Link Reader is intended to reinforce the new patterns and prepare the pupils for more advanced reading in Set Four.

The Class Library Scheme

The scheme should be continued in exactly the same way as before. (For details about how it works, see the introduction to Teacher's Book 2). It should be put into operation from Lesson 1. Throughout the year the pupils should be encouraged to read the following series:

All the titles in Longman Structural Readers, Stage 2.
All the titles in Pleasant Books in Easy English (Longman), Stages 1 and 2.
All the titles in the Practical Readers (Longman), Stages 1 and 2.

Dictation

Dictations may be given at regular intervals as before. The passages are based on patterns which the pupils have practised in their oral and written exercises. All punctuation marks should be dictated. The pupils should have a special exercise-book for dictation.

Spelling

Oral and Written Spelling exercises are based on words which have previously been introduced in the Phonic Reading Drills. (These, in turn, have been derived wholly from the pupils' active vocabulary). A portion of the exercise-book kept for dictation may be used for spelling.

Workbooks 3a and 3b
Parallel written work is again provided for each Lesson and should
be set as homework. From Lesson 17 onwards, the right-hand pages
of the Workbooks will be devoted to Guided Composition and Multiple Choice Exercises. The left-hand pages will contain structural
exercises reinforcing the patterns practised orally in the classroom.

In the Guided Composition scheme, the pupils will be trained to
write simple, compound and complex sentences through a series of
graded exercises. They will write paragraphs based on the texts which
have previously appeared in the Pupils' Book. These exercises become
increasingly difficult so that by the end of Set Four, the pupils will be
quite ready to attempt free composition. Multiple Choice exercises
are also based on the same texts. They are designed to test comprehension and the use of familiar structural words and lexical items.

Tests
Attainment tests are included at the end of each Workbook. As before,
Alternative or Supplementary Tests are given in this Handbook, as
well as Mark Scales.

Listening Tape 3
The use of the tape is optional. Teachers who have a tape-recorder
may wish to use the tape to present the dialogues and non-fiction
texts in class.

Revision Lesson **1**   Not a very good morning

Mother:	Bréakfast's réady, chíldren!	1
Sandy (sadly):	Áll ríght, múm. We're cóming.	

Mother and Father:	Good mórning, Sándy. Good mórning, Súe.	2
Children (sadly):	Good mórning, múm. Good mórning, dád.	

Father *(copying them):*	Good mórning, múm. Good mórning, dád. You dón't sóund véry háppy and you dón't lóok véry háppy!	3

Father:	Hów do you féel, Sándy? Áre you áll ríght?	4
Sandy (sadly):	Yés, dád.	

Father:	Whát's the mátter with yóu, Súe? Háve you gót a héadache?	5
Sue (sadly):	Nó, dád.	

Father:	Then whát's úp with you both this mórning?	6
Sandy:	The hólidays are óver and schóol begíns todáy!	

Content and Basic Aims

PATTERNS AND STRUCTURAL WORDS

I'm going to see him on (Monday)
at (9.0 o'clock).
(He) feels/looks (ill).
(He)'s got (a headache)/(flu).
How does (he) feel?
What's (he) got?

● **General Remarks**

The pupils will require the following books: *Pupils' Book 3, Workbook 3a,* and *Professor Boffin's Umbrella* (Longman Structural Readers, Stage 2). In addition, they will read Longman Structural Readers Stage 2 and other recommended titles throughout the year as part of the Class Library Scheme. (See Introduction, page xi).

Greet the class and say a few words in English or the mother tongue introducing this year's work. Two years have passed since the course began. Sandy and Sue, like the pupils themselves, are that much older and their appearance has changed a little. There will not only be dialogues and stories this year, but pieces of general interest as well. The first sixteen lessons will be devoted to revision.

The simple present of the verbs *look* and *feel* to describe illnesses is revised. It is related to *have got* (possession: ailments). Compare Book 2, TU 16. Now conduct the lesson in the usual way. The pupils should be instructed to detach the mask at the end of their books.

● **Aural/Oral Procedure**

(a) Listening (Books shut)
(b) Listening and Understanding (Books open; pictures only)
(c) Listening (Books shut)
(d) Listening and Chorus Repetition (Books shut)
(e) Listening and Group Repetition (Books shut)
(f) Reading Aloud: Chorus and Individual (Books open)

● **Graded Comprehension Questions**

Ask questions about the dialogue and the pictures in the following way:

(a) Yes/No Tag Answers: is/are/do/does/has. To elicit a subject followed by an auxiliary verb.

TEACHER: Is dinner ready?
PUPIL: No, it isn't.
TEACHER: Is breakfast ready?
PUPIL: Yes, it is. etc.

(b) Negative Questions. Make negative statements:

TEACHER: Breakfast isn't ready.
PUPIL: Isn't breakfast ready? etc.

(c) Questions with Who and What: is/are/do/does. To elicit a subject followed by an auxiliary.

TEACHER: Who is calling them to breakfast?
PUPIL: Mother is. etc.

(d) Double Questions. To elicit negative and affirmative statements.

TEACHER: Do Sandy and Sue look happy or sad?
PUPIL: They don't look happy. They look sad. etc.

(3) General Questions: What, How and Why. Do not elicit complete answers.

TEACHER: Why is mother calling the children?
PUPIL: Because breakfast's ready. etc.

(f) Asking questions in pairs: How, What, When.

TEACHER: Ask me if they look happy.
PUPIL: Do they look happy?
TEACHER: How . . .
PUPIL: How do they look? etc.

● **Acting the Scene**

Invite four pupils to come to the front of the class to act the scene.

● **Unprepared Reading**

Professor Boffin's Umbrella, page 2, captions 1 and 2. New Words: *clouds, sky.*
Write the new words on the blackboard and explain them. Ask one or two pupils to read.

● **Activity**

Revise: The animals went in two by two. See Book 2, Lessons 29–37.

● **Writing**

Workbook 3a, Revision Lesson 1.

Revision Lesson 2

- **Spelling Drill:** Books shut.

  cat/bath; sat/pass; lamp/class; hat/fast; black/ask.
  Ask individual pupils to spell these words orally. As soon as a word has been spelt correctly, write it on the blackboard. When all the words have been written, erase them. Then dictate them to the class.

- **Phonic Practice:** Sounds and Spellings: Books open.

  The letters ie [i:] and ee [i:]
  Chorus and Group Repetition
  Give the instructions *Open your books! Look at Lesson 2! Read together!* Ask the pupils to repeat after you the words at the top of this page, first in chorus, then in groups.

- **Pattern Drill:** Books open.

  Illustrate each exercise first by providing the stimulus and the response. Make sure the pupils really understand how they must respond. Then conduct the drills given below. If a child makes a mistake, correct him and ask him to repeat the right answer.

  To elicit: I'm going to see him on (Monday) at (9.0) o'clock.

  TEACHER: *Number 1.*
  When are you going to see him?
  PUPIL: I'm going to see him on Monday at 9.0 o'clock. etc.

- **Reading and Repetition Drill:** Books open.

  Chorus and Group Repetition
  Ask the pupils to repeat after you the following patterns, first in chorus, then in groups:

  TEACHER: *Number 13.*
  How does mother feel? *All together!*
  She feels tired. *All together!*
  She has got a headache. *All together!*
  etc.

- **Pattern Drill:** Books open.

  (a) To elicit: (Mother) is/does/has.

  TEACHER: *Number 13.*
  Who's tired?
  PUPIL: Mother is.
  TEACHER: Who feels tired?
  PUPIL: Mother does.
  TEACHER: Who has got a headache?
  PUPIL: Mother has. etc.

  (b) To elicit: (She's tired).

  TEACHER: *Number 13.*
  How's mother?
  PUPIL: She's tired. etc.

  (c) To elicit: (She) feels (tired).

  TEACHER: *Number 13.*
  How does mother feel?
  PUPIL: She feels tired. etc.

  (d) To elicit: (She) looks (tired).
  Conduct the drill in the way shown in (c) above substituting *looks* for *feels*.

  (e) To elicit: (She) feels (tired). (She) has got (a headache).

  TEACHER: *Number 13.*
  What's the matter with mother?
  PUPIL: She feels tired. She has got a headache. etc.

  (f) Asking questions: How and What.

  TEACHER: *Number 13.*
  Ask me if mother feels tired.
  PUPIL: Does mother feel tired.
  TEACHER: How . . .
  PUPIL: How does mother feel?
  TEACHER: Ask me if mother's got a headache.
  PUPIL: Has mother got a headache?
  TEACHER: What . . .
  PUPIL: What has mother got? etc.

- **Unprepared Reading**

  Professor Boffin's Umbrella, page 2, caption 3

- **Activity**

  A Guessing Game.
  Invite a pupil to come to the front of the class and whisper 'an ailment' in his ear. Any of the following may be given: a cold, an ear-ache, flu, a headache, measles, mumps, a stomach-ache, a temperature, a toothache. Members of the class must guess the correct 'ailment'. Pupils who do so are given a turn to come to the front.

  TEACHER: *(whispering to pupil):* You've got a cold.
  (addressing class): What's the matter with him?
  MEMBER OF CLASS: *(addressing pupil):* Have you got flu?
  PUPIL: No, I haven't.
  MEMBER OF CLASS: Have you got a cold?
  PUPIL: Yes, I have.
  TEACHER: Good! Sit down A. Now you B.

- **Writing**

  Workbook 3a, Revision Lesson 2.

Revision Lesson **2**

groce<u>ries</u>   fr<u>ee</u>ze   bab<u>ies</u>   kn<u>ee</u>s   carr<u>ies</u>   s<u>ea</u>s   hurr<u>ies</u>   tr<u>ee</u>s

When are you going to see him?

| 1 Monday | 2 Tuesday | 3 Wednesday | 4 Thursday | 5 Friday | 6 Saturday |

| 7 Sunday | 8 Monday | 9 Tuesday | 10 Wednesday | 11 Thursday | 12 Friday |

How does (he) feel? etc. . . . .

	Mother 13	Mrs Gasbag 14
is/feels/looks has got	tired a headache	bad an earache

	Sandy 15	Billy 16
is/feels/looks has got	terrible a toothache	sick a stomach-ache

	Sue 17	Father 18
is/feels/looks has got	hot a temperature	weak flu

	Tom 19	Simon 20
is/feels/looks has got	awful measles	ill mumps

Revision Lesson **3** Look out, boys!

Narrator: Sándy and Súe are at schóol.
Sue is háving a lésson
with her néw téacher, Mŕ Sláde.

1

Narrator: Sándy is with his fríends.
Sándy's cláss
is háving a swímming lésson.

2

Sandy: Cóme and háve a swím, Bílly!
Wé're having a góod tíme!

3

Billy: Bŕr!
The wáter's térribly cóld!

4

Sandy: Díve into the póol, Bílly!
Billy: I cán't díve.
I'm góing to júmp

5

Sandy: Lóok óut, bóys!
There's góing to bé
a bíg wáve!

6

Content and Basic Aims

PATTERNS AND STRUCTURAL WORDS	VOCABULARY	
There's going to be (a big wave). *Let's have (breakfast/a holiday).* *He/she/they must have (breakfast/a holiday).* *He/she wants to/they want to have (breakfast/a holiday).* *He's/she's/they're having (breakfast/a holiday).* *When (do they) have (breakfast)?*	*Nouns*	*Expression*
	pool (swimming) wave (sea) swimming lesson	Brr!
	Verb	
	dive	

● **General Remarks**

Have as an ordinary verb is revised here.
Compare Book 2, Teaching Units 20 and 21.

● **Aural/Oral Procedure**

(a) Listening (Books shut)
(b) Listening and Understanding (Books open; pictures only)
(c) Listening (Books shut)
(d) Listening and Chorus Repetition (Books shut)
(e) Listening and Group Repetition (Books shut)
(f) Reading Aloud: Chorus and Individual (Books open)

● **Graded Comprehension Questions**

Ask questions about the dialogue and the pictures in the following way:

(a) Yes/No Tag Answers: are and is.
To elicit a subject followed by an auxiliary verb.

TEACHER: Are Sandy and Sue at home?
PUPIL: No, they aren't.
TEACHER: Are they at school?
PUPIL: Yes, they are. etc.

(b) Negative Questions.
Make negative statements in the following way:

TEACHER: Sandy and Sue aren't at school.
PUPIL: Aren't Sandy and Sue at school? etc.

(c) Questions with Who and Whose: is and are.
To elicit a subject followed by an auxiliary verb.

TEACHER: Who's having a lesson?
PUPIL: Sue is. etc.

(d) Double Questions.
To elicit negative and affirmative statements.

TEACHER: Are Sandy and Sue at home or at school?
PUPIL: They aren't at home. They're at school. etc.

(e) General Questions: Where and Why.
Do not elicit complete answers.

TEACHER: Where are Sandy and Sue?
PUPIL: At school. etc.

(f) Asking questions in pairs: Where and Why.

TEACHER: Ask me if Sandy and Sue are at school.
PUPIL: Are Sandy and Sue at school?
TEACHER: Where . . .
PUPIL: Where are Sandy and Sue? etc.

● **Acting the Scene**

Invite two pupils to come to the front of the class to act the scene. The Narrator's part should be omitted. (Frames 1 and 2.) Billy may jump off a chair when acting Frames 5 and 6.

● **Unprepared Reading**

Professor Boffin's Umbrella, page 3, captions 1 and 2.
New Word: *holes.*

● **Activity**

Revise some or all of the following rhymes:

(a) Thirty days has September. (Book 2, Lesson 21.)
(b) The Four Seasons. (Book 2, Lesson 23.)
(c) Boys and Girls. (Book 2, Lesson 25.)
(d) Barber, barber. (Book 2, Lesson 39.)

● **Writing**

Workbook 3a, Revision Lesson 3.

Revision Lesson 4

- **Spelling Drill:** Books shut.

Oral and Written
bath/cart; pass/farmer; class/park; fast/mark;
ask /hard.

- **Phonic Practice:** Sounds and Spellings: Books open.

The letters i [ai] ie [i:] and ee [i:]
Chorus and Group Repetition

- **Repetition Drill:** Books open.

Chorus and Group Repetition

TEACHER: *Number 20.*
      Let's have breakfast. *All together!*
Repeat this pattern with each of the items shown.

- **Pattern Drill:** Books open.

(a) To elicit: Let's have (breakfast).

   TEACHER: *Number 20.*
   PUPIL: Let's have breakfast. etc.

(b) To elicit: He/she/they must have (breakfast).

   TEACHER: *Number 20.*
         What must they do?
   PUPIL: They must have breakfast. etc.

(c) To elicit: He/she/they can have (breakfast).

   TEACHER: *Number 20.*
         What can they do?
   PUPIL: They can have breakfast. etc.

(d) To elicit: He/she wants to/they want to have (breakfast).

   TEACHER: *Number 20.*
         What do they want to do?
   PUPIL: They want to have breakfast. etc.

(e) To elicit: He's/she's/they're going to have (breakfast).

   TEACHER: *Number 20.*
         What are they going to do?
   PUPIL: They're going to have breakfast. etc.

(f) To elicit: He's/she's/they're having (breakfast).

   TEACHER: *Number 20.*
         What are they doing?
   PUPIL: They're having breakfast. etc.

(g) Asking questions in pairs: When.

   TEACHER: *Number 20.*
         Ask me if they always have breakfast at a quarter to eight.
   PUPIL: Do they always have breakfast at a quarter to eight?
   TEACHER: When . . .

PUPIL: When do they always have breakfast? etc.

Time expressions (in the morning/afternoon; once a week/year, etc. must be supplied as appropriate. Omit No. 75.

- **Unprepared Reading**

Professor Boffin's Umbrella, page 3, caption 3.
New Word: *special.*

- **Activity**

Dictation.
Dictate the following passage:

It's Súnday mórning./Fáther, Sándy and Súe/ are háving bréakfast./Móther is in béd./She féels íll./She has got a bád héadache./Súe has máde some téa./She has táken/a cúp of téa to móther./Móther is háving her téa in béd.

First Reading: The teacher reads without interruption. The pupils listen only.
Second Reading: The teacher reads each group of words *once* only. The pupils listen and write.
Third Reading: The teacher reads without interruption. The pupils listen and read their work silently. After the third reading they may be given a minute or so to correct their work.

- **Writing**

Workbook 3a, Revision Lesson 4.

Revision Lesson **4**　Let's have . . .

20

breakfast

25

lunch

30

tea

35

dinner

40

a meal

45

a game

50

a bath

55

a haircut

60

a lesson

65

a party

70

a holiday

75

a good time

80

a run

85

a wash

90

a swim

95

a walk

Revision Lesson 5   With Billy's best wishes

Narrator: Sándy's néw téacher is Mŕs Hárt.
Mŕs Hárt is tálking to Sándy nów.

Mrs Hart: You aren't páying atténtion, Sándy.
Whát are you lóoking at?

Sandy: A póstcard, Mrs Hárt.
Bílly sént it to me
dúring the hólidays.
Mrs Hart: Lét me sée it.

Mrs Hart: It's a phótograph of a príson
in the Tówer of Lóndon.
Whén were yóu
at the Tówer of Lóndon, Bílly?
Billy: I was thére on Aúgust 3rd, Mŕs Hárt.

Billy: I sént a póstcard of the príson
to Sándy.

Mrs Hart: Whát did you wríte
on the cárd, Bílly?
Billy: I wróte, "I wísh you were hére."

Content and Basic Aims

PATTERNS AND STRUCTURAL WORDS	VOCABULARY	
	Nouns	*Verbs*
I wish you were here. *It was (7.50)|(Sunday)|(January 1st)|(10th March)| (May)|(1967).* *(He was) in (bed)|at (church) at (7.50) on (Monday) in (January).* *What time|day|date|month|year was it?*	card postcard Tower of London	wish
	Expressions	
	Let me see (= allow me to look) With (Billy's) best wishes	

● **General Remarks**

The forms *was/were* are revised in patterns involving the use of the prepositions *at/on/in* indicating *time* and *in/at* indicating *place*. Compare Book 2, TU 26.

● **Aural/Oral Procedure**

(a) Listening (Books shut)
(b) Listening and Understanding (Books open; pictures only)
(c) Listening (Books shut)
(d) Listening and Chorus Repetition (Books shut)
(e) Listening and Group Repetition (Books shut)
(f) Reading Aloud: Chorus and Individual (Books open)

● **Graded Comprehension Questions**

(a) Yes/No Tag Answers: is/was/does/did.
To elicit a subject followed by an auxiliary verb.

TEACHER: Is Sandy's new teacher Mrs Grant?
PUPIL: No, she isn't.
TEACHER: Is Sandy's new teacher Mrs Hart?
PUPIL: Yes, she is. etc.

(b) Negative Questions.
Make negative statements in the following way:

TEACHER: Sandy's new teacher isn't Mrs Hart.
PUPIL: Isn't Sandy's new teacher Mrs Hart? etc.

(c) Questions with Who: is/was/does/did.
To elicit a subject followed by an auxiliary verb.

TEACHER: Who's talking to Sandy?
PUPIL: Mrs Hart is. etc.

(d) Double Questions.
To elicit negative and affirmative statements.

TEACHER: Is Mrs Hart talking to Sandy or Tom?
PUPIL: She isn't talking to Tom. She's talking to Sandy. etc.

(e) General Questions: Why, When and Where.
Do not elicit complete answers.

TEACHER: Why isn't Sandy paying attention to Mrs Hart?
PUPIL: Because he's looking at a postcard. etc.

(f) Asking questions in pairs: Why, When and Where.

TEACHER: Ask me if Sandy is paying attention.
PUPIL: Is Sandy paying attention?
TEACHER: Why isn't . . .
PUPIL: Why isn't Sandy paying attention? etc.

● **Acting the Scene**

Invite a pupil to come to the front of the class to take the part of Mrs Hart. The pupils taking the part of Sandy and Billy should remain seated. An actual postcard may be used. The Narrator's part, frame 1, should be omitted.

● **Unprepared Reading**

Professor Boffin's Umbrella, page 4, captions 1 and 2.
New Words: *ordinary, test* (vb.).

● **Activity**

Revise: The grand old duke of York, Book 2, Lesson 51.

● **Writing**

Workbook 3a, Revision Lesson 5.

Revision Lesson 6

- **Spelling Drill:** Books shut.

  Oral and Written
  ball/chalk; call/talk; wall/walk; tall/always; small/already; all/bald.

- **Phonic Practice:** Sounds and Spellings: Books open.

  The letters ie [i:] ee [i:] and ea [i:]
  Chorus and Group Repetition

- **Reading and Repetition Drill:** Books open.

  Chorus and Group Repetition

  TEACHER: *Number 96.*
  Where was Sandy at ten to eight?
  All together!
  Sandy was in bed at ten to eight. *All together!*

  Practise these patterns with each of the items shown.

- **Pattern Drill:** Books open.

  (a) To elicit: (Sandy) was/(Sandy and Sue) were.

  TEACHER: *Number 96.*
  Who was in bed at ten to eight?
  PUPIL: Sandy was. etc.

  (b) To elicit: It was (7.50)/(Sunday)/(January 1st)/(10th March)/(May)/(1967).

  TEACHER: *Number 96.*
  Sandy was in bed. What time was it?
  PUPIL: It was ten to eight. etc.

  Make affirmative statements about each picture and then ask: What time/day/date/month/year was it?

  (c) To elicit: (He was in bed at ten to eight).

  TEACHER: *Number 96.*
  When was Sandy in bed?
  PUPIL: He was in bed at ten to eight. etc.

  (d) To elicit: (He was in bed at ten to eight).

  TEACHER: *Number 96.*
  Where was Sandy at ten to eight?
  PUPIL: He was in bed at ten to eight. etc.

  (e) Asking questions in pairs: What time/day/date/month/year . . .

  TEACHER: *Number 96.*
  Ask me if it was ten to eight.
  PUPIL: Was it ten to eight?
  TEACHER: What time . . .
  PUPIL: What time was it?

TEACHER: *Number 100.*
Ask me if it was Sunday.
PUPIL: Was it Sunday?
TEACHER: What day . . .
PUPIL: What day was it? etc.

- **Unprepared Reading**

  Professor Boffin's Umbrella, page 4, caption 3.
  New Words: *air, moon, stars.*

- **Activity**

  It's time for a story: The Holidays, page 256.
  Write the following words on the blackboard and explain them: *hotel, bay, beach, tummy, snorkel, towards, pinch* (= nip), *towards, grab, point* (vb.), *seagull, crab.*

- **Writing**

  Workbook 3a, Revision Lesson 6.

Revision Lesson **6** Where were they . . . ?
When were they . . . ?

chief	knees	teas		piece	sees	seas		field	trees	please

Sandy 96	Sandy and Billy 97	Mother and father 98	The thief 99
bed 7.50	class 9.15	town 10.25	prison 12.0

In AT

The children 100	The family 101	Sandy and Sue 102	Father 103
church Sunday	home Monday	school Tuesday	work Wednesday

At ON

Sue 104	The children 105	Sue 106	Father 107
the country January 1st	the village February 2nd	the classroom 10th March	the park 21st April

In ON

Sue 108	The children 109	The children 110	The children 111
the dentist's May	the stationer's June	the funfair July	the seaside August

At IN

Sandy 112	Sandy and Sue 113	Father 114	Mum and dad 115
London 1967	Paris 1968	Germany 1969	Italy 1970

In IN

Revision Lesson 7   New Neighbours

The hóuse néxt dóor to the Clárks
has been émpty for a lóng tíme.

On Mónday
a bíg ván arríved at the hóuse
and stópped outside the gáte.

The ván was fúll of fúrniture.
Twó wórkmen cárried the fúrniture
into the émpty hóuse.

Sándy and Súe wátched the mén
from their gárden.

Thén a smáll cár
stópped behínd the ván.
A mán, a wóman and thrée chíldren
got óut of it.

The wórkmen dídn't nótice the smáll cár.
They néarly cárried thát
into the hóuse, tóo!

Content and Basic Aims

PATTERNS AND STRUCTURAL WORDS	VOCABULARY
(He) didn't (post)/(he) (posted) (the letter) at (6.30) on (Thursday) on (September 4th/10th October) in (December) in (1968).	*Nouns*
	furniture neighbour van workman

- **General Remarks**

  The regular past ('-id', '-d' and '-t' endings) is revised here in patterns involving the use of mixed points of time and the prepositions *at, on* and *in*. Compare Book 2, TU 34.

- **Aural/Oral Procedure**

  (a) Listening (Books shut)
  (b) Listening and Understanding (Books open: pictures only)
  (c) Listening (Books shut)
  (d) Listening and Chorus Repetition (Books shut)
  (e) Listening and Group Repetition (Books shut)
  (f) Reading Aloud: Chorus and Individual (Books open)

- **Graded Comprehension Questions**

  (a) Yes/No Tag Answers: has/did/was.

  TEACHER: Has the house next door to the Clarks been empty for a short time?
  PUPIL: No, it hasn't.
  TEACHER: Has it been empty for a long time?
  PUPIL: Yes, it has. etc.

  (b) Negative Questions.

  TEACHER: The house hasn't been empty for a long time.
  PUPIL: Hasn't the house been empty for a long time? etc.

  (c) Questions with Who and Which: has and did.

  TEACHER: Which house has been empty for a long time?
  PUPIL: The house next door has. etc.

  (d) Double questions.

  TEACHER: Has the house been empty for a long time or a short time?
  PUPIL: It hasn't been empty for a short time. It's been empty for a long time. etc.

  (e) General Questions: How (long), When, Where, What.

  TEACHER: How long has the house next door been empty?
  PUPIL: A long time. etc.

  (f) Asking questions in pairs: How (long), When, Where, What.

  TEACHER: Ask me if the house next door has been empty for a long time.
  PUPIL: Has the house next door been empty for a long time?
  TEACHER: How long . . .
  PUPIL: How long has the house next door been empty? etc.

- **Telling the Story**

  Ask one pupil at a time to reconstruct the story by referring only to the pictures. The pupils should remain seated during this exercise.

- **Unprepared Reading**

  Professor Boffin's Umbrella, page 5, captions 1 and 2.
  New Word: *return* (vb.).

- **Activity**

  Revise: Old Macdonald, Book 2, Lessons 55–63. Animals etc. occur in the following order: chicks, ducks, turkeys, pigs, car.

- **Writing**

  Workbook 3a, Revision Lesson 7.

Revision Lesson 8

- **Spelling Drill:** Books shut.

  Oral and Written
  or/ball/chalk; call/for/talk; wall/walk/story;
  fork/tall/always; horse/small/already; all/cork/
  bald.

- **Phonic Practice:** Sounds and Spellings: Books open.

  The letters ie [i:] and [ai]
  Chorus and Group Repetition

- **Repetition Drill:** Books open.

  Chorus and Group Repetition
  Ask the pupils to repeat the following patterns
  after you first in chorus, then in groups:
  116: He posted the letter at half past six.
  117: She turned on the television at ten past eight.
  118: He finished work at twenty-five to six.
  119: They visited Mrs Gasbag on Thursday.
  120: They played football on Friday.
  121: She washed the clothes on Saturday.
  122: He paid the bill on September the 4th.
  123: They stayed at home on the 10th of October.
  124: He remembered his wife's birthday on the 27th of February.
  125: It rained in December.
  126: It snowed in January.
  127: They arrived in February.
  128: He travelled by air in 1968.
  129: They moved to a new house in 1969.
  130: He remained in England in 1970.

- **Pattern Drill:** Books open.

  (a) To elicit: No, (he) didn't. Yes, (he) did.

  TEACHER: *Number 116.*
  Did he post the letter at six o'clock?
  PUPIL: No, he didn't.
  TEACHER: Did he post the letter at half past six?
  PUPIL: Yes, he did. etc.

  (b) To elicit negative and affirmative statements.

  TEACHER: *Number 116.*
  Did he post the letter at six or at half past six?
  PUPIL: He didn't post the letter at six. He posted the letter at half past six. etc.

  (c) To elicit points of time.

  TEACHER: *Number 116.*
  When did he post the letter?
  PUPIL: At half past six. etc.

  (d) What did (he) do? What happened?
  Ask questions to elicit complete statements.

TEACHER: *Number 116.*
What did he do at half past six?
PUPIL: He posted the letter at half past six. etc.

(e) What time/day/date/month/year did (he) ...?
Ask questions to elicit points of time.

TEACHER: *Number 116.*
What time did he post the letter?
PUPIL: At half past six. etc.

(f) Asking questions in pairs: What time/day/date/month/year.

TEACHER: *Number 116.*
Ask me if he posted the letter at half past six.
PUPIL: Did he post the letter at half past six?
TEACHER: What time ...
PUPIL: What time did he post the letter?

- **Unprepared Reading**

  Professor Boffin's Umbrella, page 5, caption 3.

- **Activity**

  A Guessing Game.

  A pupil is invited to the front of the class and he tells the teacher the month he was born in. Members of the class must guess the exact date. Anyone doing so is given a turn at the front.

  TEACHER (addressing pupil): When's your birthday? What month?
  PUPIL: April.
  TEACHER (addressing class): His birthday's in April. Guess the date.
  MEMBER OF CLASS: Your birthday's on April 7th.
  PUPIL: No, it isn't.
  MEMBER OF CLASS: Your birthday's on 3rd April.
  PUPIL: Yes, it is.
  TEACHER: Good. Sit down A. Now you B.

- **Writing**

  Workbook 3a, Revision Lesson 8.

Revision Lesson **8** What time/day/date/month/ year did they . . . ?

| carr<u>ies</u> | cr<u>ies</u> | hurr<u>ies</u> | tr<u>ies</u> | stud<u>ies</u> | dr<u>ies</u> | cop<u>ies</u> | fl<u>ies</u> |

AT

116

posted
6.30

117

turned on
8.10

118

finished
5.35

ON

119

visited
Thursday

120

played
Friday

121

washed
Saturday

ON

122

paid
September 4th

123

stayed
10th October

124

remembered
27th February

IN

125

rained
December

126

snowed
January

127

arrived
February

IN

128

travelled
1968

129

moved
1969

130

remained
1970

Revision Lesson **9** The Blakes move in

Mother: Whére have you béen, chíldren?
Sue: We've been néxt dóor, múm.

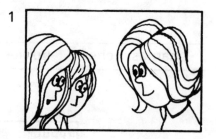

Mother: Néxt dóor?
But thát hóuse is émpty.

Sue: Nó, it ísn't, múm.
Lóok out of the wíndow.
We've gót some néw néighbours.

Sandy: Thát's Mŕ Bláke.
And thát's his wífe.
They've got thrée chíldren:
Álan, Wéndy and Tímmy.

Mother: Hów do you knów their námes?
Sue: We've álready mét them, múm.

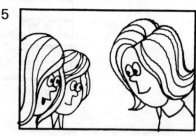

Mother: Whó are thóse twó mén?
Sandy: They're wórkmen, múm.
Their námes are Díck and Hárry.
They're véry stróng!

Content and Basic Aims

PATTERNS AND STRUCTURAL WORDS

I've just been to (church)/the (village).
I haven't been to (church)/the (village) yet.
I've already been to (church)/ the (village).
I was/went there (in the morning/last week) etc.
Where have you been?

● **General Remarks**

The present perfect form *have been* (= have gone) is revised here in patterns involving the use of *just, already* and *yet* together with place-and-time constructions. *Have been* is contrasted with the past forms *was* and *went*. Compare Book 2, TU 44.

● **Aural/Oral Procedure**

(a) Listening (Books shut)
(b) Listening and Understanding (Books open; pictures only)
(c) Listening (Books shut)
(d) Listening and Chorus Repetition (Books shut)
(e) Listening and Group Repetition (Books shut)
(f) Reading Aloud: Chorus and Individual (Books open)

● **Graded Comprehension Questions**

(a) Yes/No Tag Answers: have/is/do/are.

TEACHER: Have the children been to Professor Boffin's?
PUPIL: No, they haven't.
TEACHER: Have they been next door?
PUPIL: Yes, they have. etc.

(b) Negative Questions.

TEACHER: The children haven't been next door.
PUPIL: Haven't the children been next door? etc.

(c) Questions with Who: have/do/are.

TEACHER: Who's been next door?
PUPIL: The children have. etc.

(d) Double Questions.

TEACHER: Have the children been to Professor Boffin's, or have they been next door?
PUPIL: They haven't been to Professor Boffin's. They've been next door. etc.

(e) General Questions: Where, Which, What, How.

TEACHER: Where have the children been?
PUPIL: Next door. etc.

(f) Asking questions in pairs: Where, Which, How.

TEACHER: Ask me if the children have been next door.
PUPIL: Have the children been next door?
TEACHER: Where . . .
PUPIL: Where have the children been? etc.

● **Acting the Scene**

Invite three children to take the parts of Mother, Sandy and Sue. Seven more children may also be asked to take the silent roles. Dick and Harry could carry a table or a desk in the final frame.

● **Unprepared Reading**

Professor Boffin's Umbrella, page 6, captions 1 and 2.

● **Activity**

Revise the following rhymes:
(a) Pussy Cat, Pussy Cat. (Book 2, Lesson 87.)
(b) When I was . . . (Book 2, Lessons 45–49.)
(c) She sells sea-shells. (Book 2, Lesson 65.)

● **Writing**

Workbook 3a, Revision Lesson 9.

Revision Lesson 10

- **Spelling Drill:** Books shut.

  Oral and Written
  dirty/work/cork; bird/word/horse; first/world/story.

- **Phonic Practice:** Sounds and Spellings: Books open.

  The letters er [əː], ir [əː] and ear [əː]
  Chorus and Group Repetition

- **Repetition Drill:** Books open.

  Chorus and Group Repetition

  TEACHER: *Number 131.*
  Have you been to church? *All together!*
  I've already been to church. *All together!*
  I was there in the morning. *All together!*

  Practise these patterns with each of the items shown.

- **Pattern Drill:** Books open.

  (a) To elicit: I've just been to (church).

  TEACHER: *Number 131.*
  Where have you been?
  PUPIL: I've just been to church. etc.

  (b) To elicit: No, I didn't. I haven't been to (church) yet.

  TEACHER: *Number 131.*
  Did you go to church in the morning?
  PUPIL: No, I didn't. I haven't been to church yet. etc.

  (c) To elicit: We've already been to (church). We were there (in the morning).

  TEACHER: *Number 131.*
  Have you been to church yet?
  PUPIL: We've already been to church. We were there in the morning. etc.

  (d) To elicit: They've already been to (church). They went there (in the morning).

  TEACHER: *Number 131.*
  Have they been to church yet?
  PUPIL: They've already been to church. They went there in the morning. etc.

  (e) Asking questions in pairs:
  Where have you . . .?
  When did you . . .?

  TEACHER: *Number 131.*
  Ask me if I've been to church.
  PUPIL: Have you been to church?

TEACHER: Where . . .
PUPIL: Where have you been?
TEACHER: Ask me if I went to church in the morning.
PUPIL: Did you go to church in the morning?
TEACHER: When . . .
PUPIL: When did you go to church? etc.

- **Unprepared Reading**

  Professor Boffin's Umbrella, page 6, caption 3.

- **Activity**

  Dictation.

  Dictate the following passage:

  "Whére have you béen, múm?"/Súe ásked./
  "I've júst been to márket, Súe,"/mother ánswered./"I was thére a shórt time agó."/
  "Díd you gó to the líbrary, tóo?"/Súe ásked./
  "Yés, Súe./I was át the líbrary/at tén o'clóck./
  I have some bóoks for you./They are ín my bág."/
  "Lét me sée them,"/Súe sáid./"Óh!/I've álready réad them!"

  All punctuation marks should be dictated. For dictation procedure, consult Revision Lesson 4.

- **Writing**

  Workbook 3a, Revision Lesson 10.

Revision Lesson **10**   I've just/already been to . . .
I was/went there . . .

<u>te</u>rm   b<u>ir</u>d   l<u>ear</u>n   <u>cer</u>tain   f<u>ir</u>st   h<u>ear</u>d   h<u>er</u>   sk<u>ir</u>t   <u>ear</u>ly

---

131

church
in the morning

132

school
in the afternoon

133

town
a short time ago

134

market
ten minutes ago

135

the village
last week

136

the city
last month

137

the cinema
last night

138

the library
at half past ten

139

the country
in December

140

the seaside
in August

141

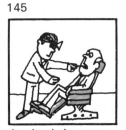

the funfair
the other day

142

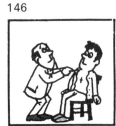

the station
at six o'clock

143

STATIONER

the stationer's
on Monday

144

WATCHMAKER

the watchmaker's
on Thursday

145

the dentist's
on Wednesday

146

the doctor's
on February 18th

Study these verbs:

be — was — have been
go — went — have gone

Revision Lesson **11** Dick and Harry

Mrs Blake:	Háve you bróught in the píano yét?
Dick and Harry:	Yés, Mŕs.

Mrs Blake:	Whére have you pút it?
Dick:	We've pút it in thére, Mŕs— in thát room.

Mrs Blake:	I dón't wánt it in *thát* room. Thát's the kítchen. Bríng it óut pléase.

Harry:	Whére do you wánt it, Mŕs?
Mrs Blake:	In hére pléase.
Dick:	Dón't dróp it on your tóes, Hárry!

Dick:	We've pút it in the córner, Mŕs. Is that áll ríght?
Mrs Blake:	I'll gó and háve a lóok.

Mrs Blake:	Mý góodness! You've túrned the píano úpside-dówn!

Revision Lesson 11

Content and Basic Aims

PATTERNS AND STRUCTURAL WORDS	VOCABULARY	
(Sandy)'s just (cut his finger). *(He) (cut) it (a while ago).* *(Sue) hasn't (set the table) yet.* *Why has (Sue set the table)?*	*Noun* corner *Verb* drop	*Expressions* in here in there turn (something) upside-down

● **General Remarks**

The simple present perfect is revised with a selection of familiar irregular verbs in patterns involving the use of *just* and *yet*. It is contrasted with the simple past and familiar points of time. Compare Book 2, TU 49.

● **Aural/Oral Procedure**

(a) Listening (Books shut)
(b) Listening and Understanding (Books open; pictures only)
(c) Listening (Books shut)
(d) Listening and Chorus Repetition (Books shut)
(e) Listening and Group Repetition (Books shut)
(f) Reading Aloud: Chorus and Individual (Books open)

● **Graded Comprehension Questions**

(a) Yes/No Tag Answers: have/does/is/will.

TEACHER: Have Dick and Harry finished work?
PUPIL: No, they haven't.
TEACHER: Have they brought in the piano?
PUPIL: Yes, they have. etc.

(b) Negative Questions.

TEACHER: They haven't brought in the piano yet.
PUPIL: Haven't they brought in the piano yet? etc.

(c) Questions with Who: have/does/will.

TEACHER: Who's brought in the piano?
PUPIL: Dick and Harry have. etc.

(d) Double Questions.

TEACHER: Have they brought in a table or a piano?
PUPIL: They haven't brought in a table. They've brought in a piano. etc.

(e) General Questions: Where and What.

TEACHER: What have Dick and Harry brought in?
PUPIL: The piano. etc.

(f) Asking questions in pairs: Where and What.

TEACHER: Ask me if they have brought in the piano.
PUPIL: Have they brought in the piano?
TEACHER: What . . .
PUPIL: What have they brought in? etc.

● **Acting the Scene**

Invite three pupils to come to the front of the class to act the scene. A table or a desk may be used to represent a piano.

● **Unprepared Reading**

Professor Boffin's Umbrella, page 7, captions 1 and 2.
New Words: *jet, aircraft, pilot, wave* (vb.).

● **Activity**

Revise: There were ten in bed, Book 2, Lessons 71 and 73.

● **Writing**

Workbook 3a, Revision Lesson 11.

Revision Lesson 12

- **Spelling Drill:** Books shut.

  Oral and Written
  hand/want; pram/wash; glad/watch; bad/what.

- **Phonic Practice:** Sounds and Spellings: Books open.

  The letters ear [ɔː] and [iə]
  Chorus and Group Repetition

- **Reading and Repetition Drill:** Books open.

  Chorus and Group Repetition

  TEACHER: *Number 247.*
      What's Sandy done? *All together!*
      Sandy's just cut his finger. *All together!*
      He cut it a while ago. *All together!*
      etc.

- **Pattern Drill:** Books open.

  (a) To elicit: (Sandy)'s just (cut his finger).

      TEACHER: *Number 247.*
          What's Sandy done?
      PUPIL: Sandy's just cut his finger. etc.

  (b) To elicit: (Sandy)'s just (cut his finger). (He) (cut) (it) (a while ago).

      TEACHER: *Number 247.*
          What's Sandy done?
      PUPIL: Sandy's just cut his finger.
      TEACHER: When did he cut it?
      PUPIL: He cut it a while ago. etc.

  (c) To elicit: (Mum) hasn't (shut the window) yet. Omit Nos. 247, 250 and 260.

      TEACHER: *Number 248.*
          What about the window?
      PUPIL: Mum hasn't shut the window yet. etc.

  (d) To elicit: (She)'s already (shut the window). Omit Nos. 247, 250 and 255.

      TEACHER: *Number 248.*
          Tell mum to shut the window.
          She's already shut the window. etc.

  (e) Asking questions in pairs: Why has . . .?
                       When did . . .?

      TEACHER: *Number 247.*
          Ask me if Sandy's cut his finger.
      PUPIL: Has Sandy cut his finger?
      TEACHER: Why . . .
      PUPIL: Why has Sandy cut his finger?
      TEACHER: Ask me if he cut his finger a while ago?
      PUPIL: Did he cut his finger a while ago?
      TEACHER: When . . .
      PUPIL: When did he cut his finger? etc.

- **Unprepared Reading**

  Professor Boffin's Umbrella, page 7, caption 3.

- **Activity**

  It's time for a story: The Blakes Move In, page 256. Write the following words on the blackboard and explain them: *other, Bang! Crash!* (interjections) *bleeding, blood, carpet.* Now read the story to the class.

- **Writing**

  Workbook 3a, Revision Lesson 12.

Revision Lesson **12** What's (he) done?
When did (he) do it?

heard hear   early near   learn ear

247
Sandy's cut his finger.
(a while ago)

248
Mum's shut the window.
(a few minutes ago)

249
Dad's put on his coat.
(three minutes ago)

250
Dad's hit his head.
(a moment ago)

251
Sue's set the table.
(at eight o'clock)

252
Dad's read his newspaper.
(a short time ago)

253
Mum's met
Mr May.
(a moment ago)

254
Sandy's spent
his pocket-money.
(during playtime)

255
Mrs Gasbag's
heard the news.
(this morning)

256
Mr May's told
them a story.
(during the lesson)

257
The professor's
found his umbrella.
(this afternoon)

258
Dad's lit
a fire.
(this evening)

259
Sandy's got
a new cap.
(this morning)

260
Sue's said
goodbye.
(a minute ago)

Study these verbs:

cut – cut – cut	meet – met – met	find – found – found
shut – shut – shut	spend – spent – spent	light – lit – lit
put – put – put	hear – heard – heard	get – got – got
hit – hit – hit	tell – told – told	say – said – said
set – set – set		
read – read – read		

Revision Lesson **13** You're a nuisance!

Narrator:	It's Sáturday mórning. Móther and fáther are shópping. Fáther is in a húrry and móther is cróss with him.	

Father:	Húrry úp, Bétty! Háven't you fínished yét?	
Mother:	Nó, I háven't.	

Father:	Whát are you góing to dó nów?	
Mother:	I'm góing to búy some frúit.	

Father:	Whý don't you búy some végetables, tóo?	
Mother:	Because I've álready bóught some.	

Father:	Whý don't you búy some péaches? You néver buy péaches.	
Mother:	Nó! They're véry expénsive!	

Mother:	Jím! Will you pléase gó hóme?	
Father:	I wánt to hélp you.	
Mother:	But you're nót hélping me! You're a núisance!	

Content and Basic Aims

PATTERNS AND STRUCTURAL WORDS	VOCABULARY	
Why don't (you/they) (blow up some balloons)? *(We've/they've) already done so.* *(We/they) (blew up some balloons) (before the party).*	*Noun*	*Verb*
	nuisance	shop
	Adj.	*Expression*
	expensive	go home

● **General Remarks**

The simple present perfect is revised with a selection of familiar irregular verbs in patterns involving the use of *just, already* and *yet.* It is contrasted with the *going to* future and simple past. Compare Book 2, TU 51.

● **Aural/Oral Procedure**

(a) Listening (Books shut)
(b) Listening and Understanding (Books open: pictures only)
(c) Listening (Books shut)
(d) Listening and Chorus Repetition (Books shut)
(e) Listening and Group Repetition (Books shut)
(f) Reading Aloud: Chorus and Individual (Books open)

● **Graded Comprehension Questions**

(a) Yes/No Tag Answers: is/are/has/does.

    TEACHER: Is it Monday morning?
    PUPIL: No, it isn't.
    TEACHER: Is it Saturday morning?
    PUPIL: Yes, it is. etc.

(b) Negative Questions.

    TEACHER: It isn't Saturday morning.
    PUPIL: Isn't it Saturday morning? etc.

(c) Questions with Who: is/has/does.

    TEACHER: Who is in a hurry?
    PUPIL: Father is. etc.

(d) Double Questions.

    TEACHER: Is it Monday morning, or Saturday morning?
    PUPIL: It isn't Monday morning. It's Saturday morning. etc.

(e) General Questions: What and Why.

    TEACHER: What day is it?
    PUPIL: (It's) Saturday. etc.

(f) Asking questions in pairs: What and Why.

    TEACHER: Ask me if it is Saturday.

    PUPIL: Is it Saturday?
    TEACHER: What day . . .
    PUPIL: What day is it? etc.

● **Acting the Scene**

Invite two pupils to come to the front of the class to act the scene. Signs reading 'Fresh Fruit', 'Fresh Vegetables' and 'Fresh Peaches' may be prepared and used as props. The Narrator's part (frame 1) should be omitted.

● **Unprepared Reading**

Professor Boffin's Umbrella, page 8, captions 1 and 2.
New Words: *space* (interstellar), *rocket, astronaut, space station, towards.*

● **Activity**

Revise: My Bonnie, Book 2, Lessons 89–95.

● **Writing**

Workbook 3a, Revision Lesson 13.

Revision Lesson 14

- **Spelling Drill:** Books shut.

  Oral and Written
  hand/slot/want; pram/cross/wash; glad/copy/
  watch; bad/soft/what.

- **Phonic Practice:** Sounds and Spellings: Books open.

  The letters ea (iː), ear [əː] and ear [iə]
  Chorus and Group Repetition

- **Reading and Repetition Drill:** Books open.
  Chorus and Group Repetition

  TEACHER: *Number 361.*
  What've you done? *All together!*
  We've blown up some balloons. *All together!*
  We blew up some balloons before the party. *All together!* etc.

- **Pattern Drill:** Books open.

  (a) To elicit: We've just (blown up some balloons).

  TEACHER: *Number 361.*
  Blow up some balloons!
  PUPIL: We've just blown up some balloons. etc.

  (b) To elicit: We're going to (blow up some balloons). We haven't (blown up any balloons) yet.

  TEACHER: *Number 361.*
  What are you going to do?
  PUPIL: We're going to blow up some balloons. We haven't blown up any balloons yet. etc.

  (c) To elicit: We've already (blown up some balloons). We (blew up some balloons) (before the party).

  TEACHER: *Number 361.*
  Blow up some balloons!
  PUPIL: We've already blown up some balloons. We blew up some balloons before the party. etc.

  (d) To elicit: Why don't they (blow up some balloons)? They've already done so. They (blew up some balloons) (before the party).

  TEACHER: *Number 361.*
  1st PUPIL: Why don't they blow up some balloons?
  2nd PUPIL: They've already done so. They blew up some balloons before the party. etc.

  (e) Asking questions in pairs: Why and When.

  TEACHER: *Number 361.*
  Ask us if we've blown up some balloons.
  PUPIL: Have you blown up some balloons?
  TEACHER: Why . . .
  PUPIL: Why've you blown up some balloons?
  TEACHER: Ask us if we blew up some balloons before the party.
  PUPIL: Did you blow up some balloons before the party?
  TEACHER: When . . .
  PUPIL: When did you blow up some balloons? etc.

- **Unprepared Reading**

  Professor Boffin's Umbrella, page 8, caption 3.
  New Expression: (100,000) *miles away.*

- **Activity**

  A Guessing Game.
  A pupil is invited to the front of the class and the teacher hands him a piece of paper with a suggestion on it. (Imperative statements derived from Revision Lesson 14 may be given.) Members of the class must find out what is on the piece of paper. Anyone guessing correctly is given a turn at the front. The game may be conducted as follows:

  TEACHER (*handing pupil a piece of paper with the words 'Throw away that waste paper' on it*):
  You haven't done this yet.
  (*addressing class*): Why doesn't he do it? Ask him.
  MEMBER OF CLASS: Why don't you blow up some balloons?
  PUPIL: Because I've already blown up some balloons.
  MEMBER OF CLASS: Why don't you throw away that waste paper?
  PUPIL: I haven't done that yet.
  TEACHER: Good! Sit down A. Now you B.

- **Writing**

  Workbook 3a, Revision Lesson 14.

Revision Lesson **14** Blow up some balloons! We've already done so!

361

We've blown up some
balloons.
(before the party)

362

We've thrown away
that waste paper.
(after the lesson)

363

We've flown our kites.

(during the afternoon)

364

We've shown mother
our new books.
(in the morning)

365

We've drawn some
pictures.
(during the lesson)

366

We've drunk our milk.

(during the morning)

367

We've eaten our
breakfast.
(at breakfast time)

368

We've taken off our
hats.
(a few minutes ago)

369

We've ridden our
bicycles.
(during the day)

370

We've bought some
sweets.
(during playtime)

371

We've brought you
some flowers.
(a while ago)

372

We've made a puppet.

(after tea)

Study these verbs:

blow—blew—blown	eat—ate—eaten
throw—threw—thrown	take—took—taken
fly—flew—flown	ride—rode—ridden
show—showed—shown	buy—bought—bought
draw—drew—drawn	bring—brought—brought
drink—drank—drunk	make—made—made

28

Revision Lesson **15** A safe place

Father: Whére's my blúe súit, déar?
Mother: It's at the cléaner's, Jím.
It'll be réady nów.
Cán you gó and gét it?

Father: Yés. I'll gó nów.
Gíve me the tícket pléase.

Mother: I'll lóok in my hándbag.
Thát's fúnny.
It ísn't hére.

Mother: I'll lóok in these dráwers.
Thát's fúnny.

Father: Cán't you fínd it, déar?
Mother: Nó, I cán't.
Father: Whére did you pút it?
Mother: I pút it in a sáfe pláce.

Mother: But nów I cán't fínd the sáfe pláce!

Content and Basic Aims

PATTERNS AND STRUCTURAL WORDS	VOCABULARY	
	Nouns	Adj.
No, it won't. Yes, it will. *(He)'ll (paint a picture)/It'll (rain) (next Friday/next August/next week etc.)*	cleaner's drawer handbag place	safe

● **General Remarks**

The *shall/will* future is revised in patterns involving the use of regular verbs and points of time (next week, etc.). The future is contrasted with the present perfect and simple past. Compare Book 2, TU 55.

Except for a few songs and rhymes, revision work is completed in this Teaching Unit.

● **Aural/Oral Procedure**

(a) Listening (Books shut)
(b) Listening and Understanding (Books open; pictures only)
(c) Listening (Books shut)
(d) Listening and Chorus Repetition (Books shut)
(e) Listening and Group Repetition (Books shut)
(f) Reading Aloud: Chorus and Individual (Books open)

● **Graded Comprehension Questions**

(a) Yes/No Tag Answers: is/can/will/does/did.

TEACHER: Does father want his coat?
PUPIL: No, he doesn't.
TEACHER: Does father want his blue suit?
PUPIL: Yes, he does. etc.

(b) Negative Questions.

TEACHER: Father doesn't want his blue suit.
PUPIL: Doesn't father want his blue suit? etc.

(c) Questions with Which and Who: is/can/will/does/did.

TEACHER: Which suit is at the cleaner's?
PUPIL: The blue suit is. etc.

(d) Double Questions.

TEACHER: Does father want his coat or his blue suit?
PUPIL: He doesn't want his coat. He wants his blue suit. etc.

(e) General Questions: What, Where, Why.

TEACHER: What does father want?
PUPIL: His blue suit. etc.

(f) Asking questions in pairs: What, Where, Why.

TEACHER: Ask me if father wants his blue suit.
PUPIL: Does father want his blue suit?
TEACHER: What . . .
PUPIL: What does father want? etc.

● **Acting the Scene**

Invite two pupils to come to the front of the class to act the scene. A handbag would be a useful prop.

● **Unprepared Reading**

Professor Boffin's Umbrella, page 9, captions 1 and 2.

● **Activity**

Revise the following rhymes:
(a) Swan swam over sea, Book 2, Lesson 79.
(b) What are you going to be? Book 2, Lesson 105. Substitute: baker, butcher, chemist, doctor, policeman, policewoman, postman, sailor, scientist, soldier.

● **Writing**

Workbook 3a, Revision Lesson 15.

Revision Lesson 16

- **Spelling Drill:** Books shut.

  Oral and Written
  pass/address; ask/assistant; class/Japan; ran/
  policeman; nasty/about; man/woman.

- **Phonic Practice:** Sounds and Spellings: Books
  open.

  The letters ear [iə] and er [ə]
  Chorus and Group Repetition

- **Repetition Drill:** Books open.

  Chorus and Group Repetition

  TEACHER: *Number 473.*
  What'll he do next month? *All
  together!*
  He'll paint a picture next month. *All
  together!*

  Repeat these patterns with the items shown.
  Note that 'What'll happen . . .' is required for
  Nos. 486 and 487. Vary the pronouns as indi-
  cated in the pictures.

- **Pattern Drill:** Books open.

  (a) To elicit: No, he/she/it/they won't. Yes, he/
  she/it/they will.

  TEACHER: *Number 473.*
  Will he paint a picture tomorrow?
  PUPIL: No, he won't.
  TEACHER: Will he paint a picture next
  month?
  PUPIL: Yes, he will. etc.

  (b) To elicit: No, I shan't. Yes, I shall. Omit
  Nos. 486 and 487.
  The pupils must identify themselves with
  the characters in the pictures.

  TEACHER: *Number 473.*
  Will you paint a picture to-
  morrow?
  PUPIL: No, I shan't.
  TEACHER: Will you paint a picture next
  month?
  PUPIL: Yes, I shall. etc.

  (c) To elicit negative and affirmative statements.

  TEACHER: *Number 473.*
  Will he paint a picture tomorrow?
  PUPIL: He won't paint a picture tomorrow. He'll paint a picture
  next month.

  (d) To elicit points of time.

  TEACHER: *Number 473.*
  When'll he paint a picture?
  PUPIL: Next month. etc.

  (e) To elicit: (He's) just (painted a picture).
  (He) (painted a picture) (last month). (He)'ll
  (paint a picture) (next month), too.

  TEACHER: *Number 473.*
  What's he done? (Or: What's
  happened?)
  PUPIL: He's just painted a picture.
  TEACHER: What about last month?
  PUPIL: He painted a picture last month.
  TEACHER: What about next month?
  PUPIL: He'll paint a picture next month,
  too. etc.

  (f) Asking questions in pairs: When.

  TEACHER: *Number 473.*
  Ask me if he'll paint a picture
  next month.
  PUPIL: Will he paint a picture next
  month?
  TEACHER: When . . .
  PUPIL: When'll he paint a picture? etc.

- **Unprepared Reading**

  Professor Boffin's Umbrella, page 9, caption 3.
  New Expression: *(flying) at 180,000 miles a
  second.*

- **Activity**

  Dictation.

  Dictate the following passage:

  "Háve you pósted/my létter yét, Súe?"/
  móther ásked./
  "Nó, I háven't, múm,"/Súe sáid./"I've gíven
  it to Sándy."/
  "Whén did you gíve it to him, Súe?"/
  "I gáve it to him/thís mórning, múm."/
  "Sándy!/Háve you pósted my létter yét?"/
  "Nó, múm./I'm sórry./I forgót./I'll póst it
  nów."/

- **Writing**

  Workbook 3a, Revision Lesson 16.

Revision Lesson **16** What'll happen? What'll they do?

near   bak<u>er</u>   h<u>ear</u>   fing<u>er</u>   <u>ear</u>   rul<u>er</u>   d<u>ear</u>   bitt<u>er</u>

last Saturday
last August
last summer
the other day
last week/ the week before last
last month/the month before last
last year/the year before last

next Saturday
next August
next summer
tomorrow or the next day
next week/the week after next
next month/the month after next
next year/the year after next

473

paint a picture
next month

474

visit Professor Boffin
next week

475

post the letter
tomorrow or the next day

476

pick some flowers
next week

477

talk about it
next month

478

wash the clothes
next Monday

479

polish the floor
next Friday

480

cook a meal
tomorrow

481

finish work early
tomorrow or the next day

482

move to a new house
next year

483

pour the tea
tomorrow

484

weigh the potatoes
tomorrow or the next day

485

call the doctor
next week

486

rain
next April

487
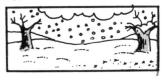
snow
next winter

Lesson **17** Please be polite!

Sandy: Máy I léave the táble pléase, dád?
Father: Nó, you máy nót, Sándy.
We háven't fínished our dínner yét.

Sue: Cán I léave the táble pléase, dád?
Mother: Nó, you cán't, Súe.
We háven't fínished our dínner yét.

Sandy: Máy I háve some chéese and bíscuits
please, dad?
Father: Of cóurse, Sándy.
Hére you áre.

Sue: Pléase lét me háve some, tóo, Sándy.
Sandy: Hére you áre, Súe.

Father: Thát was a véry góod dínner, Bétty.
I enjóyed it véry múch.

Father: Máy I léave the táble pléase?
Children: Nó, you máy nót!
Sue: We háven't fínished our dínner yet!

Content and Basic Aims

PATTERNS AND STRUCTURAL WORDS	VOCABULARY		
	Noun	*Adj.*	*Verbs*
Yes, you may. No, you may not. *May I/Can I (leave the table) please?* *Echoed Questions.*	toy	polite	burn close cross	practise sail switch on

- **General Remarks**

Formal and informal requests for permission as expressed by *may* and *can* will be practised in this unit. (Compare Book 2, TU 19.) These patterns are related to similar ones learnt earlier: *Let me* (Book 1, TU 33) and *Shall I/Do you want me to* (Book 2, TU 59).

Note that Echoed Questions will now replace Negative Questions.

It should also be noted that from this point on, the right-hand pages in the Workbooks will be devoted to guided composition exercises. There will also be multiple choice exercises to test comprehension, the use of familiar structural words and lexical items. The left-hand pages will be devoted to written reinforcement of oral patterns, as before.

- **Aural/Oral Procedure**

As for Lesson 15.

- **Graded Comprehension Questions**

(a) Yes/No Tag Answers: may. etc.
Point out that we do not normally elide *may* and *not*.

TEACHER: Does Sandy want to leave the table?
PUPIL: Yes, he does.
TEACHER: May Sandy leave the table?
PUPIL: No, he may not. etc.

(b) Echoed Questions: negative and affirmative. Make negative and affirmative statements by referring to the text to elicit echoed questions. Do not introduce *may*.

TEACHER: Sandy doesn't want to stay at the table.
PUPIL: Doesn't he?
TEACHER: He wants to leave the table.
PUPIL: Does he? etc.

(c) Questions with Who: does/has/can/did.

TEACHER: Who wants to leave the table?
PUPIL: Sandy does. etc.

(d) Double Questions.

TEACHER: Does Sandy want to stay at the table, or does he want to leave?
PUPIL: He doesn't want to stay at the table. He wants to leave. etc.

(e) General Questions: What and Why.

TEACHER: What does Sandy want to do?
PUPIL: (He wants to) leave the table.

(f) Asking questions in pairs: What and Why.

Do not introduce *may* in this exercise yet.

TEACHER: Ask me if Sandy wants to leave the table. etc.

- **Acting the Scene**

Invite four pupils to come to the front of the class to act the scene.

- **Unprepared Reading**

Professor Boffin's Umbrella, page 10, captions 1 and 2.

- **Activity**

Revise the following rhymes:

(a) Hey Diddle Diddle, Book 2, Lesson 67.
(b) I did, I did, I did, Book 2, Lesson 81–85.

- **Writing**

Workbook 3a, Lesson 17.

Workbook 3a contains twenty-two guided composition exercises which will train the pupil to write *simple* sentences. The pupils should:
1 Read each passage two or three times.
2 Answer each question with a *complete* sentence. The answers should be written consecutively to read as a *complete paragraph*.
3 Count the words in their answers and write the number beneath. Elided forms count as single words.

The answer to this guided composition exercise should read as follows:

Sandy and Sue have finished their dinner. They want to leave the table. Father won't let them. Mother and father haven't finished their dinner yet. Sandy and Sue want to eat some cheese and biscuits. Father has finished his dinner now. He wants to leave the table. The children won't let him. "We haven't finished our dinner yet," they said.

60 Words

Lesson 18

- **Spelling Drill:** Books shut.

  Oral and Written
  pay/play; say/stay; lady/baby; race/face; make/take; lake/cake; plate/date; taste/waste.

- **Phonic Practice:** Sounds and Spellings: Books open.

  The letters er [əː], [ə] and ear [iə]
  Chorus and Group Repetition

- **Reading and Repetition Drill:** Books open.

  Chorus and Group Repetition

  TEACHER: *Number 588.*
  May I play with these toys? *All together!*
  Can I play with these toys? *All together!*
  Please let me play with these toys! *All together!*
  Practise these patterns with each of the items given.

- **Pattern Drill:** Books open.

  (a) To elicit: Yes, you may. No, you may not. Provide cues by nodding, or by shaking the head.

  TEACHER: *Number 588.*
  May I play with these toys? *(Nodding)*
  PUPIL: Yes, you may.
  TEACHER: May I play with these toys? *(Shaking head)*
  PUPIL: No, you may not.

  (b) To elicit: May I (play with these toys) please?

  TEACHER: *Number 588.*
  What do you want to do?
  PUPIL: May I play with these toys please? etc.

  (c) To elicit: Can I (play with these toys)? etc. Point out that we often say 'Can I . . .?' but it is not as polite as 'May I . . .?'

  TEACHER: *Number 588.*
  What do you want to do?
  PUPIL: Can I play with these toys? etc.

  (d) To elicit: Please let me (play with these toys).

  TEACHER: *Number 588.*
  What do you want to do?
  PUPIL: Please let me play with these toys. etc.

  (e) To elicit: Shall I (play with these toys)? Remind the pupils that 'Shall I . . .?' means 'Do you want me to . . .'

  TEACHER: *Number 588.*
  What do you want to do?
  PUPIL: Shall I play with these toys? etc.

  (f) To elicit: Do you want me to (play with these toys?).

  TEACHER: *Number 588.*
  You can play with these toys.
  PUPIL: Do you want me to play with these toys? etc.

Unprepared Reading

Professor Boffin's Umbrella, page 10, caption 3.
New Word: *raising.*

- **Activity**

  It's time for a story: Father Meets the Blakes, page 257.
  Write the following words on the blackboard and explain them: *gardener, weeds, garden tools, borrow, spade, garden fork, dig, husband.* Now read the story to the class.

- **Writing**

  Workbook 3a, Lesson 18.

Lesson **18**   May I . . . ? Can I . . . ? Please let me . . .

t<u>er</u>m   farm<u>er</u>   <u>ear</u>   c<u>er</u>tain   sist<u>er</u>   d<u>ear</u>   h<u>er</u>   wat<u>er</u>   n<u>ear</u>

588

play with these toys

589

help you

590

open the parcel

591

answer the telephone

592

turn the tap off

593

try on this pair of shoes

594

pick some strawberries

595

switch on the light

596

put the letter in the
letter-box

597

taste the soup

598

cross the road

599

practise the piano

600

burn this waste paper

601

close the cupboard

602

sail my boat

Lesson **19** Isn't he a lovely baby!

Narrator:	Súe is trávelling by tráin. There's an óld mán ópposite her. He's réading a néwspaper. There's a yóung wóman besíde hím. She has a lóvely báby.

1

Sue:	Ísn't he a lóvely báby! Cán he tálk yét?
Young woman:	No, he can't, but he'll soon be able to. He can say "mummy" and "daddy"

2

Sue:	Ís he áble to wálk yét?
Young woman:	Nó, but he can alréady cráwl.

3

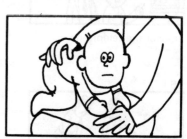

Old man:	He dóesn't smíle véry múch. Cán't you smíle, yóung féllow?

4

	The baby begins to cry loudly.
Old man:	It's áll ríght. He ísn't distúrbing me.

5

Young woman:	Nó, but I'm afráid that yóu are distúrbing hím!

6

Content and Basic Aims

PATTERNS AND STRUCTURAL WORDS	VOCABULARY	
	Noun	*Verbs*
I'm afraid that you are disturbing him. *Yes, (he) can/is (already) able to (smile).* *No, (he) can't/isn't able to (smile) yet.* *No, (he) can't, but (he)'ll soon be able to.* *Yes, (he)'ll soon be able to (smile).* *No, (he) won't be able to (smile) for a long time yet.*	fellow	be able to crawl cry (= weep) disturb

● **General Remarks**

Can/can't expressing ability and inability (see Book 1, TU 33) are reintroduced here and are practised in relation to *be able to* (present and future only).

● **Aural/Oral Procedure**

(a) Listening (Books shut)
(b) Listening and Understanding (Books open; pictures only)
(c) Listening (Books shut)
(d) Listening and Chorus Repetition (Books shut)
(e) Listening and Group Repetition (Books shut)
(f) Reading Aloud: Chorus and Individual (Books open)

● **Graded Comprehension Questions**

(a) Yes/No Tag Answers: is/has/can/will/does. To elicit a subject followed by an auxiliary verb.

TEACHER: Is Sue travelling by bus?
PUPIL: No, she isn't.
TEACHER: Is she travelling by train?
PUPIL: Yes, she is. etc.

(b) Echoed Questions: negative and affirmative. Make negative and affirmative statements to elicit echoed questions.

TEACHER: Sue isn't travelling by bus.
PUPIL: Isn't she?
TEACHER: She's travelling by train.
PUPIL: Is she? etc.

(c) Questions with Who: is/has/can/will/does. To elicit a subject followed by an auxiliary verb.

TEACHER: Who is travelling by train?
PUPIL: Sue is. etc.

(d) Double Questions.
To elicit negative and affirmative statements.

TEACHER: Is Sue travelling by bus or by train?
PUPIL: She isn't travelling by bus. She's travelling by train. etc.

(e) General Questions: How, Where, What and When.
Do not elicit complete answers.

TEACHER: How's Sue travelling?
PUPIL: By train. etc.

(f) Asking questions in pairs: How, Where, What, When.

TEACHER: Ask me if Sue's travelling by train.
PUPIL: Is Sue travelling by train?
TEACHER: How . . .
PUPIL: How's Sue travelling? etc.

● **Acting the Scene**

Invite four pupils to come to the front of the class to act the scene. It will be amusing if one of them takes the part of the baby. The Narrator's part (frame 1) should be omitted. Prompt the children as often as is necessary while they are acting their parts, though they should feel free to add words and phrases of their own if they wish to.

● **Unprepared Reading**

Professor Boffin's Umbrella, page 11, captions 1 and 2. Ask one or two pupils to read these captions without any explanation.

● **Activity**

Revise: Oranges and Lemons, Book 2, Lessons 109–115.

● **Writing**

Workbook 3a, Lesson 19.
Guided Composition: The pupils should again be instructed to work in the way indicated in Lesson 17. The correct answer should read:
Sue was in a train. An old man sat beside her. A young woman sat opposite her. The young woman had a lovely baby. She spoke to the young woman. The old man spoke to the baby. The baby began to cry.
"He isn't disturbing me," the man said.
"You are disturbing him," the young woman answered.

57 Words

Lesson 20

- **Spelling Drill:** Books shut.

Oral and Written
wait; paint; tail; afraid; train; rain; nail; remain.

Ask individual pupils to spell these words orally. As soon as a word has been spelt correctly, write it on the blackboard. When all the words have been written, erase them. Then dictate them to the class.

- **Phonic Practice:** Sounds and Spellings: Books open.

The letters er [ə] and or [ə]
Chorus and Group Repetition
Give the instructions *Open your books! Look at Lesson 20! Read together!* Ask the pupils to repeat after you the words at the top of this page, first in chorus, then in groups.

- **Reading and Repetition Drill:** Books open.

Chorus and Group Repetition
Ask the pupils to repeat after you the following patterns, first in chorus, then in groups:

TEACHER: *Number 603.*
He can already smile. *All together!*
He's already able to smile. *All together!* etc.

Point out that we can use *is able to* in place of *can*.

- **Pattern Drill:** Books open.

Illustrate each exercise first by providing the stimulus and the response. Make sure the pupils really understand how they must respond. Then conduct the drills given below. If a child makes a mistake, correct him and ask him to repeat the right answer.

(a) To elicit: Yes, he can already (smile).

TEACHER: *Number 603.*
Just look at that baby!
PUPIL: Yes, he can already smile. etc.

(b) To elicit: Yes, he's already able to (smile).

TEACHER: *Number 603.*
Can baby smile yet?
PUPIL: Yes, he's already able to smile. etc.

(c) To elicit: No, he can't (smile) yet.

TEACHER: *Number 603.*
Is baby able to smile yet?
PUPIL: No, he can't smile yet. etc.

(d) To elicit: No, he can't, but he'll soon be able to.

TEACHER: *Number 603.*
Can baby smile yet?

PUPIL: No, he can't, but he'll soon be able to. etc.

(e) To elicit: No, he isn't able to smile yet.

TEACHER: *Number 603.*
Can baby smile yet?
PUPIL: No, he isn't able to smile yet. etc.

(f) To elicit: Yes, he'll soon be able to smile.

TEACHER: *Number 603.*
Baby can nearly smile.
PUPIL: Yes, he'll soon be able to smile. etc.

(g) To elicit: No, he won't be able to smile for a long time yet.

TEACHER: *Number 603.*
Baby can't smile yet.
PUPIL: No, he won't be able to smile for a long time yet. etc.

- **Unprepared Reading**

Professor Boffin's Umbrella, page 11, caption 3.
New Word: *slow.*

- **Activity**

Action Game.
The teacher hands out a number of pieces of paper with 'actions' written on them. E.g. jump over a chair; switch on the light; cry like a baby; sing a song; polish the floor; dance; catch this ball; play hopscotch; climb on to this table; copy me; follow me; move this table; reach this book; hit me on the head; find this piece of chalk; carry my bag on his head; jump off this table; laugh loudly; fold a piece of paper like this; clean his shoes; post a letter; crawl like a baby; tell a story.

The game is conducted in the following manner:

TEACHER: Who's able to jump over a chair?
The pupils consult their pieces of paper. The pupil who has 'jump over a chair' written on it puts up his hand and says 'I am.'
TEACHER: Come out and do it then.
The pupil comes to the front of the class, mimes the action briefly, then sits down. And so on.

- **Writing**

Workbook 3a, Lesson 20.

Lesson 20   He can already . . . He's already able to . . .

farm**er**   act**or**   driv**er**   mirr**or**   teach**er**   doct**or**   rul**er**   inspect**or**

603
smile

604
laugh

605
crawl

606
count up to ten

607
write his name

608
stand up

609
reach the shelf

610
climb on to the table

611
close the door

612
switch on the light

613
understand me very well

614
BA-BA
speak very well

615
use a spoon

616
sit in his pram

617
ring the bell

40

Lesson 21 The wrong car

Father: Áh, hére we áre.
           This is óur cár.

Father: Wóuld you gét the kéy
           out of my pócket for me pléase, déar?
           My hánds are fúll.
Mother: There áren't any kéys in thís pócket.

Father: Cóuld you lóok
           in the óther pócket pléase?
Mother: Hére it ís.

Father: Now wíll you únlóck the dóor pléase?
Mother: Thát's fúnny.
           The kéy doesn't fít in the lóck.

Father: Mý góodness!
           Thís is the wróng cár!
           It's exáctly líke óurs,
           but it dóesn't belóng to ús.

Stranger: Héy!
           Whát are you dóing to mý cár?
Father: I'm sórry.
           We've máde a mistáke.

There's a hole in my bucket

There's a hole in my bucket, dear Liza, dear Liza,
There's a hole in my bucket, oh what shall I do?

Why, mend it, dear Henry, dear Henry, dear Henry,
Why, mend it, dear Henry, that's what you can do.

Lesson 21

Content and Basic Aims

PATTERNS AND STRUCTURAL WORDS	VOCABULARY				
It's (exactly) like ours. *Would you/Could you (switch on the radio) (for me) (please)?* *Can you (switch off the radio) please?*	*Nouns*	*Adj.*	*Verbs*		*Adv.*
	engine lock rubbish stranger	other wrong	clear correct deliver fit mend	mind (= look after) sweep switch off unlock	exactly
					Expression
					Here we are.

● **General Remarks**

Formal and informal suggestions and requests as expressed by *would, could* and *can* will be practised in this unit. These patterns are related to similar ones learnt earlier: *Will you/I want you to* . . . (Book 2, TU 59).

● **Aural/Oral Procedure**

(a) Listening (Books shut)
(b) Listening and Understanding (Books open: pictures only)
(c) Listening (Books shut)
(d) Listening and Chorus Repetition (Books shut)
(e) Listening and Group Repetition (Books shut)
(f) Reading Aloud: Chorus and Individual (Books open)

● **Graded Comprehension Questions**

Note that *would* and *could* cannot be introduced in any of these oral exercises.

(a) Yes/No Tag Answers: is/does/are/can/have.

TEACHER: Is this father's car?
PUPIL: No, it isn't.
TEACHER: Is this another man's car?
PUPIL: Yes, it is. etc.

(b) Echoed Questions: negative and affirmative. Make negative and affirmative statements to elicit echoed questions.

TEACHER: This isn't father's car.
PUPIL: Isn't it?
TEACHER: This is another man's car.
PUPIL: Is it? etc.

(c) Questions with Who and Whose: are/is/has.

TEACHER: Whose hands are full?
PUPIL: Father's are. etc.

(d) Double Questions.

TEACHER: Is this father's car or another man's car?
PUPIL: It isn't father's car. It's another man's (car).

(e) General Questions: Why and What.

TEACHER: Why is mother looking for father's key?
PUPIL: Because father's hands are full. etc.

(f) Asking questions in pairs: Whose, Why and What.

TEACHER: Ask me if this is father's car.
PUPIL: Is this father's car?
TEACHER: Whose . . .
PUPIL: Whose car is this? etc.

● **Acting the Scene**

Invite three pupils to come to the front of the class to act the scene. Schoolbags etc. may be used in place of parcels.

● **Unprepared Reading**

Professor Boffin's Umbrella, page 12, captions 1 and 2.
New Words: *earth, Tau Ceti* (name of star).

● **Activity**

Song: There's a hole in my bucket. See page 252 for music. Teach the first two verses of this song by getting the pupils to sing them several times after you in chorus or in groups.

● **Writing**

Workbook 3a, Lesson 21.
Guided Composition: Remind the pupils of the instructions given in Lesson 17. The correct answer should read:
Father wanted to unlock the door of his car. His hands were full. "Would you get the key out of my pocket please, dear?" he asked mother. Mother found the key. It didn't fit in the lock. It was the wrong car! A stranger saw father.
 "Hey! What are you doing to my car?" the man shouted.
 "I'm sorry," father answered. "We've made a mistake."

65 Words

Lesson 22

- **Spelling Drill:** Books shut.

  Oral and Written
  paint/plate; stay/wait; face/tail; afraid/baby;
  train/date; race/rain; make/nail; remain/lady.

- **Phonic Practice:** Sounds and Spellings: Books
  open.

  The letters or [ɔː] and [ə]
  Chorus and Group Repetition

- **Reading and Repetition Drill:** Books open.

  Chorus and Group Repetition

  TEACHER: *Number 718.*
  > Would you switch on the radio
  > please? *All together!*
  > Could you switch on the radio
  > please? *All together!*

  Point out that these are polite requests and they
  both mean the same.

- **Pattern Drill:** Books open.

  (a) To elicit: Would you (switch on the radio)
  please?

  TEACHER: *Number 718.*
  > What do you want me to do?
  PUPIL: Would you switch on the radio
  > please? etc.

  (b) To elicit: Would you (switch on the radio)
  for me please?

  TEACHER: *Number 718.*
  > What do you want me to do?
  PUPIL: Would you switch on the radio
  > for me please? etc.

  (c) To elicit: Could you (switch on the radio)
  please?

  TEACHER: *Number 718.*
  > What shall I do?
  PUPIL: Could you switch on the radio
  > please? etc.

  (d) To elicit: Will you (switch on the radio)
  please?
  Explain that we can say 'Will you . . .' and
  'Can you . . .' in place of 'Would you . . .'
  and 'Could you . . .' but that these forms
  are less polite.

  TEACHER: *Number 718.*
  > What shall I do?
  PUPIL: Will you switch on the radio
  > please? etc.

  (e) To elicit: Can you (switch on the radio)
  please?

  TEACHER: *Number 718.*
  > What do you want me to do?
  PUPIL: Can you switch on the radio
  > please? etc.

  (f) To elicit: I want you to (switch on the
  radio).

  TEACHER: *Number 718.*
  > What must I do?
  PUPIL: I want you to switch on the
  > radio. etc.

- **Unprepared Reading**

  Professor Boffin's Umbrella, page 12, caption 3.
  New Words and Expressions: *sleep* (vb.) *go(es)
  to sleep.*

- **Activity**

  Dictation.
  Dictate the following passage:

  > Súe was ón the tráin./"Máy I pláy with the
  > báby, pléase?"/ she ásked the yóung wóman
  > ópposite her./
  > "Of cóurse,"/the yóung wóman sáid./
  > "He wánts to stánd úp./Cán I hélp him?/Súe
  > ásked./
  > "He can alréady stánd úp,"/the yóung
  > móther sáid./ "He'll sóon be áble to wálk."/
  > "He's a lóvely báby,"/Súe sáid,/"and he's
  > cléver, tóo."

  For notes on delivery consult Revision Lesson
  4 if necessary.

- **Writing**

  Workbook 3a, Lesson 22.

Lesson 22 Would you . . . please?
Could you . . . please?

bottle
cork

horse   actor   fork   doctor   store   mirror   cork   inspector

718
switch on the radio

719
switch off the radio

720
burn all this rubbish

721
pay the bill

722
start the engine

723
unlock the van

724
mind the children

725
fill the wash-basin

726
wait at the corner

727
deliver this message

728
clear the table

729
pick a bunch of flowers

730

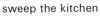
sweep the kitchen

731

mend the gate

732

correct this exercise

Lesson 23 Billy's favourite subject

Mrs Hart: You were ábsent
from schóol yésterday, Sándy.
Whére wére you?

Sandy: I cóuldn't cóme to schóol, Mrs Hárt.
My móther tóok me to the dóctor's.

Mrs Hart: Whý, Sándy?
Sandy: I húrt my fóot yésterday
and I wásn't áble to wálk próperly.

Billy: Wásn't Sándy lúcky!
He missed Máths and Hístory.
Sandy: Máths is my fávourite súbject.

Mrs Hart: Whích is yóur fávourite súbject, Bílly?
Billy: Fóotball, Mŕs Hárt.

Mrs Hart: Fóotball ísn't a súbject, Bílly.
It's a gáme.
Billy: Thát's why I líkę it, Mŕs Hárt!

With what shall I mend it, dear Liza, dear Liza,
With what shall I mend it, oh what shall I do?

With sticky, dear Henry, dear Henry, dear Henry,
With sticky, dear Henry, that's what you can do.

Content and Basic Aims

PATTERNS AND STRUCTURAL WORDS	VOCABULARY			
Maths is my favourite subject. *Yes, I could. No, I couldn't.* *(I) couldn't (fix the clock) at all.* *(He) couldn't (fix the clock) yesterday, but (he) can today.* *(He) was/wasn't able to/was unable to (fix the clock) yesterday.* *Could (he) . . .?* *(Why) could(n't) (he) . . .?*	*Nouns*	*Adj.*	*Verbs*	*Adv.*
	foot history maths subject (school)	absent favourite	be unable to miss (= fail to attend)	properly

● **General Remarks**

Could/couldn't is introduced to express past ability and inability. It is practised in relation to *was/wasn't able to* and *was unable to*.

● **Aural/Oral Procedure**

(a) Listening (Books shut)
(b) Listening and Understanding (Books open; pictures only)
(c) Listening (Books shut)
(d) Listening and Chorus Repetition (Books shut)
(e) Listening and Group Repetition (Books shut)
(f) Reading Aloud: Chorus and Individual (Books open)

● **Graded Comprehension Questions**

Could/couldn't should be introduced in these oral exercises. Illustrate on the blackboard the relationship between unelided and elided forms: could not = couldn't.

(a) Yes/No Tag Answers: was/could/did/is/does.

TEACHER: Was Sandy at school yesterday?
PUPIL: No, he wasn't.
TEACHER: Was Sandy absent yesterday?
PUPIL: Yes, he was. etc.

(b) Echoed Questions: negative and affirmative. Make negative and affirmative statements to elicit echoed questions.

TEACHER: Sandy wasn't at school yesterday.
PUPIL: Wasn't he?
TEACHER: Sandy was absent from school yesterday.
PUPIL: Was he? etc.

(c) Questions with Who: was/couldn't/did/does.

TEACHER: Who was absent from school yesterday?
PUPIL: Sandy was. etc.

(d) Double Questions.

TEACHER: Was Sandy at school yesterday, or was he absent?
PUPIL: Sandy wasn't at school yesterday. He was absent.

(e) General Questions: When, Why, Where and Which.

TEACHER: When was Sandy absent from school?
PUPIL: Yesterday. etc.

(f) Asking questions in pairs: When, Why, Where and Which.

TEACHER: Ask me if Sandy was absent from school yesterday. etc.

● **Acting the Scene**

Invite one pupil to come to the front of the class to take the part of Mrs Hart. This pupil should pretend to be marking a register.

● **Unprepared Reading**

Professor Boffin's Umbrella, page 13, captions 1 and 2.
New Expression: *I've lost my way.*

● **Activity**

Song: There's a hole in my bucket. See page 252 for music. Teach the next two verses.

● **Writing**

Workbook 3a, Lesson 23.
Guided Composition: The correct answer reads: Sandy was absent yesterday. He hurt his foot. His mother took him to the doctor's. Sandy missed Maths and History. Maths is Sandy's favourite subject. Football is Billy's favourite "subject".
    "Football isn't a subject, Billy. It's a game." Mrs Hart said.
    "That's why I like it, Mrs Hart," Billy answered.

50 Words

Lesson 24

- **Spelling Drill:** Books shut.

  Oral and Written
  wait/upstairs; paint/pair; remain/funfair; rain/hair; tail/chair.

- **Phonic Practice:** Sounds and Spellings: Books open.

  The letters b [b] and p [p]
  Chorus and Group Repetition

- **Reading and Repetition Drill:** Books open.

  Chorus and Group Repetition

  TEACHER: *Number 833.*
  Father couldn't fix the clock. *All together!*
  He wasn't able to fix the clock. *All together!*
  He was unable to fix the clock. *All together!*

  Point out that all three statements mean the same. Repeat these patterns with each of the items shown.

- **Pattern Drill:** Books open.

  (a) To elicit: No, I couldn't. Yes, I could.
      Provide clues by shaking head or nodding.

      TEACHER: *Number 833.*
      Could you fix the clock? *(shaking head)*
      PUPIL: No, I couldn't. etc.

  (b) To elicit: No, I couldn't (fix the clock) at all.
      (First person responses only.)

      TEACHER: *Number 833.*
      Were you able to fix the clock?
      PUPIL: No, I couldn't fix the clock at all. etc.

  (c) To elicit: (He) couldn't (fix the clock) yesterday, but (he) can today.

      TEACHER: *Number 833.*
      Couldn't father fix the clock yesterday?
      PUPIL: No, he couldn't fix the clock yesterday, but he can today. etc.

  (d) To elicit: (He) wasn't able to (fix the clock) yesterday.

      TEACHER: *Number 833.*
      What wasn't father able to do yesterday?
      PUPIL: He wasn't able to fix the clock yesterday. etc.

  (e) To elicit: (He) was unable to (fix the clock).

      TEACHER: *Number 833.*
      Tell me about father.
      PUPIL: He was unable to fix the clock. etc.

  (f) Asking questions in pairs: Could and Why couldn't.

      TEACHER: *Number 833.*
      Ask me if father could fix the clock.
      PUPIL: Could father fix the clock?
      TEACHER: Why couldn't . . .
      PUPIL: Why couldn't father fix the clock? etc.

- **Unprepared Reading**

  Professor Boffin's Umbrella, page 13, caption 3.

- **Activity**

  It's time for a story: The Wrong Car, page 258. Write the following word on the blackboard and explain it: *believed.* Now read the story to the class.

- **Writing**

  Workbook 3a, Lesson 24.

47

Lesson 24 (He) couldn't . . .
(He) wasn't able to . . .
(He) was unable to . . .

<u>b</u>all <u>p</u>ull | <u>b</u>ut <u>p</u>ut | <u>b</u>us <u>p</u>ass | <u>b</u>ack <u>p</u>acket

Father
833

fix the clock

Sandy and Sue
834

do their homework

Billy
835

pass the ball to Tom

Sue
836

see the film

Father
837

drive the truck

The children
838

sail across the lake

Sue
839

dive into the pool

The children
840

cross the street

The baby
841

crawl across the room

The postman
842

deliver the postcards

Sandy
843

mend the puncture

Mother
844

sing the song

The policeman
845

catch the thief

Sue
846

clear the table

Mother
847

sweep the floor

Lesson 25　Television Day: The *Flyer*

Narrator:

The children's favourite subject is General Knowledge. They watch a programme on television every week. There is a television in their classroom.

TV Commentary:

Today our programme is about the first aeroplane with an engine. For thousands of years men couldn't fly. It was too difficult. Birds are able to fly with their wings. It is very easy for them to fly. But men haven't got wings. The first aeroplanes were gliders—planes without engines. The first plane with an engine was the *Flyer*. Two brothers, Wilbur and Orville Wright, built it. On December 17th, 1903, Orville lay on the bottom wing of his plane and started the engine. The *Flyer* was able to take off with its own power. It rose 10 feet and flew 120 feet. This was a great moment in the history of flying.

But there isn't any sticky, dear Liza, dear Liza,
But there isn't any sticky, oh what shall I do?

Well, make some, dear Henry, dear Henry, dear Henry,
Well, make some, dear Henry, that's what you can do.

With what shall I make it, dear Liza, dear Liza?
With what shall I make it, oh what shall I do?

Lesson 25

Content and Basic Aims

PATTERNS AND STRUCTURAL WORDS	VOCABULARY			
For thousands of years . . . *Yes, (he) could. No, (he) couldn't.* *(I) could (copy this sentence).* *It was very easy* *(I) couldn't (bake a cake). It was* *too difficult.* *That's why (I) could/couldn't do it.* *That's why (I) was/wasn't able to do it.* *Because it was very easy/too difficult.* *(Why) was/wasn't (he) able to . . .?*	*Nouns*		*Adv.*	*Verbs*
	(TV) commentary sentence feet (measure) (gram.) flying TV glider wing knowledge moment power programme		too	lie (= rest) take off (= rise)
			Adj.	
			bottom difficult general great	*Prep.* without

General Remarks

Non-fiction pieces will appear at regular inter-vals from now on in order to expose the pupil to different language registers. Their intro-duction marks an important transition phase to audio-lingual techniques (intensive reading). The Aural/Oral Procedure is therefore modified: repetition work is excluded. The mask will not be required when presenting these pieces. Note that across-the-page line-length is used in these pieces and that stress marks are not employed. There is usually a high concentration of lexical items.

Could/couldn't and *was/wasn't able to* are practised again in this unit in patterns involving the use of the adverbs *very/too* and the ad-jectives *easy/difficult*.

Aural/Oral Procedure

(a) Listening (Books shut)
(b) Intensive Reading (Books open)
    The passage should be played or read to the class in small units. During each pause, explain unfamiliar words. Rather than give direct explanations, try to elicit as much information as possible from the pupils.
(c) Listening (Books shut)
(d) Reading Aloud: Individual (Books open)

Graded Comprehension Questions

(a) Yes/No Tag Answers: is/do/could/was/have/were/did.

    TEACHER: Is the children's favourite sub-ject Maths?
    PUPIL: No, it isn't.
    TEACHER: Is the children's favourite sub-ject General Knowledge?
    PUPIL: Yes, it is. etc.

(b) Echoed Questions.

    TEACHER: Their favourite subject isn't Maths.
    PUPIL: Isn't it? etc.

(c) Double Questions.

(d) General Questions: Which/When/Where/What/Why/How.

(e) Asking questions in pairs: Which/When/Where/What/Why/How.

Oral Composition

Write the following notes on the blackboard:

Programme—first aeroplane.
Men couldn't fly: too difficult.
Birds can, wings: very easy.
First planes: gliders.
First plane, engine: the *Flyer*.
Wilbur and Orville Wright.
Dec. 17th, 1903:
Rose 10 feet; flew 120.

Now ask one or two pupils to reconstruct the passage by referring to the notes.

Unprepared Reading

Professor Boffin's Umbrella, page 14, captions 1 and 2.
New words: *flying saucer, creatures.*

Activity

Song: There's a hole in my bucket. See page 252 for music. Teach the next three verses and repeat the song from the beginning.

Writing

Workbook 3a, Lesson 25.
Guided Composition: The correct answer reads:

For thousands of years men couldn't fly. It was too difficult. The first aeroplanes were gliders. These planes haven't got engines. The first plane with an engine was the *Flyer*. Two men built it. Their names were Wilbur and Orville Wright. On December 17th, 1903 it flew 120 feet.

49 Words

Lesson 26

- **Spelling Drill:** Books shut.

Oral and Written
term/bird/pair; certain/first/funfair; her/girl/hair.

- **Phonic Practice:** Sounds and Spellings: Books open.

The letters b [b] and p [p]
Chorus and Group Repetition

- **Reading and Repetition Drill:** Books open.

Chorus and Group Repetition

TEACHER: *Number 948.*
I could copy this sentence. It was very easy. *All together!*
Number 949.
Sue couldn't bake a cake. It was too difficult. *All together!* etc.

- **Pattern Drill:** Books open.

(a) To elicit: Yes, (I) could. No, (I) couldn't.

TEACHER: *Number 948.*
Could you copy this sentence?
PUPIL: Yes, I could.
TEACHER: *Number 949.*
Could Sue bake a cake?
PUPIL: No, she couldn't. etc.

(b) To elicit: (I) could (copy this sentence). It was very easy. (Sue) couldn't (bake a cake). It was too difficult.

TEACHER: *Number 948.*
Were you able to copy this sentence?
PUPIL: I could copy this sentence. It was very easy.
TEACHER: *Number 949.*
Was Sue able to bake a cake?
PUPIL: She couldn't bake a cake. It was too difficult. etc.

(c) To elicit: That's why (I) could/couldn't do it.

TEACHER: *Number 948.*
It was easy to copy this sentence.
PUPIL: That's why I could do it.
TEACHER: *Number 949.*
It was too difficult to bake a cake.
PUPIL: That's why Sue couldn't do it. etc.

(d) To elicit: That's why (I) was/wasn't able to do it.
Conduct the drill in the way shown in (c) above.

(e) To elicit: Because it was very easy/too difficult.

TEACHER: *Number 948.*
Why were you able to copy this sentence?
PUPIL: Because it was very easy.
TEACHER: *Number 949.*
Why wasn't Sue able to bake a cake?
PUPIL: Because it was too difficult. etc.

(f) To elicit: (Why) was/wasn't/were/weren't ...?

TEACHER: *Number 948.*
Ask me if I was able to copy this sentence.
PUPIL: Were you able to copy this sentence?
TEACHER: Why ...
PUPIL: Why were you able to copy this sentence?
TEACHER: *Number 949.*
Ask me if Sue wasn't able to bake a cake.
PUPIL: Wasn't Sue able to bake a cake?
TEACHER: Why ...
PUPIL: Why wasn't Sue able to bake a cake? etc.

- **Unprepared Reading**

Professor Boffin's Umbrella, page 14, caption 3.
New Word: *dark.*

- **Activity**

A Game: Easy and Difficult.
The teacher writes a number of actions (possible and impossible) on small pieces of paper and puts them into a hat or bag.
Possible actions: ride my bicycle; pump up the tyres; jump off the table; write my name in English; light a fire; draw a picture; shut the window; climb a tree; carry my bag.
Impossible: read (Russian); carry ten desks; drive a car; sing in (Russian); ride (a horse); drink ten bottles of milk; swim ten miles; run to London; blow out a big fire.
One pupil at a time draws a piece of paper out of the hat and declares what he could or couldn't do.

PUPIL *(consulting piece of paper):* I was able to ride my bicycle. It was very easy.
Or: I wasn't able to read Russian. It was too difficult.

- **Writing**

Workbook 3a, Lesson 26.

Lesson 26
(I) could do it. It was very easy.
(I) couldn't do it. It was too difficult.

tap   ru<u>b</u>   <u>pi</u>pe   tu<u>be</u>   <u>pupp</u>et   ru<u>bb</u>er   ni<u>pp</u>y   ro<u>bb</u>ery

Could/was able to

948

I could copy this sentence.

950

We could learn English.

952

Liz could remember the poem.

954

The boys could swim across the lake.

956

Sue could practise this piece of music.

Couldn't/wasn't able to

949

Sue couldn't bake a cake.

951

Father couldn't push the car.

953

The baby couldn't switch off the light.

955

Mother couldn't unlock the door.

957

The glider couldn't fly over the mountains.

Lesson 27 The music lesson

Narrator: Sándy's cláss is háving a músic lésson.
The músic téacher
is shówing the chíldren a víolín.

1

Teacher: Whó can pláy
a músical ínstrument?
Sandy: Í cán, sír.

2

Teacher: Cóme and pláy this víolín, Sándy.
Pláy a nóte líke thís. *(He plays.)*
(Sandy makes a terrible noise.)
Sandy: It's tóo dífficult
for mé to pláy, sír.

3

Teacher: Whích ínstrument
can yóu play, Sándy?
Sandy: The píano, sír.

4

Teacher: Cán you pláy thís píece?
Sandy: Yés, sír.
It's éasy enóugh for mé to pláy.

5

Teacher: Whát about yóu, Bílly?
Billy: I cán't pláy an ínstrument, sír.
Í can only play grámophone récords.

6

With flour and water, dear Henry, dear Henry,
With flour and water, that's what you can do.

But there isn't any water, dear Liza, dear Liza,
But there isn't any water, oh what shall I do?

Well fetch some, dear Henry, dear Henry, dear Henry,
Well fetch some, dear Henry, that's what you can do.

Lesson 27

Content and Basic Aims

PATTERNS AND STRUCTURAL WORDS	VOCABULARY		
	Nouns	*Adj.*	*Verb*
It was/they were (easy) enough (for him) *to (answer).* *It was/they were too (difficult) (for him)* *to (answer).* *Because it was/they were (easy) enough.*	gramophone record instrument (mus.) note (of music) violin	low (not high/loud) musical	lift
			Adv.
			enough

● **General Remarks**

Could/couldn't and *was/wasn't able to* are practised again in patterns involving the use of *too*, *very* and *enough* in connection with adjectives describing objects.

● **Aural/Oral Procedure**

(a) Listening (Books shut)
(b) Listening and Understanding (Books open; pictures only)
(c) Listening (Books shut)
(d) Listening and Chorus Repetition (Books shut)
(e) Listening and Group Repetition (Books shut)
(f) Reading Aloud: Chorus and Individual (Books open)

● **Graded Comprehension Questions**

(a) Yes/No Tag Answers: is/can/does.

TEACHER: Is Sandy's class having a history lesson?
PUPIL: No, it isn't.
TEACHER: Is the class having a music lesson?
PUPIL: Yes, it is. etc.

(b) Echoed Questions.

TEACHER: They aren't having a history lesson.
PUPIL: Aren't they?
TEACHER: They're having a music lesson.
PUPIL: Are they? etc.

(c) Questions with Who: is/can/does.

TEACHER: Who is showing the class a violin?
PUPIL: The music teacher is. etc.

(d) Double Questions.

TEACHER: Are they having a history lesson or a music lesson?
PUPIL: They aren't having a history lesson. They're having a music lesson. etc.

(e) General Questions: Which and What.

TEACHER: Which teacher is giving them a lesson?
PUPIL: The music teacher. etc.

(f) Asking questions in pairs: Which and What.

TEACHER: Ask me if the music teacher is giving them a lesson.
PUPIL: Is the music teacher giving them a lesson?
TEACHER: Which teacher . . .
PUPIL: Which teacher is giving them a lesson? etc.

● **Acting the Scene**

Three pupils may act this scene. Sound effects may be provided vocally if no instrument is available.

● **Unprepared Reading**

Professor Boffin's Umbrella, page 15, captions 1 and 2.
New Word: *bodies.*

● **Activity**

Song: There's a hole in my bucket. See page 252 for music. Teach the next three verses and repeat the song from the beginning.

● **Writing**

Workbook 3a, Lesson 27.

Guided Composition. The correct answer reads: Sandy's class had a music lesson. The music teacher showed the children a violin. "Come and play this violin, Sandy," he said. Sandy couldn't play the violin. It was too difficult for him to play. He played a piece on the piano instead. Sandy's friend, Billy, can't play a musical instrument. He can only play gramophone records.

57 Words

Lesson 28

- **Spelling Drill:** Books shut.

  Oral and Written
  give/drive; live/arrive; notice/nice; opposite/bite.

- **Phonic Practice:** Sounds and Spellings: Books open.

  The letters b [b] and p [p]
  Chorus and Group Repetition

- **Reading and Repetition Drill:** Books open.

  Chorus and Group Repetition

  TEACHER: He could answer the questions. *All together!*
  They were easy enough for him to answer. *All together!*
  Number 959.
  He couldn't answer the questions. *All together!*
  They were too difficult for him to answer. *All together!* etc.

- **Pattern Drill:** Books open.

  (a) To elicit affirmative and negative statements involving the use of *adjective+ enough* and *too+adjective*. (Omit 'for him' etc. throughout.)

  TEACHER: *Number 958.*
  Could he answer the questions?
  PUPIL: Yes, he could answer the questions. They were easy enough to answer.
  TEACHER: *Number 959.*
  Could he answer the questions?
  PUPIL: No, he couldn't answer the questions. They were too difficult to answer. etc.

  (b) To elicit affirmative and negative statements involving the use of *adjective+enough* and *too+adjective*. ('For him' etc. should now be included.)

  TEACHER: *Number 958.*
  Could he answer the questions?
  PUPIL: Yes, he could answer the questions. They were easy enough for him to answer.
  TEACHER: *Number 959.*
  Could he answer the questions?
  PUPIL: No, he couldn't answer the questions. They were too difficult for him to answer. etc.

  (c) To elicit: that's why (he) was/wasn't able to (answer) them/it.

  TEACHER: *Number 958.*
  The questions were very easy.
  PUPIL: That's why he was able to answer them.

  TEACHER: *Number 959.*
  The questions were too difficult.
  PUPIL: That's why he wasn't able to answer them. etc.

  (d) To elicit: Because it/they was/were (easy) enough/too difficult.

  TEACHER: *Number 958.*
  Why could he answer the questions?
  PUPIL: Because they were easy enough.
  TEACHER: *Number 959.*
  Why couldn't he answer the questions?
  PUPIL: Because they were too difficult. etc.

  (e) To elicit: Because it/they was/were very easy/too difficult. Conduct the drill in the way shown in (d) above.

- **Unprepared Reading**

  Professor Boffin's Umbrella, page 15, caption 3.
  New Words: *planet, point at.*

- **Activity**

  Dictation
  Dictate the following passage:

  Sándy had a músic lésson yésterday./
  "Wóuld you pláy this píece pléase?"/his téacher sáid./
  Sándy pláyed it véry bádly/and his téacher was cróss./
  "I'm sórry,"/Sándy sáid./"I wásn't áble to práctise it./It was tóo difficult."
  "Perháps you were tóo lázy/to práctise it,"/ his téacher sáid.

- **Writing**

  Workbook 3a, Lesson 28.

Lesson 28

(He) could answer (the questions).
(They were) easy enough for (him)
to answer.
(He) couldn't answer (the questions).
(They were) too difficult for (him)
to answer.

---

ball   puppet   but   tap   rubber   put   bus   nippy   rub

Could	Couldn't	Could	Couldn't
958	959	960	961

answer the questions
easy

difficult

buy the lollipops
cheap

expensive

962	963	964	965

eat the bar of chocolate
sweet

bitter

lift the desk
light

heavy

966	967	968	969

climb the wall
high

low

hear the commentary
loud

low

970	971	972	973

carry the packet
small

large

cut the piece of paper
thin

thick

974	975	976	977

wear the socks
dry

wet

drink the milk
cool

hot

Lesson **29** The weight-lifter

Lást wéek
fáther tóok the chíldren
to a círcus.

Fírst they sáw a wéight-lífter.
He was véry stróng.
He pícked úp a héavy wéight.

He was stróng enóugh to líft it
abóve his héad.

Thén a clówn appéared.
He tríed to líft the wéight,
but he cóuldn't!
He was tóo wéak to líft it!

Súddenly, the clówn pícked úp
anóther bíg wéight.
He lífted it éasily.

But the clówn's wéight
was ónly a bár
and twó ballóons!

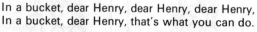

In what shall I fetch it, dear Liza, dear Liza,
In what shall I fetch it, oh what shall I do?

In a bucket, dear Henry, dear Henry, dear Henry,
In a bucket, dear Henry, that's what you can do.

But there's a hole in my bucket, dear Liza, dear Liza,
There's a hole in my bucket, oh what *shall* I do!

Content and Basic Aims

PATTERNS AND STRUCTURAL WORDS	VOCABULARY			
(He was) (strong) enough to (lift) (it). *(He) could (lift) (the weight) because (he was) (strong) enough.* *(He) couldn't (lift) (the weight) because (he was) too (weak).* *(He) was/wasn't able to (lift) (the weight) because (he was) so (strong/weak).* *(He was) very (strong/weak), so (he) could/couldn't . . .*	*Nouns*	*Adj.*	*Verbs*	*Adv.*
	bar (= rod) circus clown price river test weight weight-lifter	brave rich poor (= not rich)	appear become win	slowly so
				Prep.
				above

● General Remarks

Could/couldn't and *was/wasn't able to* are practised again in patterns involving the use of *too, very, enough* and *so* in connection with adjectives describing people. Verb/adverbial constructions are also introduced briefly.

● Aural/Oral Procedure

(a) Listening (Books shut)
(b) Listening and Understanding (Books open; pictures only)
(c) Listening (Books shut)
(d) Listening and Chorus Repetition (Books shut)
(e) Listening and Group Repetition (Books shut)
(f) Reading Aloud: Chorus and Individual (Books open)

● Graded Comprehension Questions

(a) Yes/No Tag Answers: did/was/could.

TEACHER: Did father take the children to a funfair?
PUPIL: No, he didn't.
TEACHER: Did he take them to a circus?
PUPIL: Yes, he did. etc.

(b) Echoed Questions.

TEACHER: Father didn't take them to a funfair.
PUPIL: Didn't he?
TEACHER: He took them to a circus.
PUPIL: Did he? etc.

(c) Questions with Who: did/was/could.

TEACHER: Who took the children to a circus?
PUPIL: Father did. etc.

(d) Double Questions.

TEACHER: Did father take them to the funfair or the circus?

PUPIL: He didn't take them to the funfair. He took them to the circus. etc.

(e) General Questions: Where and Why.

TEACHER: Where did father take the children?
PUPIL: To a circus. etc.

(f) Asking questions in pairs: Where and Why.

TEACHER: Ask me if father took the children to a circus. etc.

● Telling the Story

Ask one pupil at a time to reconstruct the story by referring only to the pictures. The pupils should remain seated during this exercise.

● Unprepared Reading

Professor Boffin's Umbrella, page 16, captions 1 and 2.
New Word: *picnic*.

● Activity

Song: There's a hole in my bucket. See page 252 for music. Teach the final three verses and repeat the song from the beginning. Divide the class into two groups. One group may take the part of Henry and the other the part of Liza.

● Writing

Workbook 3a, Lesson 29.
Guided Composition. Note that hyphenated words count as single words. The correct answer reads:
The children went to a circus last week. A strong weight-lifter picked up a heavy weight. After that a clown appeared. He wasn't able to lift the heavy weight. He was too weak. He picked up another big weight instead. It was easy for him to lift. This "weight" was only a bar and two balloons.

56 Words

Lesson 30

- **Spelling Drill:** Books shut.

  Oral and Written
  ride/right; hide/fight; kite/night; bite/tight;
  time/light.

- **Phonic Practice:** Sounds and Spellings: Books
  open.

  The letters t [t] and d [d]
  Chorus and Group Repetition

- **Repetition Drill:** Books open.

  Chorus and Group Repetition

  TEACHER: *Number 978.*
  He could lift the weight. *All together!*
  He was strong enough to lift it. *All together!*
  Number 979.
  He couldn't lift the weight. *All together!*
  He was too weak to lift it. *All together!* etc.

  Note the verb/adverbial constructions in Nos.
  994–997.

- **Pattern Drill:** Books open.

  (a) To elicit affirmative and negative constructions involving the use of *adjective+
  enough* and *too+adjective*.

  TEACHER: *Number 978.*
  Could he lift the weight?
  PUPIL: Yes, he could. He was strong
  enough to lift it.
  TEACHER: *Number 979.*
  Could he lift the weight?
  PUPIL: No, he couldn't. He was too
  weak to lift it. etc.

  (b) To elicit: (He) could . . . because . . ./(He)
  couldn't . . . because . . .

  TEACHER: *Number 978.*
  Why could he lift the weight?
  PUPIL: He could lift the weight because
  he was strong enough.
  TEACHER: *Number 979.*
  Why couldn't he lift the weight?
  PUPIL: He couldn't lift the weight
  because he was too weak. etc.

  (c) To elicit: (He) was/wasn't able to . . .
  because (he was) so . . .

  TEACHER: *Number 978.*
  Why was he able to lift the
  weight?
  PUPIL: He was able to lift the weight
  because he was so strong.
  TEACHER: *Number 979.*
  Why wasn't he able to lift the
  weight?

  PUPIL: He wasn't able to lift the weight
  because he was too weak. etc.

  (d) To elicit:
  (He was) very strong, so he could . . .
  (He was) too weak, so he couldn't . . .

  TEACHER: *Number 978.*
  He was very strong.
  PUPIL: He was very strong so he could
  lift the weight.
  TEACHER: *Number 979.*
  He was too weak.
  PUPIL: He was too weak, so he couldn't
  lift the weight. etc.

  (e) To elicit: That's why he was/wasn't able
  to . . .

  TEACHER: *Number 978.*
  He was strong enough.
  PUPIL: That's why he was able to lift
  the weight.
  TEACHER: *Number 979.*
  He was too weak.
  PUPIL: That's why he wasn't able to
  lift the weight. etc.

- **Unprepared Reading**

  Professor Boffin's Umbrella, page 16, caption 3.
  New Word: *backwards.*

- **Activity**

  It's time for a story: At the Circus, page 258.
  Write the following words and expressions on
  the blackboard and explain them: *ground, flip
  flop* (sound imitation), *fell over, real, pretended
  that, surprised, handkerchief, felt sorry, spanked,
  Boo hoo!* (sound imitation), *bucket, clapped.*
  Now read the story to the class.

- **Writing**

  Workbook 3a, Lesson 30.

Lesson **30**
(He) could lift the weight.
(He) was strong enough to lift it.
(He) couldn't lift the weight.
(He) was too weak to lift it.

<u>to</u>   <u>do</u>   <u>try</u>   <u>dry</u>   <u>tap</u>   <u>dad</u>   we<u>t</u>   re<u>d</u>

Could	Couldn't	Could	Couldn't
978	979	980	981

lift the weight
strong

weak

win the prize
pretty

ugly

982	983	984	985

pay half price
young

old

buy the car
rich

poor

986	987	988	989

pass the test
clever

stupid

play in the match
well

ill

990	991	992	993

become a policeman
tall

short

dive into the river
brave

afraid

994	995	996	997

get a seat
(arrived/didn't arrive)
early

late

win the race
(ran/didn't run)
fast

slowly

Lesson 31 Holiday photographs

Narrator: Fáther took lóts of phótographs
dúring the hólidays.
He's sítting in an ármchair.
He's lóoking at them.

Mother: Whát are those phótographs líke, déar?
Father: Nót tóo bád.

Father: Thís one's fáirly góod.
Mother: Lóok at Súe!
Shé looks quíte grówn-úp!

Father: Thís one's véry góod.
It's bétter than the lást one.
Mother: Sándy's éating cándy-flóss.

Father: Thís one's véry góod indéed!
It's the bést.
Yóu look véry prétty, déar.
Mother: Yóu took some góod phótos, Jím.

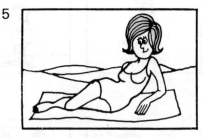

Father: Thís one of mé is the wórst!
It's véry bád indéed.
Whó tóok it?
Mother: Í did, déar!

Content and Basic Aims

PATTERNS AND STRUCTURAL WORDS	VOCABULARY		
It was (very good indeed). *It was better/worse than (Sue's).* *It was the best/worst in the class.* *It wasn't as good as (Sue's).* *It was/wasn't good enough.* *(He) came (top).*	*Nouns*	*Verb*	*Expressions*
	armchair candy-floss photo	compare	He came top/bottom. Not too bad. Take a photo.
		Adv.	
	Adj.	bottom fairly	
	better good grown-up (the) last worse worst	indeed poor (quality) quite (less than good) rather top	

● **General Remarks**

Patterns involving the use of the comparison of adjectives are introduced here. The pupils will practise two irregular comparisons only: *good* and *bad*. Adverbs of degree *(fairly, indeed, quite* and *rather)* will also be practised.

● **Aural/Oral Procedure**

As for Lesson 29.

● **Graded Comprehension Questions**

(a) Yes/No Tag Answers: did/is/are/does

TEACHER: Did father take lots of photographs yesterday?
PUPIL: No, he didn't.
TEACHER: Did he take lots of photographs during the holidays?
PUPIL: Yes, he did. etc.

(b) Echoed Questions.

TEACHER: Father didn't take any photographs yesterday.
PUPIL: Didn't he?
TEACHER: He took lots of photographs during the holidays.
PUPIL: Did he? etc.

(c) Questions with Who: did/is/does.

TEACHER: Who took lots of photographs during the holidays?
PUPIL: Father did. etc.

(d) Double Questions.

TEACHER: Did father take these photographs yesterday, or during the holidays?
PUPIL: He didn't take them yesterday. He took them during the holidays. etc.

(e) General Questions: When, Where, What, Which.

TEACHER: When did father take these photographs?
PUPIL: During the holidays. etc.

(f) Asking questions in pairs: When, Where, What, Which.

TEACHER: Ask me if he took the photographs during the holidays. etc.

● **Acting the Scene**

Ask two pupils to come to the front of the class to act the scene. Cards may be used in place of photographs. The Narrator's part (frame 1) should be omitted.

● **Unprepared Reading**

Professor Boffin's Umbrella, page 17, captions 1 and 2.

● **Activity**

Song: There's a hole in my bucket. See page 252 for music. Repeat the entire song.

● **Writing**

Workbook 3a, Lesson 31.
Guided Composition. The correct answer reads: Father took lots of photographs during the holidays. He looked at them yesterday. The photograph of Sue was fairly good. Sandy's photograph was very good. It was better than Sue's. Mother's photograph was very good indeed. It was the best. Father's photograph was the worst.
"Who took it?" father asked.
"I did, dear," mother said.

55 Words

Lesson 32

- **Spelling Drill:** Books shut.

  Oral and Written
  thief/seat/sheet; chief/neat/sleep; piece/peach/
  street; field/speak/feel.

- **Phonic Practice:** Sounds and Spellings: Books open.

  The letters t [t] and d [d]
  Chorus and Group Repetition

- **Reading and Repetition Drill:** Books open.

  Chorus and Group Repetition

  TEACHER: *Number 992.*
  What was Simon's report like? *All together!*
  It was very good indeed. *All together!*
  It was the best in the class. *All together!*
  He came top. *All together!*
  Number 993.
  What was Sue's report like? *All together!*
  It was very good. *All together!*
  It was better than Lillie's. *All together!*
  She came second. *All together!* etc.

- **Pattern Drill:** Books open.

  (a) Questions with Whose and Who.

  TEACHER: Whose report was very good indeed?
  PUPIL: Simon's was.
  TEACHER: Who came top?
  PUPIL: Simon did. etc.

  (b) To elicit: It was (very good). It was worse/better than . . .

  TEACHER: *Number 993.*
  What was Sue's report like?
  PUPIL: It was very good.
  TEACHER: How does it compare with Simon's?
  PUPIL: It was worse than Simon's.
  TEACHER: How does it compare with Lillie's?
  PUPIL: It was better than Lillie's. etc.

  (c) To elicit:
  It was (very good). It was better than . . .
  It was not as good as . . .

  TEACHER: *Number 993*
  What was Sue's report like?
  PUPIL: It was very good.
  TEACHER: How does it compare with Lillie's?
  PUPIL: It was better than Lillie's.
  TEACHER: How does it compare with Simon's?

  PUPIL: It was not as good as Simon's. etc.

  (d) To elicit: It was/wasn't good enough.
  Note on the blackboard that Nos. 992–996 are *good enough;* and Nos. 997–1000 are *not good enough.*

  TEACHER: How was Simon's report?
  PUPIL: It was good enough. etc.

  (e) Asking questions in pairs: Whose.

  TEACHER: *Number 992.*
  Ask me if Simon's report was very good indeed.
  PUPIL: Was Simon's report very good indeed?
  TEACHER: Whose report . . .
  PUPIL: Whose report was very good indeed? etc.

- **Unprepared Reading**

  Professor Boffin's Umbrella, page 17, caption 3.

- **Activity**

  A Game: What's your report like?
  The teacher writes the following on pieces of paper:
  very good indeed; very good; good; quite good; fairly good; rather poor; bad; very bad; very bad indeed. Nine pupils are then invited to come to the front of the class to choose a piece of paper (or 'report') from a hat or a bag. Members of class must guess what is written on these pieces of paper and 'grade' the pupils accordingly by changing their position in a line.

  MEMBER OF CLASS *(addressing one of nine pupils):* Bob! Your report is very bad indeed.
  PUPIL *(consulting piece of paper):* No, it's not.
  MEMBER OF CLASS: Your report is very good indeed.
  PUPIL *(consulting piece of paper):* Yes, it is.
  MEMBER OF CLASS: Stand at the front of the line. You are first. etc.

- **Writing**

  Workbook 3a, Lesson 32.
  Explain the instructions if necessary.

Lesson 32   What was (Simon's) report like?

<u>too</u>   <u>dirty</u>   <u>tidy</u>   <u>ticket</u>   <u>today</u>   <u>daddy</u>   <u>tight</u>   <u>date</u>

Simon's   992

very good indeed
the best in the class
He came top.

Sue's   993

very good
better than Lillie's
She came second.

Lillie's   994

good
She came third.

Sandy's   995

quite good
He came fourth.

Alan's   996

fairly good
He came fifth.

Tom's   997

rather poor
He came sixth.

Liz's   998

bad
She came seventh.

Wendy's   999

very bad
worse than Liz's
She came eighth.

Billy's   1000

very bad indeed
the worst in the class
He came bottom.

Study these adjectives:

good—better—the best
bad—worse—the worst

64

Lesson **33** The best garden in the neighbourhood

Narrator: Tímmy is hélping his fáther
in the gárden.
Tímmy is the yóungest
in the Bláke fámily.

Mr Blake: You can díg a hóle thére, Tímmy.
Í'll dig one hére.
We can plánt thése twó trées.

Timmy: Ís this déep enóugh, dád?
Mr Blake: Nó. Díg a déeper hóle, Tímmy.
Timmy: Ríght you áre, dád.

Mr Blake: Thére we áre!
Thése trées will sóon g20grów táll.
Timmy: Míne's táller than yóurs, dád.

Timmy: Óur gárden looks véry níce nów.
Mr Blake: Nó, it dóesn't, Tímmy.
It's fúll of wéeds.

Timmy: Stíll, it's the nícest gárden
in the néighbourhood.
Mr Blake: The nícest gárden?
Timmy: Yés.
Nóbody's gráss is lónger than óurs!

Sing this grave and simple strain

Sing this grave and simple strain,
Sing it faster, sing it faster,
round and round again.

Content and Basic Aims

PATTERNS AND STRUCTURAL WORDS	VOCABULARY			
Nobody's grass is longer than ours. *(Simon)'s (taller)|(hotter)|(larger)| (tidier) than (you are).* *(He)'s|(It)'s the (tallest)|(hottest)| (largest)|(tidiest) in (our class)|of them all|I have ever seen.*	*Nouns*	*Adj.*	*Verbs*	*Expressions*
	grass hole neighbourhood weed(s)	deep	dig grow plant	Right you are! Still (= all the same)

- **General Remarks**

  Patterns involving the regular comparison of adjectives are introduced here. Both *-er|-est* and *-ier|-iest* endings will be practised with familiar adjectives.

- **Aural/Oral Procedure**

  (a) Listening (Books shut)
  (b) Listening and Understanding (Books open; pictures only)
  (c) Listening (Books shut)
  (d) Listening and Chorus Repetition (Books shut)
  (e) Listening and Group Repetition (Books shut)
  (f) Reading Aloud: Chorus and Individual (Books open)

- **Graded Comprehension Questions**

  (a) Yes/No Tag Answers: is/will/does.

     TEACHER: Is Timmy helping mother?
     PUPIL: No, he isn't.
     TEACHER: Is he helping father?
     PUPIL: Yes, he is. etc.

  (b) Echoed Questions.

     TEACHER: Timmy isn't helping his mother.
     PUPIL: Isn't he?
     TEACHER: He's helping his father.
     PUPIL: Is he? etc.

  (c) Questions with Who and Whose: is/can/will/does.

     TEACHER: Who is helping Mr Blake?
     PUPIL: Timmy is. etc.

  (d) Double Questions.

     TEACHER: Is Timmy helping his mother or his father?
     PUPIL: He isn't helping his mother. He's helping his father. etc.

  (e) General Questions: Where, What and Why.

     TEACHER: Where are Timmy and father?
     PUPIL: In the garden. etc.

  (f) Asking questions in pairs: Where, What and Why.

TEACHER: Ask me if Timmy and his father are in the garden.
PUPIL: Are Timmy and his father in the garden?
TEACHER: Where . . .
PUPIL: Where are Timmy and his father? etc.

- **Acting the Scene**

  Ask two pupils to come to the front of the class to act the scene. They must pretend to dig and plant trees. The Narrator's part (frame 1) should be omitted.

- **Unprepared Reading**

  Professor Boffin's Umbrella, page 18, captions 1 and 2.

- **Activity**

  Song: Sing this grave and simple strain. See page 252 for music. Ask the class to repeat the song several times after you. Then divide the class into two and perform the song as a two-part round.

- **Writing**

  Workbook 3a, Lesson 33.
  Guided Composition. The correct answer reads: Yesterday Timmy helped his father in the garden. Timmy is the youngest in the Blake family. Timmy and his father dug two holes. They planted two trees. "Our garden looks very nice," Timmy said.
   "It's full of weeds," his father answered.
   "It's the nicest garden in the neighbourhood," Timmy said.
   "The nicest garden?" his father asked.
   "Yes," Timmy answered. "Nobody's grass is longer than ours."

                                          65 Words

Lesson 34

- **Spelling Drill:** Books shut.

  Oral and Written
  boy/boys; day/days; key/keys; donkey/donkeys;
  play/plays; pay/pays; buy/buys.
  A spelling rule may be given: we add 's' to a
  noun or verb if there is a vowel (a, e, i, o, u)
  before 'y'.

- **Phonic Practice:** Sounds and Spellings: Books
  open.

  The letters t [t] and d [d] (Regular verb endings)
  Chorus and Group Repetition

- **Reading and Repetition Drill:** Books open.

  Chorus and Group Repetition
  The captions beneath the pictures should be
  repeated.

  TEACHER: *Number 1000.*
  Sandy is tall. *All together!* etc.

- **Pattern Drill:** Books open.

  Books will not be required during these exercises. However, they may be kept open for
  reference purposes. Draw the pupils' attention
  to the adjectives at the bottom of the page.
  Briefly point out differences in spelling:
  tall/taller/tallest *(-er/-est)*; hot/hotter/hottest
  (double consonant); large/larger/largest *(-r/-st)*;
  tidy/tidier/tidiest ('y' becomes 'i').

  (a) To elicit: He's (younger) than I am. He's
  the (youngest) boy in our class.

  TEACHER: Tom is very young.
  PUPIL: He's younger than I am. He's
           the youngest boy in our class.
           etc.

  Substitute: fat, big, thin, clever, heavy,
  lucky, tidy, naughty, busy, tall, neat, old,
  strong.

  (b) To elicit: I'm (younger) than you are. I'm
  the (youngest) in our class.

  TEACHER: I'm very young.
  PUPIL: I'm younger than you are. I'm
           the youngest in our class. etc.

  Substitute the adjectives given in (a) above.

  (c) To elicit: It was (hotter) yesterday. The day
  before yesterday was the (hottest) day in
  the year.

  TEACHER: It's very hot today.
  PUPIL: It was hotter yesterday. The day
           before yesterday was the hottest
           day in the year. etc.

  Substitute: cool, cold, warm, nice, windy,
  sunny, dry, cloudy, fine.

  (d) To elicit: That (policeman) is (taller). (He)'s
  the (tallest policeman) I have ever seen.

  TEACHER: This policeman is tall.
  PUPIL: That policeman is taller. He's
           the tallest policeman I have ever
           seen. etc.

  Substitute: river/long; wall/high; man/
  strong; man/weak; river/muddy; boy/
  naughty; girl/silly; girl/pretty; man/fat;
  boy/brave; book/cheap; house/ugly; car/
  dirty; girl/neat; radio/small.

  (e) To elicit: No, (he) isn't. (He)'s (younger).

  TEACHER: He's older than I am.
  PUPIL: No, he isn't. He's younger. etc.

  Substitute: it's hotter today; it's cooler
  today; he's taller than I am; my car's older
  than yours; this box is lighter than that one;
  he arrived earlier this morning; he's richer
  than I am; this cushion's softer than that
  one; the floor's dirtier now; the clothes are
  wetter now; he's thinner than I am.

  (f) To elicit: No, (he) isn't. (He)'s the
  (youngest).

  TEACHER: He's the oldest pupil in the class.
  PUPIL: No, he isn't. He's the youngest.
           etc.

  Substitute: it's the hottest day in the year;
  it's the coolest day in the year; he's the
  tallest in the class; this car's the oldest;
  this man's the oldest; my house is the
  biggest; these towels are the cleanest; these
  clothes are the wettest; he's the thinnest of
  them all.

- **Unprepared Reading**

  Professor Boffin's Umbrella, page 18, caption 3.

- **Activity**

  Dictation
  Dictate the following passage:

  Yésterday we hád a tést./It was véry dífficult./
  We cóuldn't ánswer áll the quéstions./They
  were tóo dífficult./Only óne bóy was áble to
  fínish the tést./Thát was Símon./Hís wórk was
  the bést/in the cláss./He came tóp./Bílly's
  wórk/was the wórst in the cláss./Hé came
  bóttom.

- **Writing**

  Workbook 3a, Lesson 34.

Lesson 34   How do they compare?

1000

Sandy is tall.

1001

Simon is taller than Sandy.

1002

Tom is the tallest boy in our class.

1003

It's hot today.

1004

It was hotter yesterday.

1005

The day before yesterday was the hottest day in the year.

1006

Mr Brown's car is large.

1007

Mr Hill's car is larger than Mr Brown's.

1008

Mr Bell's car is the largest I have ever seen.

1009

Liz's desk is quite tidy.

1010

Lillie's desk is tidier than Liz's.

1011

Sue's desk is the tidiest of them all.

Study these adjectives:

tall—taller—the tallest   You know these, too:
cheap, clean, clever, cold, cool, fast, full, great, hard, high, kind, light, loud, neat, new, poor, quick, quiet, rich, short, slow, small, smart, soft, strong, sweet, thick, tight, warm, weak.

hot—hotter—the hottest   You know these, too:
big, fat, flat, glad, sad, thin.

large—larger—the largest   You know these, too:
brave, fine, nice, safe, strange.

tidy—tidier—the tidiest   You know these, too:
busy, cloudy, dirty, dry, early, easy, empty, funny, happy, heavy, hungry, lazy, lucky, muddy, nasty, naughty, nippy, pretty, silly, sleepy, sunny, thirsty, windy, ugly.

Lesson 35 Television Day: Mass-production

TV Commentary:

Henry Ford built the world's first mass-produced car in 1908.
Before 1908 cars were very expensive. Look at these two
cars. Which is the older? That's an easy question. Of course,
the car on the left is older than the one on the right. The car
on the left was expensive, difficult to drive, and it wasn't
very reliable. Only a few people could buy a car like this.
The car on the right is cheaper, lighter, faster and easier to
drive. Millions of people can buy a car like this. Why are
modern cars so cheap and reliable? Because the makers
build millions of cars and make them all exactly the same.
We call this "mass-production". Mass-produced things
are usually cheap.

The more we are together

The more we are together, together, together,
The more we are together, the merrier we shall be.
For your friends are my friends
And my friends are your friends,
So the more we are together, the merrier we shall be.

Lesson 35

Content and Basic Aims

PATTERNS AND STRUCTURAL WORDS	VOCABULARY		
Millions of people . . . The (bicycle) on the left is (cheaper) than the one on the right. The (bicycle) on the right is not as/so (cheap) as the one on the left. They're both (cheap), but which is the (cheaper)? They're all (cheap), but which is the (cheapest)? Which of the two is the (cheaper)?	*Nouns* maker mass-production *Adj.* left (cp. right) reliable mass-produced same modern	*Verb* build *Expression* on the left on the right	

● **General Remarks**

The second non-fiction passage is introduced here. The teacher's attention is again drawn to the modified Aural/Oral Procedure. (Compare Lesson 25).

There will be further practice involving the regular comparison of adjectives, including the use of *not so/as . . . as.*

● **Aural/Oral Procedure**

(a) Listening (Books shut)
(b) Intensive Reading (Books open)
    The passage should be played or read to the class in small units. During each pause, explain unfamiliar words. Rather than give direct explanations, try to elicit as much information as possible from the pupils.
(c) Listening (Books shut)
(d) Reading Aloud: Individual (Books open)

● **Graded Comprehension Questions**

(a) Yes/No Tag Answers: did/were/is/was/could/can/are/do.

> TEACHER: Did Henry Ford build the first mass-produced car in 1920?
> PUPIL: No, he didn't.
> TEACHER: Did he build it in 1908?
> PUPIL: Yes, he did. etc.

(b) Echoed Questions.

> TEACHER: Henry Ford didn't build the first mass-produced car in 1920.
> PUPIL: Didn't he?
> TEACHER: He built it in 1908.
> PUPIL: Did he? etc.

(c) Double Questions.

> TEACHER: Did Henry Ford build the first mass-produced car in 1920, or in 1908?
> PUPIL: He didn't build it in 1920. He built it in 1908. etc.

(d) General Questions: When, What . . . like, Why.

> TEACHER: When did Henry Ford build the world's first mass-produced car?
> PUPIL: In 1908. etc.

(e) Asking questions in pairs: When, Why, Which.

● **Oral Composition**

Write the following notes on the blackboard:

Henry Ford—first mass-produced car, 1908.
Before 1908: cars: expensive, difficult to drive, not reliable. Few could buy.
Modern cars: cheap, light, fast, easy to drive, reliable. Millions can buy.
Why? Mass-production. Cheap things.

Now ask one or two pupils to reconstruct the passage by referring to the notes.

● **Unprepared Reading**

Professor Boffin's Umbrella, page 19, captions 1 and 2.
New Word: *habit.*

● **Activity**

Song: The more we are together. See page 252 for music. Teach this song to the class by asking them to repeat it several times after you.

If there is time, repeat: Sing this grave and simple strain (Lesson 33) as a two-part round.

● **Writing**

Workbook 3a, Lesson 35.

Guided Composition. The correct answer reads: Henry Ford built the world's first mass-produced car in 1908. Before 1908 cars were very expensive. Only a few people could buy them. Lots of people can buy cars today. Modern cars are cheap. They are reliable, too. Modern cars are mass-produced. Mass-produced things are usually cheap.

47 Words

Lesson 36

- **Spelling Drill:** Books shut.

  Oral and Written
  lady/ladies; baby/babies; country/countries;
  family/families; try/tries; cry/cries; fly/flies;
  diary/diaries.
  A spelling rule may be given: 'y' is replaced by
  'ies' when preceded by a consonant.

- **Phonic Practice:** Sounds and Spellings: Books
  open.

  The letter d [d] (Regular verb endings)
  Chorus and Group Repetition

- **Repetition Drill:** Books open.

  Chorus and Group Repetition

  TEACHER: *Number 1012.*
              Which of the two is the cheaper?
              All together!
              The bicycle on the left is cheaper,
              All together!
              than the one on the right. *All
              together!*
  Practise these patterns with the items given.

- **Pattern Drill:** Books open.

  (a) To elicit: The (bicycle) on the left is
      (cheaper) than the one on the right.

      TEACHER: *Number 1012.*
               How do they compare?
      PUPIL: The bicycle on the left is cheaper
               than the one on the right. etc.

  (b) To elicit: The (bicycle) on the right is not as
      (cheap) as the one on the left.

      TEACHER: *Number 1012.*
               What about the bicycle on the
               right?
      PUPIL: The bicycle on the right is not
               as cheap as the one on the left.
               etc.

  (c) To elicit: The (bicycle) on the right is not
      so (cheap) as the one on the left.
      Point out that we can say *not so . . . as* in
      place of *not as . . . as.* They both mean the
      same.

      TEACHER: *Number 1012.*
               What about the bicycle on the
               right?
      PUPIL: The bicycle on the right is not so
               cheap as the one on the left. etc.

  (d) To elicit: They're both (cheap), but which
      (is) the (cheaper)?

  Point out that we must always use the *-er*
  ending when comparing two people or things.

      TEACHER: *Number 1012.*
               Tell me about those two bicycles.

  PUPIL: They're both cheap, but which
           is the cheaper? etc.

  (e) To elicit: They're all (cheap), but which (is)
      the (cheapest)?

      The pupils must imagine there are lots of
      objects etc. Point out that we must always
      use the *-est* ending when comparing more
      than two objects.

      TEACHER: *Number 1012.*
               Tell me about all those bicycles.
      PUPIL: They're all cheap, but which is
               the cheapest? etc.

  (f) To elicit: Which of the two (is) the (cheaper)?

      TEACHER: *Number 1012.*
               They're both cheap.
      PUPIL: Which of the two is the cheaper?
               etc.

- **Unprepared Reading**

  Professor Boffin's Umbrella, page 19, caption 3.

- **Activity**

  It's time for a story: The Dancing Competition,
  page 259.

  Write the following words and expressions on
  the blackboard and explain them: *important,
  entered a dancing competition, Good luck!, silver,
  judges* (competition), *agree, winners, clapped,
  shook hands, certificate, silver cup, congratulations, champagne, proud.* Now read the story
  to the class.

- **Writing**

  Workbook 3a, Lesson 36.
  The adjective *different* is not introduced until
  Lesson 45. It will have to be explained here
  before this exercise can be attempted.

Lesson 36

Which (of the two) is (the) cheaper?
The bicycle on the left is cheaper than the one on the right.
The bicycle on the right is not as cheap as the one on the left.

---

listene<u>d</u>   opene<u>d</u>   cleane<u>d</u>   playe<u>d</u>   fille<u>d</u>   turne<u>d</u>

1012

bicycle (cheap)

1013

cushion (soft)

1014

hill (high)

1015

clown (funny)

1016

window (dirty)

1017

machine (new)

1018

weight-lifter (strong)

1019

weight (heavy)

1020

dress (nice)

1021

hole (deep)

1022

ruler (long)

1023

uniform (smart)

1024

lamp-post (tall)

1025

postman (old)

1026

actress (pretty)

Lesson **37** Don't be, so greedy!

Mother: Hére are some strawberries for you, Súe.
And hére's some créam.

Sandy: Thát's not fáir, múm!
Súe's got móre stráwberries
than Í have.
And she's got móre créam, tóo.

Sandy: Lóok!
Í've got véry féw stráwberries
and véry líttle créam.
She álways gets móre than Í do.

Mother: Hére you áre, Sándy.
Sue: Now Í've got féwer stráwberries
than Sándy
and léss créam!
Thát's not fáir.

Mother: Cóunt your stráwberries.
Sandy: 1, 2, 3, 4, 5, 6, 7, 8, 9, 10 stráwberries.
Sue: 1, 2, 3, 4, 5, 6, 7, 8, 9, 10 stráwberries.
Mother: Sée? You've bóth got the sáme.

Father: Dón't be so gréedy bóth of you!
You álways recéive the móst
and your móther and Í
álways recéive the léast!

Content and Basic Aims

PATTERNS AND STRUCTURAL WORDS	VOCABULARY			
I haven't got much. I've got very little. I haven't got many. I've got very few. I've got more/less/fewer than you have. I've got the most/the least/the fewest.	*Noun*	*Verb*	*Expression*	*Adj.*
	marble(s)	receive	That's not fair!	fair less greedy more least most

● **General Remarks**

Patterns involving the irregular comparison of *much, many* and *little* are introduced here. *Little* and *few* are contrasted in patterns involving the use of familiar countable and uncountable nouns. This unit amplifies patterns introduced earlier. Compare Book 1, TU's 44 and 45 and Book 2, TU's 10, 11 and 42.

● **Aural/Oral Procedure**

(a) Listening (Books shut)
(b) Listening and Understanding (Books open; pictures only)
(c) Listening (Books shut)
(d) Listening and Chorus Repetition (Books shut)
(e) Listening and Group Repetition (Books shut)
(f) Reading Aloud: Chorus and Individual (Books open)

● **Graded Comprehension Questions**

(a) Yes/No Tag Answers: is/has/does/are/have/do.

TEACHER: Is mother giving Sue some apples?
PUPIL: No, she isn't.
TEACHER: Is she giving her some strawberries?
PUPIL: Yes, she is. etc.

(b) Echoed Questions.

TEACHER: Mother isn't giving Sue any apples.
PUPIL: Isn't she?
TEACHER: She's giving her some strawberries.
PUPIL: Is she? etc.

(c) Questions with Who: is/has/does.

TEACHER: Who is giving Sue some strawberries?
PUPIL: Mother is. etc.

(d) Double Questions.

TEACHER: Is mother giving Sue some apples or some strawberries?
PUPIL: She isn't giving her any apples.

She's giving her some strawberries. etc.

(e) General Questions: What, Why, How (many/much).

TEACHER: What is mother giving Sue?
PUPIL: Some strawberries (and cream). etc.

(f) Asking questions in pairs: What, Why, How (many/much).

TEACHER: Ask me if mother is giving Sue some strawberries.
PUPIL: Is mother giving Sue some strawberries?
TEACHER: What . . .
PUPIL: What is mother giving Sue? etc.

● **Acting the Scene**

Invite four pupils to sit round the teacher's table and act the scene.

● **Unprepared Reading**

Professor Boffin's Umbrella, page 20, captions 1 and 2.
New Word: *dreaming*.

● **Activity**

Repeat:
(a) The more we are together. (Lesson 35)
(b) Sing this grave and simple strain (Lesson 33)
(c) There's a hole in my bucket. (Lessons 21–29)

● **Writing**

Workbook 3a, Lesson 37.
Guided Composition. The correct answer reads: Mother gave Sue some strawberries and cream. Sandy felt cross. Sue had more than he had. Mother gave him some more. "Now I've got fewer strawberries than Sandy and less cream!" Sue said. The children counted their strawberries. They both had ten. "You always receive the most and your mother and I always receive the least!" father said.

58 Words

Lesson 38

- **Spelling Drill:** Books shut.

  Oral and Written
  carries/boys; donkeys/babies; countries/keys; flies/days; plays/ladies; buys/strawberries.
  If necessary, remind the pupils of the spelling rules given in Lessons 34 and 36.

- **Phonic Practice:** Sounds and Spellings: Books open.

  The letter d [t] (Regular verb endings)
  Chorus and Group Repetition

- **Reading and Repetition Drill:** Books open.

  Chorus and Group Repetition
  The captions beneath the pictures should be repeated.

  TEACHER: *Number 1000.*
  Have you got any candy-floss? *All together!*
  I haven't got much. *All together!* etc.

- **Pattern Drill:** Books open.

  (a) To elicit: I haven't got much/many. I've got very little/few.

  TEACHER: Have you got any bread?
  PUPIL: I haven't got much. I've got very little.
  TEACHER: Have you got any apples?
  PUPIL: I haven't got many. I've got very few. etc.
  Substitute the selection of uncountable and countable nouns given in the Pupil's Book.

  (b) To elicit: I've got more (bread) than you have.

  TEACHER: I've got some bread.
  PUPIL: I've got more bread than you have.
  TEACHER: I've got some apples.
  PUPIL: I've got more apples than you have. etc.

  Substitute all the nouns given.

  (c) To elicit: I've got less (bread)/fewer (apples) than you have.

  TEACHER: I've got very little bread.
  PUPIL: I've got less bread than you have.
  TEACHER: I've got very few apples.
  PUPIL: I've got fewer apples than you have. etc.

  Substitute all the nouns given.

  (d) To elicit: I've got less/fewer than you have.

  TEACHER: I've got some bread.
  PUPIL: I've got less than you have.
  TEACHER: I've got some apples.
  PUPIL: I've got fewer than you have. etc.

Substitute all the nouns given.

  (e) To elicit: I've got the least/the fewest.

  TEACHER: I haven't got much bread.
  PUPIL: I've got the least.
  TEACHER: I haven't got many apples.
  PUPIL: I've got the fewest. etc.

Substitute all the nouns given.

  (f) To elicit: I've got the least/the fewest.

  TEACHER: I've got a lot of bread.
  PUPIL: I've got the least.
  TEACHER: I've got a lot of apples.
  PUPIL: I've got the fewest. etc.

Substitute all the nouns given.

- **Unprepared Reading**

  Professor Boffin's Umbrella, page 20, caption 3.

- **Activity**

  A Game: Lists.
  The pupils are given a limited amount of time to write as many words as they can beginning with a particular letter. The pupil with the longest list is the winner.

  TEACHER: Think of words beginning with 'a'. Write as many as you can in three minutes: beginning from . . . now!

  When the time is up, the pupils read their lists aloud to the teacher.

  TEACHER: Very good A. You have the most. You have the least B.

- **Writing**

  Workbook 3a, Lesson 38.

Lesson 38 Not much/Not many/Very little/ Very few

baked	fixed	helped	skipped	stopped	worked

1000

Have you got
any candy-floss?
I haven't got much.

1100

I've got
more than you have.

1200

I've got
the most!

1300

Have you got
any lemonade?
I've got very little.

1400

I've got
less than you have.

1500

I've got
the least!

1600

Have you won
any marbles?
I haven't won many.

1700

I've won
more than you have.

1800

I've won
the most!

1900

Have you bought
any records?
I've bought very few.

2000

I've bought
fewer than you have.

2100

I've bought
the fewest!

Study these adjectives:
much/many—more—the most little—less—the least few—fewer—the fewest

Not much/Very little
bread chalk food honey ink jam chocolate   *Uncountable nouns*

Not many/Very few
apples biscuits cards dresses jars matches peaches   *Countable*

76

Lesson **39** The protest march

Sue:	Lénd me some móney please, Sándy. I'm bróke.	1

Sandy: I'm bróke, tóo.
Sue: Lét's ásk múm.

Sue: We háven't gót enóugh móney, múm.
Sandy: Máy we háve some móre pléase?
Mother: Ásk your fáther, chíldren.

Sue: We háven't gót enóugh móney, dád.
Sandy: Máy we háve some móre pléase?

Father: Yóu get plénty of pócket-móney. You dón't néed ány móre.

Sandy: Whát can we dó nów, Súe?
Sue: Í knów, Sándy.

Mother: Lóok at the chíldren! They're on a prótest-márch!
Father (reading): MÓRE PÓCKET-MÓNEY— OR WE WILL GÓ ON STRÍKE!

Solomon Grundy

Solomon Grundy,
Born on Monday,
Christened on Tuesday,
Married on Wednesday,
Ill on Thursday,
Worse on Friday,
Died on Saturday,
Buried on Sunday,
And that was the end
Of Solomon Grundy!

Content and Basic Aims

PATTERNS AND STRUCTURAL WORDS	VOCABULARY				
	Nouns	Adj.	Verb	Expressions	Conj.
I've got too little/enough/only a little/a little/plenty of/too much (lather). *I've got too few/enough/only a few/a few/plenty of/too many (marbles).* *I need some more.* *I don't need any more/so much/ so many.*	lather protest- march	enough plenty (of)	lend	I'm broke. go on strike	or (= if not)

● **General Remarks**

Patterns involving the use of *little/a little/few/ a few/enough/plenty (of)/much/many* to describe quantity will be practised in this unit. Contrast is again drawn between countable and un-countable nouns.

● **Aural/Oral Procedure**

(a) Listening (Books shut)
(b) Listening and Understanding (Books open; pictures only)
(c) Listening (Books shut)
(d) Listening and Chorus Repetition (Books shut)
(e) Listening and Group Repetition (Books shut)
(f) Reading Aloud: Chorus and Individual (Books open)

● **Graded Comprehension Questions**

(a) Yes/No Tag Answers: does/is/are/have/do/ will.

TEACHER: Does Sue want Sandy to lend her a pen?
PUPIL: No, she doesn't.
TEACHER: Does she want him to lend her some money?
PUPIL: Yes, she does. etc.

(b) Echoed Questions: negative and affirmative.

TEACHER: Sue doesn't want Sandy to lend her a pen.
PUPIL: Doesn't she?
TEACHER: She wants him to lend her some money.
PUPIL: Does she? etc.

(c) Questions with Who: does/can't/won't/will.

TEACHER: Who wants some money from Sandy?
PUPIL: Sue does. etc.

(d) Double Questions.

TEACHER: Does Sue want Sandy to lend her a pen or some money?

PUPIL: She doesn't want him to lend her a pen. She wants him to lend her some money. etc.

(e) General Questions: What, Who and Why.

TEACHER: What does Sue want Sandy to do?
PUPIL: To lend her some money. etc.

(f) Asking questions in pairs: What, Who and Why.

TEACHER: Ask me if Sue wants Sandy to lend her some money.
PUPIL: Does Sue want Sandy to lend her some money?
TEACHER: What . . . etc.

● **Acting the Scene**

Invite four pupils to come to the front of the class to act the scene. A makeshift banner would be a useful prop.

● **Unprepared Reading**

Professor Boffin's Umbrella, page 21, captions 1 and 2.

● **Activity**

Teach the new rhyme, Solomon Grundy, by getting the children to repeat it several times after you in chorus and in groups.

● **Writing**

Workbook 3a, Lesson 39.

Guided Composition.
New Word: *banner*.
The correct answer reads as follows:
Sue wanted Sandy to lend her some money. "I'm broke," she said. Sandy couldn't lend her any. The children asked mother for some money. "Ask your father," mother said. The children asked father. He didn't give them any. Sandy and Sue went on a protest-march. Their banner said: MORE POCKET-MONEY— OR WE'LL GO ON STRIKE!

55 Words

Lesson 40

- **Spelling Drill:** Books shut.

  Oral and Written
  babies/donkeys/trees; knees/carries/keys; monkeys/sees/strawberries.

  Ask individual pupils to spell these words orally. As soon as a word has been spelt correctly, write it on the blackboard. When all the words have been written, erase them. Then dictate them to the class.

- **Phonic Practice:** Sounds and Spellings: Books open.

  The letter d [d] and [t] (Regular verb endings)
  Chorus and Group Repetition
  Give the instructions *Open your books! Look at Lesson 40! Read together!* Ask the pupils to repeat after you the words at the top of this page, first in chorus, then in groups.

- **Reading and Repetition Drill:** Books open.

  Chorus and Group Repetition
  The captions beneath the pictures should be repeated, first in chorus, then in groups.

  TEACHER: *Number 1000.*
         I've got too little lather. All together!
        etc.

- **Pattern Drill:** Books open.

  Illustrate each exercise first by providing the stimulus and the response. Make sure the pupils really understand how they must respond. Then conduct the drills given below. If a child makes a mistake, correct him and ask him to repeat the right answer.

  (a) To elicit: No, I've got too little/too few. I need some more.

  TEACHER: Have you got enough butter?
  PUPIL: No, I've got too little. I need some more.
  TEACHER: Have you got enough toys?
  PUPIL: No, I've got too few. I need some more. etc.

  Substitute the selection of uncountable and countable nouns given in the Pupil's Book.

  (b) To elicit: No, I haven't got enough. I've got only a little/a few. I need some more.

  TEACHER: Have you got enough butter?
  PUPIL: No, I haven't got enough. I've got only a little. I need some more.
  TEACHER: Have you got enough toys?
  PUPIL: No, I haven't got enough. I've got only a few. I need some more. etc.

  Substitute all the nouns given.

  (c) To elicit: Yes, I've got a little/a few. I've got enough. I don't need any more.

  Point out that *a little* and *a few* mean *some/as much as I need.*

  TEACHER: Have you got enough butter?
  PUPIL: Yes, I've got a little. I've got enough. I don't need any more.
  TEACHER: Have you got enough toys?
  PUPIL: Yes, I've got a few. I've got enough. I don't need any more. etc.

  Substitute all the nouns given.

  (d) To elicit: I've got plenty of butter/toys. I've got enough. I don't need any more.

  TEACHER: What about butter?
  PUPIL: I've got plenty of butter. I've got enough. I don't need any more.
  TEACHER: What about toys?
  PUPIL: I've got plenty of toys. I've got enough. I don't need any more. etc.

  Substitute all the nouns given.

  (e) To elicit: I've got too much/many. I don't need so much/many.

  TEACHER: Have you got enough butter?
  PUPIL: I've got too much. I don't need so much.
  TEACHER: Have you got enough toys?
  PUPIL: I've got too many. I don't need so many. etc.

  Substitute all the nouns given.

- **Unprepared Reading**

  Professor Boffin's Umbrella, page 21, caption 3.

- **Activity**

  Dictation
  Dictate the following passage:

  Whó is the tállest bóy/in our cláss?/Tóm is the tállest bóy./He's táller than Sándy and Bílly./Bílly is nót as táll as Sándy./Whó is the fáttest bóy/in our cláss?/We áll knów thát./Áll the bóys éat a lót,/but Bílly éats the móst/and hé's the héaviest./Símon éats the léast/and hé's the líghtest.

- **Writing**

  Workbook 3a, Lesson 40.

Lesson 40　Little/A little/Few/A few/ Enough/Plenty

listene<u>d</u>　bake<u>d</u>　opene<u>d</u>　fixe<u>d</u>　cleane<u>d</u>　helpe<u>d</u>　fille<u>d</u>　stoppe<u>d</u>

Less than enough/less than I need

1000

I've got
too little lather.
I need some more.

2000

I've got
too few marbles.
I need some more.

3000

I haven't got
enough lather.
I've got
only a little.

4000

I haven't got
enough marbles.
I've got
only a few.

Enough/plenty/as much as I need

5000

I've got
a little lather.
I've got enough.
I don't need
any more.

6000

I've got
a few marbles.
I've got enough.
I don't need
any more.

7000

I've got
plenty of lather.
I've got enough.
I don't need
any more.

8000

I've got
plenty of marbles.
I've got enough.
I don't need
any more.

More than enough/more than I need

9000

I've got too much lather.
I don't need so much.

10,000

I've got too many marbles.
I don't need so many.

Too little/enough/only a little/a little/plenty of/too much
butter　cheese　cream　fruit　sugar　wool　furniture
Too few/enough/only a few/a few/plenty of/too many
toys　aspirins　bananas　bricks　chocolates　skirts　vegetables

Lesson **41**   On strike

Sue:	The prótest-márch dídn't wórk!
Sandy:	Whát can we dó nów, Súe?
Sue:	Lét's ásk agáin.

Sue:	Pléase gíve us a ríse, dád.
Sandy:	Thíngs are móre expénsive thése dáys.
Father:	I'm sórry, chíldren.

Sue:	But, dád!
	We're álways bróke.
	Óther chíldren recéive móre than wé do.
Father:	The ánswer is NÓ!

Sandy:	Whát can we dó nów, Súe?
Sue:	Dón't wórry, Sándy.

	(Later)
Father:	Whát's úp with the chíldren, Bétty?
Mother:	You wón't gíve them móre pócket-móney, so they're bóth ángry with you, Jím.

Father:	Whý aren't you dóing your hómework?
Sue:	Becáuse we're ón stríke!

I love sixpence

I love sixpence, jolly little sixpence,
I love sixpence better than my life,
I'll spend a penny of it, and I'll lend a penny of it,
And I'll take fourpence home for my wife.

Content and Basic Aims

PATTERNS AND STRUCTURAL WORDS	VOCABULARY	
They receive more than we do. *(It)'s more/less (beautiful) than . . .* *(It)'s the most/least (beautiful) I've ever (seen).* Tag Rejoinders.	*Nouns*	*Verb*
	answer person	worry
	Adj.	*Expressions*
	angry wonderful	Give (us) a rise. It didn't work. (= It wasn't successful.) these days

● **General Remarks**

The pupils will practise comparing adjectives of two or more syllables with *more/less* and *the most/the least*. Two-syllable adjectives which can be compared with *-er/-est* as well as *more/most* are not dealt with.

Note that Tag Rejoinders will now replace Echoed Questions.

● **Aural/Oral Procedure**

(a) Listening (Books shut)
(b) Listening and Understanding (Books open; pictures only)
(c) Listening (Books shut)
(d) Listening and Chorus Repetition (Books shut)
(e) Listening and Group Repetition (Books shut)
(f) Reading Aloud: Chorus and Individual (Books open)

● **Graded Comprehension Questions**

(a) Yes/No Tag Answers: did/will/do/are.

TEACHER: Did the children ask for more money?
PUPIL: Yes, they did.
TEACHER: Did they get it?
PUPIL: No, they didn't. etc.

(b) Tag Rejoinders: affirmative/negative; negative/affirmative. Make affirmative and negative statements to elicit tag rejoinders.

TEACHER: They asked for more money.
PUPIL: They did, didn't they?
TEACHER: They didn't get any more money.
PUPIL: They didn't, did they? etc.

(c) Questions with Who: did/are/won't/aren't.

TEACHER: Who asked for more money?
PUPIL: The children did. etc.

(d) Double Questions.

TEACHER: Did the children ask for less money or for more money?
PUPIL: They didn't ask for less money. They asked for more money. etc.

(e) General Questions: What and Why.

TEACHER: What didn't work?
PUPIL: The protest-march. etc.

(f) Asking questions in pairs: What and Why.

TEACHER: Ask me if the protest-march worked.
PUPIL: Did the protest-march work?
TEACHER: Why didn't . . .
PUPIL: Why didn't the protest-march work? etc.

● **Acting the Scene**

Invite four pupils to come to the front of the class to act the scene.

● **Unprepared Reading**

Professor Boffin's Umbrella, page 22, captions 1 and 2.

● **Activity**

(a) Song: I love sixpence. See page 252 for music. Teach the first verse of this song.
(b) Rhyme: Solomon Grundy. Repeat this rhyme. (See Lesson 39.)

● **Writing**

Workbook 3a, Lesson 41.

Guided Composition. The correct answer reads: The protest-march didn't work. Sandy and Sue spoke to father again. They asked for a rise. Father didn't give them a rise. Later that evening mother said to father, "You won't give them more pocket-money, so they're both angry with you, Jim." Sandy and Sue didn't do their homework. They were on strike!

53 Words

Lesson 42

- **Spelling Drill:** Books shut.

  Oral and Written
  cries/hurries/trees/donkeys; tries/knees/studies/
  keys; sees/flies/monkeys/nationalities.

- **Phonic Practice:** Sounds and Spellings: Books
  open.

  The letters t [t] and th [θ]
  Chorus and Group Repetition

- **Reading and Repetition Drill:** Books open.

  Chorus and Group Repetition
  The captions beneath the pictures should be
  repeated. Point out that we must use *more/most/
  less/least* to compare adjectives of more than
  two syllables. All the longer adjectives the pupils
  have learnt so far have been collected together
  in Lesson 42 of the Pupil's Book.

  TEACHER: *The 1st picture.*
  Doreen's an actress. *All together!*
  She's beautiful. *All together!* etc.

- **Pattern Drill:** Books open.

  (a) To elicit: It's the most (beautiful) story I've
  ever read.

  TEACHER: How did you find the story?
  Wasn't it beautiful?
  PUPIL: It's the most beautiful story I've
  ever read.

  Substitute: interesting, unusual, wonderful,
  difficult.

  (b) To elicit: Yes, she's the most (beautiful)
  person I've ever met.

  TEACHER: How did you find her? Wasn't
  she beautiful?
  PUPIL: Yes, she's the most beautiful
  person I've ever met.

  Substitute: careful, careless, dangerous,
  difficult, famous, interesting, musical, reliable, unusual, well-behaved, wonderful.

  (c) To elicit: Yes, it's the most beautiful film
  I've ever seen.

  TEACHER: How did you find the film?
  Wasn't it beautiful?
  PUPIL: Yes, it's the most beautiful film
  I've ever seen.

  Substitute: interesting, modern, unusual,
  wonderful.

  (d) To elicit: It's the most (difficult) test I've
  ever done.

  TEACHER: How did you find the test?
  Wasn't it difficult?
  PUPIL: Yes, it's the most difficult test
  I've ever done.

Substitute: interesting, reliable, unusual,
wonderful.

(e) To elicit mixed superlatives. Explain to the
pupils that before answering they must
decide whether to use *most + adjective* or
-est.

TEACHER: How did you find (her)? Wasn't
(she) (beautiful)?
PUPIL: Yes, (she)'s the most (beautiful)
person I've ever met.
TEACHER: How did you find (him)? Wasn't
(he) (tall)?
PUPIL: Yes, (he)'s the (tallest) person
I've ever met.

Substitute: careful, neat, careless, greedy,
nice, well-behaved, fat, interesting, thin,
famous, short, musical, lazy, reliable, funny,
difficult, wonderful, good, bad, rich,
dangerous.

(f) To elicit: No, (it) isn't. (It)'s more (interesting).

TEACHER: My book's less interesting than
yours.
PUPIL: No, it isn't. It's more interesting.

Substitute: Simon's less well-behaved than
Tom; this test is less difficult than that one;
this floor is less slippery than that one;
my car is less reliable than yours; he's less
famous than his brother; he's less musical
than his sister; he's less careless than his
brother; it's less expensive than yours; it's
less modern than yours.

(g) To elicit: No, (it) isn't. (It)'s less
(interesting).

Conduct the drill in the way shown in (f)
above, reversing each statement.

- **Unprepared Reading**

  Professor Boffin's Umbrella, page 22, caption 3.

- **Activity**

  It's time for a story: Mr Blake's Car, page 260.
  Write the following words and expressions on
  the blackboard and explain them: *think so,
  garage petrol, air* (for tyres), *oil* (petroleum),
  *beach, competition, a long way from, rope, chain,
  broke down* (car). Now read the story to the
  class.

- **Writing**

  Workbook 3a, Lesson 42.

Lesson **42** More/Less/The most/The least

tin	thin		tree	three		seat	south		boat	bath

1st

Doreen's an actress.
She's beautiful

2nd

Veronica's an actress.
She's more beautiful
than Doreen.

3rd

Elizabeth's an actress.
She's the most beautiful
actress I have ever seen.

4th

Sandy's a schoolboy.
He's well-behaved.

5th

Tom's a schoolboy.
He's more well-behaved
than Sandy.

6th

Simon's a schoolboy.
He's the most well-behaved
boy I have ever met.

7th

This car's reliable.

8th

This car's less
reliable than the
first one.

9th

This is the least reliable
car I have ever driven.

10th

This story's
interesting.

11th

This story's less
interesting than the
first one.

12th

This is the least
interesting story I have
ever read.

More/Less/The Most/The least . . .
beautiful, careful, careless, dangerous, difficult, expensive, famous, interesting, modern, musical, reliable, slippery, unusual, well-behaved, wonderful.

Lesson **43** The strike is over

It snówed héavily lást Sáturday.
There was déep snów in the gárden.

1

Sándy and Súe got some spádes
from the shéd in the gárden.
They wánted to cléar the páth.

2

They bóth wórked véry hárd.
Sándy dug fáster than Súe,
but Súe wórked more cárefully.

3

Sóon the páth was cléar.
Fáther smíled háppily
at the chíldren.

4

"You've wórked véry wéll," he sáid.
"You've wórked véry chéerfully.
You've hélped me véry múch."

5

"I'm glád that
the stríke is óver.
I'm góing to gíve you
some éxtra pócket-móney,
because you've bóth éarned it!"

6

I love fourpence, jolly little fourpence,
I love fourpence better than my life,
I'll spend a penny of it, and I'll lend a penny of it,
And I'll take twopence home for my wife.

Lesson 43

Content and Basic Aims

PATTERNS AND STRUCTURAL WORDS	VOCABULARY			
	Nouns	*Adj.*	*Verbs*	*Adv.*
I'm glad that . . . *(Sandy) (dug) (faster/more quickly) than (Sue).* *(He dug) very (fast)/very (quickly)/very much* *(faster)/very much more (quickly).* *(Sandy) (dug/didn't dig) as (fast/quickly) as (Sue).*	path shed spade strike (= protest)	clear extra	dress earn whisper	cheerfully further

● **General Remarks**

Patterns involving the comparison of adverbs (regular and irregular forms) will be practised here.

● **Aural/Oral Procedure**

(a) Listening (Books shut)
(b) Listening and Understanding (Books open; pictures only)
(c) Listening (Books shut)
(d) Listening and Chorus Repetition (Books shut)
(e) Listening and Group Repetition (Books shut)
(f) Reading Aloud: Chorus and Individual (Books open)

● **Graded Comprehension Questions**

(a) Yes/No Tag Answers: did/was/have.

TEACHER: Did it rain last Saturday?
PUPIL: No, it didn't.
TEACHER: Did it snow heavily last Saturday?
PUPIL: Yes, it did. etc.

(b) Tag Rejoinders: affirmative/negative; negative/affirmative.

Make affirmative and negative statements to elicit tag rejoinders.

TEACHER: It snowed heavily last Saturday.
PUPIL: It did, didn't it?
TEACHER: It didn't rain last Saturday.
PUPIL: It didn't, did it? etc.

(c) Questions with Who: did/was/have.

TEACHER: Who got some spades from the shed?
PUPIL: Sandy and Sue did. etc.

(d) Double Questions.

TEACHER: Did it rain last Saturday, or did it snow?
PUPIL: It didn't rain last Saturday. It snowed. etc.

(e) General Questions: When, Where, Why, How.

TEACHER: When did it snow heavily?
PUPIL: Last Saturday. etc.

(f) Asking questions in pairs: When, Where, Why, How.

TEACHER: Ask me if it snowed last Saturday.
PUPIL: Did it snow last Saturday?
TEACHER: When . . .
PUPIL: When did it snow? etc.

● **Telling the Story**

Ask one or two pupils to tell the story by referring only to the pictures. The pupils should remain seated during this exercise.

● **Unprepared Reading**

Professor Boffin's Umbrella, page 23, captions 1 and 2.

● **Activity**

(a) Song. I love sixpence. See page 252 for music. Teach the next verse of this song.
(b) Rhyme: Solomon Grundy. Repeat this rhyme. (See Lesson 39.)
(c) Song. The more we are together. (See Lesson 35.)

● **Writing**

Workbook 3a, Lesson 43.

Guided Composition. The correct answer reads: It snowed heavily last Saturday. Sandy and Sue got some spades from the shed in the garden. They cleared the path. They worked very well. They worked cheerfully, too. They helped father very much. The strike was over. Father gave them some extra pocket-money. They both earned it.

48 Words

Lesson 44

- **Spelling Drill:** Books shut.

  Oral and Written
  term/bird/learn; certain/first/heard; her/skirt/
  early.

- **Phonic Practice:** Sounds and Spellings: Books open.

  The letters d [d] and th [θ]
  Chorus and Group Repetition

- **Reading and Repetition Drill:** Books open.

  Chorus and Group Repetition
  The captions beneath the pictures should be
  repeated. Point out to the pupils that they will
  now be comparing *actions,* not *people* and
  things. Adverbs compare in the same way as
  adjectives.

  TEACHER: *The 13th picture.*
  Sandy dug faster than Sue. *All
  together!* etc.

- **Pattern Drill:** Books open.

  (a) To elicit: (Sandy) (dug) (faster) than (Sue).

  TEACHER: *The 13th picture.*
  Who dug faster? Sandy or Sue?
  PUPIL: Sandy dug faster than Sue. etc.

  Note that 'Which' must be used in the 14th
  picture.

  (b) To elicit:
  Oh yes, (he dug) very (fast).
  Oh yes, (she danced) very (beautifully).

  TEACHER: *The 13th picture.*
  Did Sandy dig faster than Sue?
  PUPIL: Oh yes, he dug very fast.

  Note: 15th: very far; 16th: very much;
  17th: very well.

  TEACHER: *The 19th picture.*
  Did Sue dance more beautifully
  than Lillie?
  PUPIL: Oh yes, she danced very beautifully. etc.

  (c) To elicit: Oh yes, very much (faster)/more
  (beautifully).

  TEACHER: *The 13th picture.*
  Did Sandy dig faster than Sue?
  PUPIL: Oh yes, very much faster.
  TEACHER: *The 19th picture.*
  Did Sue dance more beautifully
  than Lillie?
  PUPIL: Oh yes, very much more beauti-
  fully. etc.

  (d) To elicit: (Sue) didn't (dig) as (fast)/
  (beautifully) as (Sandy).

  TEACHER: *The 13th picture.*
  Tell me about Sue.
  PUPIL: Sue didn't dig as fast as Sandy.
  TEACHER: *The 19th picture.*
  Tell me about Lillie.
  PUPIL: Lillie didn't dance as beautifully
  as Sue. etc.

  (e) To elicit: (Sandy) (dug) as (fast/beautifully)
  as (Sue).

  TEACHER: *The 13th picture*
  Tell me about Sandy and Sue.
  PUPIL: Sandy dug as fast as Sue.
  TEACHER: *The 19th picture.*
  Tell me about Sue and Lillie.
  PUPIL: Sue danced as beautifully as
  Lilly. etc.

- **Unprepared Reading**

  Professor Boffin's Umbrella, page 23, caption 3.
  New Word: *China.*

- **Activity**

  A Guessing Game: Tell me how . . .
  The teacher invites a pupil to the front of the
  class and hands him a piece of paper with an
  adverb written on it. Members of the class
  must guess the correct adverb in the following
  way:

TEACHER:	He's writing. Tell me how he's writing.
MEMBER OF CLASS	*(addressing pupil):* You're writing neatly.
PUPIL	*(consulting piece of paper):* No, I'm not.
MEMBER OF CLASS:	You're writing fast.
PUPIL:	Yes, I am.
MEMBER OF CLASS	*(addressing teacher):* He's writing fast.
TEACHER:	Good. Sit down A. Now you B.

  The following verbs and adverbs may be put
  together:
  (He's) writing: fast, well, beautifully, carefully,
  neatly.
  (The bird's) flying: fast, high, far, well,
  beautifully.
  (He's) speaking: fast, well, beautifully, politely,
  quietly, cleverly.
  (She's) dancing: fast, well, beautifully, cleverly,
  neatly.

- **Writing**

  Workbook 3a, Lesson 44.

Lesson 44   How do they compare?

<u>d</u>rink   <u>th</u>ink   <u>d</u>raw   <u>th</u>row   lou<u>d</u>   mou<u>th</u>   nee<u>d</u>   tee<u>th</u>

13th

Sandy dug faster
than Sue.

14th

The plane flew higher
than the glider.

15th

Tom climbed further
than Billy.

16th

Billy weighed more
than Tom.

17th

Sue played better
than Sandy.

18th

Sue studied harder
than Sandy.

19th

Sue danced
more beautifully
than Lillie.

20th

Sue wrote
more carefully
than Sandy.

21st

Sandy spoke
more politely
than Billy.

22nd

Sandy fought
more bravely
than Simon.

23rd

Sue dressed
more neatly
than Wendy.

24th

Sue whispered
more quietly
than Lillie.

25th

Father sang
more sweetly
than Mother

26th
Billy ate
more greedily
than Sandy.

27th
Liz skipped
more cleverly
than Lillie.

Lesson **45** Television Day: How an artist works

TV Commentary:

In our programme today, we want you to compare two
pictures. On the left, you can see some objects. Our artist
used these as a model. On the right, you can see a picture.
Our artist drew it for you. Did the artist copy the objects
exactly? Of course, not. The pictures are different from each
other. For instance, the bowl in the picture on the left isn't
the same shape as the one on the right. Artists often use real
people and real things as models, but they don't always copy
them exactly. Compare the two pictures carefully. There are
five more differences. Can you find them all?

I love twopence, jolly little twopence,
I love twopence better than my life,
I'll spend a penny of it, and I'll lend a penny of it,
And I'll take nothing home for my wife.

Content and Basic Aims

PATTERNS AND STRUCTURAL WORDS	VOCABULARY			
	Nouns		*Adj.*	*Expressions*
They use them as models. *They're the same (quality)/ different in (quality). The (suit/suits) on the left is/are the same as/different from the one/ones on the right. They're the same as/different from each other.*	artist (= painter) depth difference height length model	object (thing) quality record-player shape size swimming-pool width	bright different real wide	each other for instance

● **General Remarks**

Patterns involving the use of the adjectives *the same (as)* and *different (from)* in relation to quality, colour, size, shape, price, etc. are introduced here.

● **Aural/Oral Procedure**

(a) Listening (Books shut)
(b) Intensive Reading (Books open)
The passage should be played or read to the class in small units. During each pause, explain unfamiliar words. Rather than give direct explanations, try to elicit as much information as possible from the pupils.
(c) Listening (Books shut)
(d) Reading Aloud: Individual (Books open)

● **Graded Comprehension Questions**

(a) Yes/No Tag Answers: can/did/are/is/do.

TEACHER: Can you see some people on the left?
PUPIL: No, I can't.
TEACHER: Can you see some objects?
PUPIL: Yes, I can. etc.

(b) Tag Rejoinders: affirmative/negative; negative/affirmative. Make affirmative and negative statements to elicit tag rejoinders.

TEACHER: I can see some objects in the picture.
PUPIL: You can, can't you?
TEACHER: I can't see any people in the picture.
PUPIL: You can't, can you? etc.

(c) Double Questions.

TEACHER: Can you see any people or objects in the picture?
PUPIL: I can't see any people. I can see some objects.

(d) General Questions: What, How and Where.

TEACHER: What can you see in the picture?
PUPIL: (Some objects). etc.

(e) Asking questions in pairs: What, How, Where and Why.

TEACHER: Ask me if I can see any objects in the picture.
PUPIL: Can you see any objects in the picture?
TEACHER: What . . .
PUPIL: What can you see in the picture? etc.

● **Oral Composition**

Write the following notes on the blackboard:

Compare the two pictures.
On the left: objects: model.
On the right: a picture.
Did the artist copy exactly? No.
Pictures are different: for instance, bowls: shape.
Compare carefully: five differences.

Now ask one or two pupils to reconstruct the passage by referring to the notes.

● **Unprepared Reading**

Professor Boffin's Umbrella, page 24, captions 1 and 2.

● **Activity**

(a) Song: I love sixpence. See page 252 for music. Teach the next verse and repeat the song from the beginning.
(b) Repeat: Sing this grave and simple strain. (See Lesson 33.)

● **Writing**

Workbook 3a, Lesson 45.

Guided Composition. The correct answer reads: Our artist drew a picture. He used some objects as a model. He didn't copy the objects exactly. The two pictures are different from each other. For instance, the bowls aren't the same shape. Artists don't always copy their models exactly.

41 Words

Lesson 46

- **Spelling Drill:** Books shut.

  Oral and Written
  hear/heard; ear/early; dear/learn; year/wear; ears/pears.

- **Phonic Practice:** Sounds and Spellings: Books open.

  The letters th [θ] t [t] and d [d]
  Chorus and Group Repetition

- **Reading and Repetition Drill:** Books open.

  Chorus and Group Repetition

  TEACHER: *The 12th picture.*
  Those two suits are the same quality.
  All together!
  The 13th picture.
  Those two suits are different in quality. *All together!*

  Practice these patterns with each of the items given.

- **Pattern Drill:** Books open.

  (a) To elicit: They're the same (quality)/different in (quality).

  TEACHER: *The 12th picture.*
  How do those two suits compare?
  PUPIL: They're the same quality.
  TEACHER: *The 13th picture.*
  How do those two suits compare?
  PUPIL: They're different in quality. etc.

  (b) To elicit: The (suit) on the left is the same as/different from the one on the right.

  TEACHER: *The 12th picture.*
  How do those two suits compare?
  PUPIL: The suit on the left is the same as the one on the right.
  TEACHER: *The 13th picture.*
  How do those two suits compare?
  PUPIL: The suit on the left is different from the one on the right. etc.

  (c) To elicit: They're the same as/different from each other.

  TEACHER: *The 12th picture.*
  How do those two suits compare?
  PUPIL: They're the same as each other.
  TEACHER: *The 13th picture.*
  How do those two suits compare?
  PUPIL: They're different from each other. etc.

  (d) To elicit: The (suits) on the right are (better) than the ones on the left.

  TEACHER: *The 12th and 13th pictures.*
  How do the suits on the right differ from the ones on the left?
  PUPIL: The suits on the right are better than the ones on the left.
  TEACHER: *The 14th and the 15th pictures.*
  How do the marbles on the right differ from the ones on the left?
  PUPIL: The marbles on the right are brighter than the ones on the left. etc.

  (e) To elicit: The (suits) on the left are not as (good) as the ones on the right.

  TEACHER: *The 12th and 13th pictures.*
  How do the suits on the left compare with the ones on the right?
  PUPIL: The suits on the left are not as good as the ones on the right. etc.

- **Unprepared Reading**

  Professor Boffin's Umbrella, page 24, caption 3.

- **Activity**

  Dictation
  Dictate the following passage:

  Sándy and Súe/were véry húngry yésterday./They bóth áte a lót/but Sándy ate móre quíckly than Súe./"Dón't éat só gréedily,"/móther sáid./"Dó you wánt ány móre fóod?/There's plénty in the pót."/
  "Nó thánks,"/they ánswered./"We've bóth hád enóugh./We've éaten tóo múch/and we cán't móve."

- **Writing**

  Workbook 3a, Lesson 46.

Lesson **46**   The same (quality)
Different in (quality)
The same as each other
Different from each other

| th<u>in</u>   t<u>in</u>   <u>dr</u>ink | <u>th</u>ree   <u>tr</u>ee   <u>dr</u>aw | sou<u>th</u>   sea<u>t</u>   lou<u>d</u> |

The same	Different	The same	Different
12th	13th	14th	15th
suits/quality	better	marbles/colour	brighter
16th	17th	18th	19th
violins/size	bigger	sheds/shape	larger
20th	21st	22nd	23rd
record-players/price	more expensive	boys/weight	heavier
24th	25th	26th	27th
towers/height	higher	swimming-pools/length	longer
28th	29th	30th	31st
drawers/width	wider	holes/depth	deeper

Lesson **47**   Lots of coins, but no money!

Narrator: Sándy and Tóm bóth colléct
fóreign cóins.
Tóm has a góod colléction,
and só has Sándy.

Tom: Háve you gót any Méxican cóins, Sándy?
Sandy: Nó, I've gót nóne.
Tom: Néither have Í.

Tom: Háve you gót any Gérman cóins?
Sandy: Yés, I've gót twó.
Tom: Só have Í.

Tom: Áre yours the sáme?
Sandy: Nó, they're dífferent in síze
and dífferent in válue.

Sandy: I've got Frénch cóins, Gérman cóins,
Itálian cóins and Américan cóins.
But whát's the úse?

Sandy: I *néver* háve any Énglish cóins!
Tom: Néither have Í.
We've got lóts of cóins,
but nó móney!

I love nothing, jolly little nothing;
What can nothing buy for my wife?
I have nothing to spend and nothing to lend
And I love nothing better than my wife.

Content and Basic Aims

PATTERNS AND STRUCTURAL WORDS	VOCABULARY				
	Nouns	Adj.	Verb	Conj.	Expression
I've got/bought no (money/toys). I've got/bought none. I haven't got any (money) either. Neither have I. So have I.	coin collection value	foreign Mexican	collect	either neither	What's the use?

● **General Remarks**

Patterns involving the use of *any, no* and *none* in connection with familiar countable and uncountable nouns will be practised here. The use of *either, neither* and *so* in negative and affirmative responses with *have* will also be practised. Other auxiliary verbs will be practised in TU 29.

● **Aural/Oral Procedure**

(a) Listening (Books shut)
(b) Listening and Understanding (Books open; pictures only)
(c) Listening (Books shut)
(d) Listening and Chorus Repetition (Books shut)
(e) Listening and Group Repetition (Books shut)
(f) Reading Aloud: Chorus and Individual (Books open)

● **Graded Comprehension Questions**

(a) Yes/No Tag Answers: do/has/are/have.

TEACHER: Do Sandy and Tom both collect English coins?
PUPIL: No, they don't.
TEACHER: Do they both collect foreign coins?
PUPIL: Yes, they do. etc.

(b) Tag Rejoinders: affirmative/negative; negative/affirmative.

TEACHER: They both collect foreign coins.
PUPIL: They do, don't they?
TEACHER: They don't collect English coins.
PUPIL: They don't, do they? etc.

(c) Questions with Who: do/has/hasn't/doesn't.

TEACHER: Who collects foreign coins?
PUPIL: Sandy and Tom *do*. etc.

(d) Double Questions.

TEACHER: Do they collect English coins or foreign coins?
PUPIL: They don't collect English coins. They collect foreign coins. etc.

(e) General Questions: What and How.

TEACHER: What do Sandy and Tom collect?
PUPIL: Foreign coins. etc.

(f) Asking questions in pairs: What, Why, How.

TEACHER: Ask me if they collect foreign coins.
PUPIL: Do they collect foreign coins?
TEACHER: What . . .
PUPIL: What do they collect? etc.

● **Acting the scene**

Invite two pupils to come to the front of the class to act the scene. A few coins could serve as useful props. The Narrator's part (Frame 1) should be omitted.

● **Unprepared Reading**

Professor Boffin's Umbrella, page 25, captions 1 and 2.

● **Activity**

Song: Teach the final verse of 'I love sixpence'. See page 252 for music. Then repeat the complete song from the beginning. If necessary, explain the last line of the song: i.e. he loves his wife best of all.

● **Writing**

Workbook 3a, Lesson 47.

Guided Composition. The correct answer reads: Sandy and Tom both collect foreign coins. They've both got good collections. They haven't got any Mexican coins. They've got some German coins. Sandy and Tom have got some French, Italian and American coins, too. They never have any English coins. They've got lots of coins. They haven't got any money.

51 Words

Lesson 48

- **Spelling Drill:** Books shut.

  Oral and Written
  peach/hear/heard; ear/each/early; learn/reach/
  dear; wear/clean/year.

- **Phonic Practice:** Sounds and Spellings: Books open.

  The letters t [t] and s [s]
  Chorus and Group Repetition.

- **Reading and Repetition Drill:** Books open.

  Chorus and Group Repetition

  The captions beneath the pictures should be repeated. Point out that we can use *no* in place of *not . . . any*. We can never use a noun after *none*.

  TEACHER: *Number 3.*
  Have you got any money? *All together!* etc.

- **Pattern Drill:** Books open.

  Books will not be required during these exercises but may be kept open for reference purposes.

  (a) To elicit: I haven't got any (money). I've got no (money). I've got none.

    TEACHER: Have you got any money?
    PUPIL: I haven't got any money. I've got no money.
    I've got none.

  Substitute the selection of countable and uncountable nouns given in the Pupil's Book.

  (b) To elicit: I haven't got any (money) either.

    TEACHER: I haven't got any money.
    PUPIL: I haven't got any money either.

  Substitute the nouns given.

  (c) To elicit: Neither have I. I haven't got any (money) either.

    TEACHER: I haven't got any money.
    PUPIL: Neither have I. I haven't got any money either.

  Substitute the nouns given.

  (d) To elicit: So have I. I've got some (money) too.

    TEACHER: I've got some money.
    PUPIL: So have I. I've got some money too.

  Substitute the nouns given.

  (e) To elicit: I haven't (bought) any (sweets).
    I've (bought) no (sweets).
    I've (bought) none.

    TEACHER: Have you bought any sweets?
    PUPIL: I haven't bought any sweets.
    I've bought no sweets.
    I've bought none.

  Substitute the following: lent him any money; won any prizes; corrected any exercise-books; received any presents; earned any pocket-money; folded any paper; met any people; eaten any apples; read any books; made any mistakes; baked any cakes; noticed any strangers; told any stories; used any ink.

- **Unprepared Reading**

  Professor Boffin's Umbrella, page 25, caption 3.

- **Activity**

  It's time for a story: Gramophone Records, page 260. Write the following words on the blackboard and explain them: *old-fashioned classical* (music), *pop* (music). Now read the story to the class.

- **Writing**

  Workbook 3a, Lesson 48.

Lesson **48** Any Some No None

3

Have you got any money?

13

I haven't got any money.
I've got no money.
I've got none.

30

I haven't got any either.
Neither have I.

4

Have you got any toys?

14

I haven't got any toys.
I've got no toys.
I've got none.

40

I haven't got any either.
Neither have I.

5

Have you got any fruit?

15

I've got some.

50

So have I.

6

Have you got any model cars?

16

I've got some.

60

So have I.

Have you got any . . . ?/I haven't got any . . ./I've got no . . .
sandwiches, water, oranges, soap, tomatoes, paper, friends, news, tea, ideas, wood, buttons, rice, neighbours.

Lesson 49 Window-shopping is free

Narrator: Móther and Súe
are lóoking at a lóvely wíndow-displáy.
There are lóts of níce thíngs
in the shóp-window.

1

Mother: Hów múch is thát blóuse, Súe?
Sue: It's £1.50 pénce.
It's quíte chéap.
Mother: Yés, but it's póor quálity.

2

Mother: Hów múch does that fúnny hát cóst?
Sue: It cósts £3.18 pénce.
Mother: It's not tóo expénsive,
but I could néver wéar a hát like thát!

3

Sue: Lóok at that lóvely fúr cóat, múm.
Mother: It's béautiful, Súe.
It's máde of mínk.

4

Sue: But lóok at the príce.
It cósts £1250.
Mother: It's véry expénsive indéed!

5

Mother: We cán't affórd to go shópping, Súe.
Shópping's expénsive.
Sue: But wíndow-shópping is frée, múm!

6

Tongue-twister: Ducks and drakes

A duck
And a drake
And a ha'penny cake
And a penny to pay the old baker,
A hop and a scotch is another notch,
Slitherum, slatherum, take her.

Lesson 49

Content and Basic Aims

PATTERNS AND STRUCTURAL WORDS	VOCABULARY			
Shopping's expensive. *How much is it/are they . . . ? How much does it/do they cost? What did you pay for that/those . . . ? What's the price of that/those . . . ? It is/they are/it costs/they cost/I paid (£1.50/$2.95) (each)/for . . .*	*Nouns*		*Adj.*	*Expression*
	camera cent(s) dollar(s) mink pence	pound(s) (£) shop-window window-display window-shopping	free (no money)	(We) can't afford . . .
			Verbs	
			afford cost	

● **General Remarks**

Patterns involving the use of *How much/many* in connection with price are practised here. (Compare TU 26.) All prices are expressed in British and American decimal currency.

● **Aural/Oral Procedure**

(a) Listening (Books shut)
(b) Listening and Understanding (Books open; pictures only)
(c) Listening (Books shut)
(d) Listening and Chorus Repetition (Books shut)
(e) Listening and Group Repetition (Books shut)
(f) Reading Aloud: Chorus and Individual (Books open)

● **Graded Comprehension Questions**

(a) Yes/No Tag Answers: are/is/does/could/can.

   TEACHER: Are mother and Sue looking at a car?
   PUPIL: No, they aren't.
   TEACHER: Are they looking at a window-display?
   PUPIL: Yes, they are. etc.

(b) Tag Rejoinders.

   TEACHER: They're looking at a window-display.
   PUPIL: They are, aren't they?
   TEACHER: They aren't looking at a car.
   PUPIL: They aren't, are they? etc.

(c) Questions with Who, Which and What: are/is/does/couldn't/can't.

   TEACHER: Who is looking at the window-display?
   PUPIL: Mother and Sue *are*.

(d) Double Questions.

   TEACHER: Are they looking at a car, or at a window-display?

   PUPIL: They aren't . . . etc.

(e) General Questions: What, Where, How (much), Why.

   TEACHER: What are mother and Sue looking at? etc.

(f) Asking questions in pairs: What, Where, How (much), Why.

● **Acting the Scene**

Invite two pupils to come to the front of the class to act the scene. The objects mentioned in the window-display could be drawn on the blackboard and the pupils could face the blackboard while acting the scene. The Narrator's part (frame 1) should be omitted.

● **Unprepared Reading**

Professor Boffin's Umbrella, page 26, captions 1 and 2. New Word: *land* (vb.).

● **Activity**

Teach the tongue-twister, 'Ducks and Drakes', by getting the class to repeat it after you, first in chorus, then in groups. Once it has been learned, individual pupils should try to say it as quickly as possible.
   The game Ducks and Drakes involves making a flat stone skim across calm water. This is a very old English rhyme, each line of which represents the number of times the stone is made to leap out of the water (six in all).

● **Writing**

Workbook 3a, Lesson 49.

Guided Composition. The correct answer reads: Mother and Sue looked at a lovely window-display. First they looked at a cheap blouse. It was poor quality. Then they looked at a funny hat. It wasn't too expensive. After that they looked at a very expensive mink coat.
   "We can't afford to go shopping, Sue. Shopping's expensive," mother said.
   "But window-shopping is free, mum!" Sue answered.

58 Words

Lesson 50

- **Spelling Drill:** Books shut.

  Oral and Written
  sister; brother; mother; father; ladder; water; paper; baker; butcher; barber.
  Special attention should be paid to the -er [ə] endings.

- **Phonic Practice:** Sounds and Spellings: Books open.

  The letters k [k] and ck [k]
  Chorus and Group Repetition

- **Repetition Drill:** Books open.

  Chorus and Group Repetition

  TEACHER: *Number 6.*
  How much do those lollipops cost?
  All together!
  They cost one penny each. *All together!*
  They're very cheap indeed. *All together!*

  Practise these patterns with the items given. Use *that* in place of *those* with singular nouns.

- **Pattern Drill:** Books open.

  (a) To elicit: Look at that/those . . .
  How much is it/are they?
  It is/they are (one penny each).
  It's/they're (very cheap indeed).

  TEACHER: *Number 6.*
  1st PUPIL: Look at those lollipops. How much are they?
  2nd PUPIL: They're one penny each. They're very cheap indeed. etc.

  (b) To elicit: Look at that/those . . .
  How much does it/do they cost?
  It costs/they cost (one penny each).
  It's/they're (very cheap indeed).

  TEACHER: *Number 6.*
  1st PUPIL: Look at those lollipops. How much do they cost?
  2nd PUPIL: They cost one penny each. They're very cheap indeed. etc.

  (c) To elicit: How much do (those lollipops)/ does (that camera) cost?
  They cost/it costs (one penny each)

  TEACHER: *Number 6.*
  1st PUPIL: How much do those lollipops cost?
  2nd PUPIL: They cost one penny each. etc.

  (d) To elicit: How many pence/pounds/cents/ dollars do (those lollipops)/does (that camera) cost?
  They cost/it costs (one penny each).

  TEACHER: *Number 6.*
  1st PUPIL: How many pence do those lollipops cost?
  2nd PUPIL: They cost one penny each. etc.

  (e) To elicit: How much did you pay for (those lollipops)?
  I paid (one penny each).

  TEACHER: *Number 6.*
  1st PUPIL: How much did you pay for those lollipops?
  2nd PUPIL: I paid one penny each. etc.

  (f) To elicit: What's the price of (those lollipops)?
  The price is (one penny each).

  TEACHER: *Number 6.*
  1st PUPIL: What's the price of those lollipops?
  2nd PUPIL: The price is one penny each. etc.

- **Unprepared Reading**

  Professor Boffin's Umbrella, page 26, caption 3.
  New Word: *branch.*

- **Activity**

  A Guessing Game: How much is it?

  The teacher writes the price of an object (say, a bicycle) on a piece of paper and puts it in his pocket. He gives the class a clue about its price, telling them whether it is very expensive, very cheap, etc. All the members of the class then write a price on a piece of paper and read their guesses to the teacher, one by one. The pupil who comes nearest the teacher's price is the winner.

  TEACHER: How much is the bicycle in pounds and pence/dollars and cents? It's rather expensive. Write your answers on a piece of paper.
  The pupils write their answers.
  Now read your answers to me.
  How much is the bicycle, (Bob)?
  PUPIL: It's (£)28.40. etc.

- **Writing**

  Workbook 3a, Lesson 50.

Lesson **50**

How much is it/are they?
How much does it/do they cost?
How many pence/cents/pounds/
dollars does it cost?
How much did you pay for that/
those . . .?
What's the price of that/those . . .?

---

break   bri<u>ck</u>   loo<u>k</u>   lo<u>ck</u>er   li<u>ke</u>   ki<u>ck</u>   steak   sti<u>ck</u>

English Money

6

lollipops
1 penny each
very cheap indeed

16

model cars
25 pence each
cheap

60

camera
£1.50
fairly cheap

7

bicycle
£25.17
rather expensive

17

piano
£450
expensive

70

car
£2000
very expensive indeed

American Money

8

postcards
3 cents each
very cheap indeed

18

toy robots
25 cents each
cheap

80
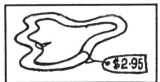
bicycle tube
$2.95
quite cheap

9

record-player
$180.50
rather expensive

19

van
$2500
expensive

90

house
$25,000
very expensive indeed

Lesson **51**   Sandy serves lunch

Narrator: It's Sándy's túrn
to sérve lúnch todáy.
He néver sérves véry wéll!

Billy: Hów many píeces of méat are there, Sándy?
Sandy: í, 2́, 3́, 4́, 5́, 6́, 7́, 8́, 9́, 1́0.
There are tén píeces in the dísh.
There are enóugh for tén péople.

Tom: Hów much máshed potáto is there, Sándy?
Sandy: There's quíte a lót.
The bówl's álmost fúll.
There's enóugh for tén péople.

Sandy: Whó wánts some móre?
Children: Í do! I do! Í do!

Sandy: Nów the dísh is álmost émpty.
There's hárdly ány méat for mé.
Billy: Ís there ány máshed potáto?
Sandy: Nó, there's nóne at áll.

Billy: Lét's give Sándy sóme of our fóod.
Sandy: Nów I've gót tóo múch!

Tongue-twister: A lame tame crane

My dame has a lame tame crane,
My dame has a crane that is lame,
Pray gentle Jane, let my dame's lame tame crane
Feed and come home again.

Content and Basic Aims

PATTERNS AND STRUCTURAL WORDS	VOCABULARY	
	Noun	*Adv.*
How much/many (mashed potato/sweets) is there/are there in that (bowl/jar)?		
There is/are a lot/plenty/quite a lot/only a little/only a few/hardly any/none at all.	dish	almost hardly
(Because) it's full/almost full/less than half full/almost empty/empty.	*Adj.*	*Verb*
There is/are enough for (ten people/ one person).	mashed (potato)	serve (food)

● **General Remarks**

Patterns involving the use of *How much/many* in connection with quantity are practised here. This unit further amplifies patterns which have previously been introduced. Compare Book 1, TU's 24 and 44 and Book 2, TU's 10, 11, 27.

● **Aural/Oral Procedure**

(a) Listening (Books shut)
(b) Listening and Understanding (Books open; pictures only)
(c) Listening (Books shut)
(d) Listening and Chorus Repetition (Books shut)
(e) Listening and Group Repetition (Books shut)
(f) Reading Aloud: Chorus and Individual (Books open)

● **Graded Comprehension Questions**

(a) Yes/No Tag Answers: is/does/are/do/has.

TEACHER: Is it Billy's turn to serve today?
PUPIL: No, it isn't.
TEACHER: Is it Sandy's turn to serve?
PUPIL: Yes it is. etc.

(b) Tag Rejoinders.

TEACHER: It's Sandy's turn to serve today.
PUPIL: It is, isn't it?
TEACHER: It isn't Billy's turn to serve today.
PUPIL: It isn't, is it? etc.

(c) Questions with Who: is/doesn't/do/hasn't.

TEACHER: Who is going to serve today?
PUPIL: Sandy is. etc.

(d) Double Questions.

TEACHER: Is it Billy's turn or Sandy's turn to serve today?
PUPIL: It isn't Billy's turn. It's Sandy's (turn).

(e) General Questions: Whose, How (many/ much), Why.

TEACHER: Whose turn is it to serve today?
PUPIL: (It's) Sandy's. etc.

(f) Asking questions in pairs: Whose, How (many/much), Why.

TEACHER: Ask me if it is Sandy's turn to serve today.
PUPIL: Is it Sandy's turn to serve today?
TEACHER: Whose . . .
PUPIL: Whose turn is it to serve today? etc.

● **Acting the Scene**

Invite about ten children to come to the front of the class to act the scene. The Narrator's part (frame 1) should be omitted.

● **Unprepared Reading**

Professor Boffin's Umbrella, page 27, captions 1 and 2.

● **Activity**

Teach the tongue-twister, 'A lame tame crane', by getting the class to repeat it after you, first in chorus, then in groups. Once it has been learned, individual pupils should try to say it as quickly as possible.

● **Writing**

Workbook 3a, Lesson 51.

Guided Composition. The correct answer reads: It was Sandy's turn to serve lunch yesterday. He usually serves very badly. There was enough meat and potato for ten people. Sandy served the children. Then he gave them some more. There wasn't enough food for Sandy.
"Let's give Sandy some of our food," Billy said.
All the children gave Sandy some of their food.
"Now I've got too much!" Sandy said.
63 Words

Lesson 52

- **Spelling Drill:** Books shut.

Oral and Written

driver; finger; stationer; bitter; shower; rubber; winter; locker; dinner; remember.
Special attention should again be paid to the -er [ə] endings.

- **Phonic Practice:** Sounds and Spellings: Books open.

The letters g [g] and k [k]
Chorus and Group Repetition

- **Repetition Drill:** Books open.

Chorus and Group Repetition

TEACHER: *The 1st picture.*
How much mashed potato is there in that bowl? *All together!*
There's a lot. *All together!*
The bowl's full. *All together!*
There's enough for 10 people. *All together!* etc.

Note that the pattern 'There's enough for . . .' will be omitted from the 5th, 10th, 15th and 20th frames.

- **Pattern Drill:** Books open.

(a) To elicit: How much (mashed potato)/many (sweets) is/are there in that (bowl)?
There is/are (a lot). The (bowl)'s (full).

TEACHER: *The 1st picture.*
1st PUPIL: How much mashed potato is there in that bowl?
2nd PUPIL: There's a lot. The bowl's full. etc.

(b) To elicit: There is/are plenty of (mashed potato/sweets).
There's enough for (10) people/1 person.

Elicit *plenty* throughout. Omit the 5th, 10th, 15th and 20th pictures.

TEACHER: *The 1st picture.*
Is there much mashed potato?
PUPIL: There's plenty of mashed potato.
There's enough for 10 people. etc.

(c) To elicit: There isn't aren't much/many (mashed potato/sweets). There isn't/aren't enough for (12) people/1 person.

Omit the 5th, 10th, 15th and 20th pictures.

TEACHER: *The 1st picture.*
Is there enough mashed potato for 12 people?
PUPIL: There isn't much mashed potato.
There isn't enough for 12 people. etc.

(d) To elicit: There's too little/there are too few (mashed potato/sweets). There isn't/aren't enough for (12) people/1 person.

Omit the 5th, 10th, 15th, and 20th pictures.

TEACHER: *The 1st picture.*
Is there enough mashed potato for 12 people?
PUPIL: There's too little mashed potato.
There isn't enough for 12 people. etc.

(e) To elicit: Because the (bowl)'s (full).

TEACHER: *The 1st picture.*
How do you know there's enough mashed potato for 10 people?
PUPIL: Because the bowl's full. etc.

Use *not enough for 1 person* in the 5th, 10th, 15th and 20th pictures.

- **Unprepared Reading**

Professor Boffin's Umbrella, page 27, caption 3.

- **Activity**

Dictation

√ Dictate the following passage:

"Hów múch/does your módel cár cóst, Sándy?"/Bílly ásked./
"It cósts 25 pénce,"/Sándy sáid./
"Lóok at míne,"/Bílly sáid./"It's the sáme síze as yóurs./Í can gíve you míne/and yóu can gíve me yóurs."/
"Nó, thánk you,"/Sándy sáid./"Théy're the sáme síze/but nót the sáme príce./Mý cár's máde of métal./Yóurs is ónly máde of plástic."

- **Writing**

Workbook 3a, Lesson 52.

Lesson 52   How much is there . . . ?
How many are there . . . ?
There's (a lot/enough for . . .)
There are (a lot/enough for . . .)
It's (full).

bi**g**   **k**itchen   do**g**   **k**ey   di**g**   **k**ite   ba**g**   ba**k**e

How much mashed potato is there in that bowl?

1st	2nd	3rd	4th	5th

a lot full	quite a lot almost full	only a little less than half full	hardly any almost empty	none at all empty
10 people	8 people	3 people	1 person	

How many sweets are there in that jar?

6th	7th	8th	9th	10th
a lot full	quite a lot almost full	only a few less than half full	hardly any almost empty	none at all empty
10 people	8 people	3 people	1 person	

How much toothpaste is there in that tube?

11th	12th	13th	14th	15th

a lot full	quite a lot almost full	only a little less than half full	hardly any almost empty	none at all empty
10 people	8 people	3 people	1 person	

How many biscuits are there in that tin?

16th	17th	18th	19th	20th

a lot full	quite a lot almost full	only a few less than half full	hardly any almost empty	none at all empty
10 people	8 people	3 people	1 person	

Lesson **53** A nice maths lesson

Narrator: The children in Sándy's cláss
enjóyed their máths lésson todáy.
They dídn't do any súms.
They pláyed a gáme.

Mrs Hart: Cóme to the frónt of the cláss, Sándy.
Stánd agáinst the wáll pléase.

Mrs Hart: Nów I'll pút a márk
agáinst the wáll
with a piece of chálk.

Mrs Hart: Hów táll is Sándy?
Guéss!
Wéll, Bílly?
Billy: He's óne métre
twénty céntimetres táll, Mŕs Hárt.

Mrs Hart: Whát's Sándy's héight?
Lét's méasure the dístance
from the flóor
to the márk on the wáll.

Mrs Hart: You were álmost ríght, Bílly.
Sándy's quíte táll.
He's óne métre twénty-twó
céntimetres táll.

Content and Basic Aims

PATTERNS AND STRUCTURAL WORDS	VOCABULARY			
How (tall) is that (boy)? *(He)'s quite (tall).* *(He)'s (1 metre 29 centimetres tall).* *(He)'s quite (a tall boy/tall).* *(He)'s about (1.29).*	*Nouns*			
	age Centigrade centimetre degree (temperature) distance front	gramme kilo(gramme) kilometre metre sum (maths)	right (cp. wrong) square	
			Verbs	*Adv.*
			guess measure	away
	Expressions		*Prep*	
	(kilometres) away degrees (centigrade)		about (= approx.) against (leaning)	

● **General Remarks**

Patterns involving the use of *How + adjective* are practised in connection with weights, measures, size, etc. Only metric units will be practised. This unit amplifies the *How + adverb* pattern introduced in Book 2, TU 40.

● **Aural/Oral Procedure**

As for Lesson 51.

● **Graded Comprehension Questions**

(a) Yes/No Tag Answers: did/will/is/was.

TEACHER: Did Sandy's class have a history lesson?
PUPIL: No, they didn't.
TEACHER: Did they have a maths lesson?
PUPIL: Yes, they did. etc.

(b) Tag Rejoinders.

TEACHER: Sandy's class had a maths lesson today.
PUPIL: They did, didn't they?
TEACHER: They didn't have a history lesson today.
PUPIL: They didn't, did they? etc.

(c) Questions with Whose and Who: did/will/is/does.

TEACHER: Whose class had a maths lesson today?
PUPIL: Sandy's did. etc.

(d) Double Questions.

TEACHER: Did Sandy's class have a history lesson or a maths lesson today?
PUPIL: They didn't have a history lesson today. They had a maths lesson. etc.

(e) General Questions: When, What, Where, How.

TEACHER: When did Sandy's class have a maths lesson?
PUPIL: Today. etc.

(f) Asking questions in pairs: When, What, Where, How.

TEACHER: Ask me if Sandy's class had a maths lesson today.
PUPIL: Did Sandy's class have a maths lesson today?
TEACHER: When . . . etc.

● **Acting the Scene**

The scene may be acted out in the normal way or played as a game. The Narrator's part (frame 1) should be omitted.

● **Unprepared Reading**

Professor Boffin's Umbrella, page 28, captions 1 and 2.

● **Activity**

Repeat the following tongue-twisters:

(a) Ducks and Drakes, Lesson 49.
(b) A lame tame crane. Lesson 51.

● **Writing**

Workbook 3a, Lesson 53.

Guided Composition. The correct answer reads: The children in Sandy's class had a maths lesson yesterday. They played games. Sandy stood against the wall at the front of the class. Mrs Hart put a mark against the wall. "How tall is Sandy?" she said. "Guess'!' Billy guessed first. Then Mrs Hart measured the distance. Billy was nearly right. Sandy is one metre, twenty-two centimetres tall.

59 Words

Lesson 54

- **Spelling Drill:** Books shut.

  Oral and Written

  hear/actor; dear/inspector; near/mirror; ear/motor; year/doctor.
  Special attention should be paid to the -*or* [ə] endings.

- **Phonic Practice:** Sounds and Spellings: Books open.

  The letters g [g] and c [k]
  Chorus and Group Repetition

- **Repetition Drill:** Books open.

  Chorus and Group Repetition

  TEACHER: *The 1st picture.*
  How tall is that boy? *All together!*
  He's quite tall. *All together!*
  What height is he? *All together!*
  He's 1 metre 29 centimetres tall. *All together!* etc.

- **Pattern Drill:** Books open.

  (a) To elicit: How (tall is that boy)?
  (He's) quite (tall).

  TEACHER: *The 1st picture.*
  1st PUPIL: How tall is that boy?
  2nd PUPIL: He's quite tall. etc.

  (b) To elicit: How (tall is that boy)?
  (He's) (1 metre 29 centimetres tall).

  TEACHER: *The 1st picture.*
  1st PUPIL: How tall is that boy?
  2nd PUPIL: He's 1 metre 29 centimetres tall. etc.

  Omit the 4th frame.

  (c) To elicit very short answers to questions beginning with *How*.

  TEACHER: *The 1st picture.*
  How tall is that boy?
  PUPIL: 1 (metre) 29 (centimetres).
  TEACHER: *The 2nd picture.*
  How high is that building?
  PUPIL: 50 metres. etc.

  Omit the 4th frame.

  (d) To elicit: What (height is that boy?)
  (He's 1 metre 29 centimetres tall).

  TEACHER: *The 1st picture.*
  1st PUPIL: What height is that boy?
  2nd PUPIL: He's 1 metre 29 centimetres tall. etc.

  (e) To elicit: (He's) quite a (tall boy).
  (He's) about (1 metre 29 centimetres tall).

  TEACHER: *The 1st picture.*
  Describe that boy.
  PUPIL: He's quite a tall boy.
  He's about 1 metre 29 centimetres tall. etc.

  Omit the 3rd, 10th, 11th, and 12th frames.

  (f) To elicit: (He's) quite (tall).
  (He's) about (1 metre 29 centimetres tall).

  TEACHER: *The 1st picture.*
  Tell me about the boy.
  PUPIL: He's quite tall.
  He's about 1 metre 29 centimetres tall. etc.

- **Unprepared Reading**

  Professor Boffin's Umbrella, page 28, caption 3.
  New Word: *back* (part of body).

- **Activity**

  It's time for a story: Mother and Sue Go Shopping, page 261. Write the following words and expressions on the blackboard and explain them: *choose/chose, get ready, (shoe) department, insisted, argument, I don't care.* Now read the story to the class.

- **Writing**

  Workbook 3a, Lesson 54.

Lesson 54 How (tall) is (that boy)?
What (height) is (he)?

<u>g</u>oal <u>c</u>oat <u>g</u>lass <u>c</u>lass <u>g</u>ame <u>c</u>ame e<u>gg</u>-<u>c</u>up

---

1st

How:
What:

tall — boy
quite tall
height — 1 metre
29 centimetres tall

2nd

high — building
quite high
height — 50 metres
high

3rd

big — shoes
quite big
size — size 40

4th

How:
What:

large — swimming-pool
quite large
shape — square

5th

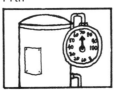

much — camera
quite cheap
price — £1.50

6th

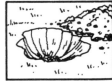

heavy — parcel
quite heavy
weight — 2 kilos 250
grammes

7th

How:
What:

long — path
quite long
length — 25 metres
long

8th

wide — shed
quite wide
width — 3 metres
wide

9th

deep — hole
quite deep
depth — 1 metre
deep

10th

How:
What:

old — girl
quite old
age — 12 years old

11th

hot — water
quite hot
temperature — 70
degrees Centigrade

12th

far — city
quite far
distance — 125
kilometres away

Lesson 55 Television Day: The search for oil

TV Commentary:

Almost everyone in the world uses oil in some way. Without oil, the world will stop, so men look for it everywhere. In our film today, you can see some oilmen. They are drilling for oil. They drill for oil in deserts, in mountains and under the sea. Quite often they find nothing, but the search for oil always continues. Oil is very important because none of our machines can run without it. Big ships carry oil everywhere. Perhaps the oil in your bicycle or in your father's car has come from somewhere far away. Perhaps it has come from Texas, Iraq, or Venezuela. Cars and bicycles need oil, but so do many other things. How many things can you name?

Sally in our alley

Of all the girls that are so smart there's none like pretty Sally,
She is the darling of my heart, and lives in our alley.
There is no lady in the land that's half so sweet as Sally,
She is the darling of my heart and lives in our alley.

Content and Basic Aims

PATTERNS AND STRUCTURAL WORDS	VOCABULARY		
Every/No/Any/Some Compounds. *Everyone's/everybody's (playing football).* *I didn't (see) anyone/anybody.* *I've already (bought) something.* *Have you (bought) anything?* *I (bought) nothing.* *Neither did I/So did I.* *I didn't (buy) anything either.*	*Nouns*		*Verbs*
	desert search Iraq ship oil Texas (petroleum) Venezuela oilman way (manner) sea		continue look for drill (bore) lose hide name
	Adj.		*Expressions* a machine runs (on oil) far away in some way
	important		

● **General Remarks**

Compounds of *every/no/any/some* will be practised here. The use of *either, neither* and *so* in negative and affirmative responses with *did* will also be practised. This unit amplifies patterns first introduced in TU 24. Compare also TU 29.

● **Aural/Oral Procedure**

(a) Listening (Books shut)
(b) Intensive Reading (Books open)
   The passage should be played or read to the class in small units. During each pause, explain unfamiliar words. Rather than give direct explanations, try to elicit as much information as possible from the pupils.
(c) Listening (Books shut)
(d) Reading Aloud: Individual (Books open)

● **Graded Comprehension Questions**

(a) Yes/No Tag Answers: does/will/do/can/are/has.

   TEACHER: Does almost everyone in the world use (coal)?
   PUPIL: No, *they don't.*
   TEACHER: Does everyone use oil?
   PUPIL: Yes, they do. etc.

(b) Tag Rejoinders.

   TEACHER: Everyone in the world uses oil.
   PUPIL: They do, don't they?
   TEACHER: They don't use coal.
   PUPIL: They don't, do they? etc.

(c) Double Questions.

   TEACHER: Does everyone in the world use coal or oil?
   PUPIL: They don't use coal. They use oil. etc.

(d) General Questions: Why, What, Where, How.

(e) Asking questions in pairs: Why, What, Where, How.

● **Oral Composition**

Write the following notes on the blackboard:

Everyone uses oil.
Without it, the world will stop—so men search.
Oilmen drill—deserts, mountains, under sea.
Sometimes find nothing.
Oil important: machines run on it.
Ships carry it everywhere.
Oil in bicycle, father's car—perhaps from Texas, Iraq, Venezuela.
Cars, bicycles need oil—name other things.

Now ask one or two pupils to reconstruct the passage by referring to the notes.

● **Unprepared Reading**

Professor Boffin's Umbrella, page 29, captions 1 and 2.

● **Activity**

Song: Sally in our alley. See page 253 for music. Teach the first verse of this song by getting the pupils to repeat it several times after you in chorus and in groups.

● **Writing**

Workbook 3a, Lesson 55.

Guided Composition. The correct answer reads: Almost everyone in the world uses oil in some way. Oilmen drill for oil in deserts, in mountains and under the sea. They don't always find it. They look for oil all the time. Oil is very important. None of our machines can run without it. Big ships carry oil everywhere. Oil comes from places like Texas, Iraq and Venezuela.

60 Words

Lesson 56

- **Spelling Drill:** Books shut.

  Oral and Written
  driver/hear/actor; dear/mother/inspector; near/rubber/mirror; motor/ear/barber; year/doctor/finger.
  Special attention should be paid to the -er/-or [ə] endings.

- **Phonic Practice:** Sounds and Spellings: Books open

  The letter c [k] and [s]
  Chorus and Group Repetition

- **Reading and Repetition Drill:** Books open.

  Chorus and Group Repetition
  The captions beneath the pictures should be repeated. Point out that we can use -body in place of -one in these compounds.

  TEACHER: *The 13th picture.*
  They're all singing. *All together!* etc.

- **Pattern Drill:** Books open.

  Books will not be required for the drills but may be kept open for reference purposes.

  (a) To elicit: Everyone's (playing football).

  TEACHER: They're all playing football.
  PUPIL: Everyone's playing football.

  Substitute: diving into the pool; talking; practising the piano; sailing across the lake; crying; clearing the table; correcting their mistakes; mending the car; sweeping the floor; planting flowers; whispering; dressing; crawling on the grass; looking for you.

  (b) To elicit: Everybody's (playing football).

  Conduct the drill in the way shown in (a) using the same substitutions.

  (c) To elicit: I didn't (see) anyone. I (saw) no one.

  TEACHER: Did you see anyone?
  PUPIL: I didn't see anyone. I saw no one.

  Substitute: talk to; tell; hear; find; get; show; ask; bring; call; notice; play with.

  (d) To elicit: I didn't (see) anybody. I (saw) nobody.

  Conduct the drill in the way shown in (c) above using the same substitutions.

  (e) To elicit: I've already (bought) something. Have you (bought) anything?

  TEACHER: Why don't you buy something?
  PUPIL: I've already bought something. Have you bought anything?

  Substitute: build; lend him; win; collect; earn; read; eat; draw; do; wash; spend; drink; bake; make.

  (f) To elicit: Yes, I (bought) something. So did I. I (bought) something, too.

  TEACHER: Did you buy anything?
  1st PUPIL: Yes, I bought something.
  2nd PUPIL: So did I. I bought something, too.

  Use the substitutions given in (e) above.

  (g) To elicit: No, I bought nothing. Neither did I. I didn't buy anything either.

  TEACHER: Did you buy anything?
  1st PUPIL: No, I bought nothing.
  2nd PUPIL: Neither did I. I didn't buy anything either.

  Use the substitutions given in (e) above.

- **Unprepared Reading**

  Professor Boffin's Umbrella, page 29, caption 3.

- **Activity**

  A Guessing Game: I spy with my little eye.

  A pupil is invited to come to the front of the class. He thinks of an object which is familiar to everybody (and is preferably in the classroom). Then he provides the first letter as a clue. Members of the class must guess the object. Anyone doing so is given a turn to come to the front.

  PUPIL: I spy with my little eye something beginning with 'p'.
  MEMBER OF CLASS: It's a pen.
  PUPIL: No, it isn't.
  MEMBER OF CLASS: It's a picture.
  PUPIL: Yes, it is.
  TEACHER: Good. Sit down A. Now you B.

- **Writing**

  Workbook 3a, Lesson 56.

Lesson 56 Every No Any Some

cold cinema cool city bicycle concert

Every	No/None	Any	Some
Everyone ⎤	No one ⎤	Anyone ⎤	Someone ⎤
Everybody ⎦	Nobody ⎦	Anybody ⎦	Somebody ⎦
Everything	Nothing	Anything	Something
Everywhere	Nowhere	Anywhere	Somewhere

People

13th

They're all singing.
Everyone is singing.
Everybody is singing.

16th

Knock at the door!
Is there anyone in?
Is there anybody in?

19th

There's no one in.
There's nobody in.

22nd

There's someone at the
window.
There's somebody at the
window.

Things

14th

The room's neat and tidy.
Everything is in its place.

17th

Is there anything in that box?

20th

The box is empty.
There's nothing in it.

23rd

There's something in
that box.
It's a Jack-in-the-box!

Places

15th

I lost my pen yesterday.
I looked for it everywhere.

18th

I couldn't find my pen
anywhere.

21st

Where did you go yesterday?
Nowhere. I stayed here.

24th

They're hiding somewhere.
They're under the bed.

Lesson **57** Copycat!

Sandy:	Whát are you dóing, Súe?	1
Sue:	I'm cómbing my háir.	
Sandy:	Só am Í.	

Sue:	I shán't cómb my háir ány móre.	2
Sandy:	Néither shall Í.	
Sue:	Stóp it, Sándy!	
	Cópycat!	

Mother:	Whý are you quárrelling, chíldren?	3
Sue:	It's Sándy, múm.	
	He's cópying me áll the tíme.	
Sandy:	Dón't tell táles!	

Sue:	I'm nót!	4
Sandy:	You áre!	

Sue:	Whére's my skípping-rópe?	5
	I'm góing to skíp in the gárden.	
Sandy:	Só am Í.	

Sue:	Sée! You *áre* cópying me!	6
Sandy (falling):	Óuch!	
Sue:	It sérves you ríght!	

Of all the days within the week I dearly love but one day,
And that's the day that comes between the Saturday and Monday,
For then I'm dressed in all my best to go to call on Sally,
She is the darling of my heart and lives in our alley.

Content and Basic Aims

PATTERNS AND STRUCTURAL WORDS	VOCABULARY	
I am/was/can/must/shall/do, too.	*Nouns*	*Expressions*
So am/was/can/must/shall/do I.		
I'm not/wasn't/can't/mustn't/shan't/	skipping-rope	all the time
don't either.	tale	any more (= any longer)
Neither am/was/can/must/shall/do I.		Copycat!
	Verbs	Don't tell tales.
		It serves you right.
	comb	See! (= I told you so)
	fall	Stop it.
	quarrel	

● **General Remarks**

Negative and affirmative responses involving the use of *either, neither, so* and *too* in connection with familiar auxiliary verbs will be practised in this unit. Compare TU's 24 and 29.

● **Aural/Oral Procedure**

(a) Listening (Books shut)
(b) Listening and Understanding (Books open; pictures only)
(c) Listening (Books shut)
(d) Listening and Chorus Repetition (Books shut)
(e) Listening and Group Repetition (Books shut)
(f) Reading Aloud: Chorus and Individual (Books open)

● **Graded Comprehension Questions**

(a) Yes/No Tag Answers: is/will/are/does.

TEACHER: Is Sue cleaning her teeth?
PUPIL: No, she isn't.
TEACHER: Is she combing her hair?
PUPIL: Yes, she is. etc.

(b) Tag Rejoinders.

TEACHER: Sue is combing her hair.
PUPIL: She is, isn't she?
TEACHER: She isn't cleaning her teeth.
PUPIL: She isn't, is she? etc.

(c) Questions with Who: is/won't/are/will/does.

TEACHER: Who is combing her hair?
PUPIL: Sue is. etc.

(d) Double Questions.

TEACHER: Is Sue cleaning her teeth, or combing her hair?
PUPIL: She isn't cleaning her teeth. She's combing her hair. etc.

(e) General Questions: What, Why, Where.

TEACHER: What is Sue doing?

PUPIL: She's combing her hair. etc.

(f) Asking questions in pairs: Why and Where.

TEACHER: Ask me if Sue is combing her hair.
PUPIL: Is Sue combing her hair?
TEACHER: Why . . .
PUPIL: Why is Sue combing her hair? etc.

● **Acting the Scene**

Invite three pupils to come to the front of the class to act the scene.

● **Unprepared Reading**

Professor Boffin's Umbrella, page 30, captions 1 and 2.

● **Activity**

Song: Sally in our alley. See page 253 for music. Teach the next verse. Explain 'in all my best', i.e. his best clothes.

● **Writing**

Workbook 3a, Lesson 57.

Guided Composition. The correct answer reads: Sue was angry with Sandy this morning. He was a copycat. The children quarrelled. "He's copying me all the time," Sue told mother. Sue skipped in the garden. Sandy copied her again. He fell down. He hurt himself. "It serves you right!" Sue said.

44 Words

Lesson 58

- **Spelling Drill:** Books shut.

  Oral and Written
  term/farmer/actor/horse; sister/certain/driver/
  fork; her/water/for/inspector.

- **Phonic Practice:** Sounds and Spellings: Books open.

  The letters c [k] and [s] and k [k]
  Chorus and Group Repetition

- **Reading and Repetition Drill:** Books open.

  Chorus and Group Repetition
  The captions beneath the pictures should be repeated.

  TEACHER: *The 25th picture.*
  I'm freezing. *All together!*
  I am, too. *All together!*
  So am I. *All together!* etc.

- **Pattern Drill:** Books open.

  Books will not be required for the drills but may be kept open for reference purposes.

  (a) To elicit: So am I/Neither am I.

  TEACHER: I'm tired.
  PUPIL: So am I.
  TEACHER: I'm not tired.
  PUPIL: Neither am I. etc.

  Substitute: polite; musical; brave; rich;
  poor; greedy; angry; untidy; unlucky;
  cross; wrong; right.

  (b) To elicit: So was I/Neither was I.

  Conduct the drill in the way shown in (a)
  above using the same substitutions.

  (c) To elicit: So can I/Neither can I.

  TEACHER: I can play the piano.
  PUPIL: So can I.
  TEACHER: I can't play the piano.
  PUPIL: Neither can I. etc.

  Substitute: dive into the pool; switch on the
  light; clear the table; deliver this parcel;
  mind the baby; unlock the door; sweep the
  floor; lift this weight; drill a hole; serve the
  food; measure you; hide under the bed.

  (d) To elicit: So must I/Neither must I.

  Conduct the drill in the way shown in (c)
  above using the same substitutions.

  (e) To elicit: So shall I/Neither shall I.

  Conduct the drill in the way shown in (d)
  above using the same substitutions.

  (f) To elicit: So do I/Neither do I.

  TEACHER: I feel sleepy.
  PUPIL: So do I. etc.

  TEACHER: I don't feel sleepy.
  PUPIL: Neither do I. etc.

  Substitute: like ice-cream; play football;
  need a haircut; run fast; understand English;
  remember him; weigh 35 kilos; know him;
  write very well; collect stamps; work hard;
  earn some money every week.

  (g) To elicit mixed responses of the types
  practised in (a) to (f). Make mixed statements using the same substitutions.

  TEACHER: I'm right.
  PUPIL: So am I.
  TEACHER: I don't remember him.
  PUPIL: Neither do I.
  TEACHER: I mustn't lift this weight.
  PUPIL: Neither must I. etc.

- **Unprepared Reading**

  Professor Boffin's Umbrella, page 30, caption 3.

- **Activity**

  Dictation
  Dictate the following passage:

  "Í've got some márbles,"/Sándy sáid./
  "Só have Í,"/Bílly ánswered./
  "Óur márbles/are the sáme síze and shápe,"/
  Sándy sáid./
  The twó bóys pláyed/and Billy won áll Sándy's
  márbles./Sándy went hóme./His bág was émpty./
  There was nóthing in it./He had lóts of márbles/
  an hóur agó/but nów he has nóne.

- **Writing**

  Workbook 3a, Lesson 58.

Lesson 58   I (am), too/So (am) I
I('m) not, either/Neither (am) I

<u>c</u>old   <u>k</u>itchen   <u>c</u>inema   <u>c</u>ool   <u>k</u>ey   <u>c</u>ity   <u>c</u>amera   <u>k</u>ite   <u>c</u>ement

Am and was

25th

I'm freezing.
I am, too. ⎱
So am I. ⎰

26th

I'm not ready.
I'm not, either. ⎱
Neither am I. ⎰

27th

I was upside-down.
I was, too. ⎱
So was I. ⎰

28th

I wasn't hurt.
I wasn't, either. ⎱
Neither was I. ⎰

Can and must

29th

I can play the piano.
I can, too. ⎱
So can I. ⎰

30th

I can't afford £10.
I can't, either. ⎱
Neither can I. ⎰

31st

I must drink this medicine.
I must, too. ⎱
So must I. ⎰

32nd

I mustn't play with matches.
I mustn't either. ⎱
Neither must I. ⎰

Shall and have

33rd

I shall go by bus.
I shall, too. ⎱
So shall I. ⎰

34th

I shan't go by train.
I shan't, either. ⎱
Neither shall I. ⎰

35th

I've got an egg.
I have, too. ⎱
So have I. ⎰

36th

I haven't got a plate.
I haven't, either. ⎱
Neither have I. ⎰

Do and did

37th

I feel sleepy.
I do, too ⎱
So do I. ⎰

38th

I don't like it.
I don't either. ⎱
Neither do I. ⎰

39th

I threw it away.
I did, too. ⎱
So did I. ⎰

40th

I didn't enjoy it.
I didn't, either. ⎱
Neither did I. ⎰

Lesson **59** Absent-minded

Narrator:	It's bréakfast tíme. Móther and the chíldren are háving bréakfast. Fáther's réading his néwspaper. He's véry ábsent-mínded!	1

Mother:	Wóuld you líke any tóast, déar?
Father:	Ḿm?
Mother:	Tóast, dear?
Father:	Ḿm?

2

Mother:	Wóuld you líke any téa déar?
Father:	Ḿm?
Mother (crossly):	Óh, Jím! You're nót lístening to mé!
Father:	Ḿm?

3

Mother:	Wóuld you líke any tóast, chíldren?
Sandy:	We'd lóve some, múm.
Mother:	Háve some bútter and mármalade, tóo.

4

(They have finished breakfast.)

Sue:	Thát was a lóvely bréakfast. Thánks, múm.

5

Father:	Have yóu fínished alréady? Í haven't had my bréakfast yét!
Mother:	I'm sórry, Jím. There's nóne léft.

6

My master and the neighbours all make fun of me and Sally,
And but for her I'd rather be a slave and row a galley,
But when my seven long years are up, Oh, then, I'll marry Sally,
And then how happily we'll live, but not in our alley.

Content and Basic Aims

PATTERNS AND STRUCTURAL WORDS	VOCABULARY			
I'd like some (soup). *Would you like any (soup)?* *Yes, please. I'd love some.* *(Is) there any (soup) left?* *Yes/No, there's some/none left.* *I'd like to have some (soup).*	*Nouns*	*Verb*	*Adj.*	*Expression*
	marmalade toast	love	absent-minded	Mm? (= What?)

- **General Remarks**

  Polite invitations involving the use of *Would* with *like/love* and familiar countable and uncountable nouns will be practised here. Compare TU's 9 and 11. Related patterns were first introduced in Book 1, TU's 46 and 48.

  Note that Link Reader 3, *Marley Castle,* will be required in Lesson 61.

  At the end of Lesson 60, the pupils should be set the Attainment Test which appears on the final pages of Workbook 3a. The teacher may set the 'Alternative or Supplementary Test' (see page 121) *instead of* or *in addition to* the Attainment Test in the Pupil's Workbook if he wishes to. For Mark Scales, see page 249.

- **Aural/Oral Procedure**

  As for Lesson 57.

- **Graded Comprehension Questions**

  (a) Yes/No Tag Answers: is/are/does/was/have.

  To elicit a subject followed by an auxiliary verb. Do not use *would.*

  TEACHER: Is it dinner time?
  PUPIL: No, it isn't.
  TEACHER: Is it breakfast time?
  PUPIL: Yes, it is. etc.

  (b) Tag Rejoinders.

  Make affirmative and negative statements to elicit tag rejoinders.

  TEACHER: It's breakfast time.
  PUPIL: It is, isn't it?
  TEACHER: It isn't dinner time.
  PUPIL: It isn't, is it? etc.

  (c) Questions with Who: are/is/isn't/would/hasn't.

  To elicit a subject followed by an auxiliary verb.

  TEACHER: Who is having breakfast?
  PUPIL: Mother and the children *are.*

  (d) Double Questions.

  To elicit negative and affirmative statements.

  TEACHER: Is it dinner time or breakfast time?
  PUPIL: It isn't dinner time. It's breakfast time. etc.

  (e) General Questions: What and Why.

  TEACHER: What are mother and the children doing?
  PUPIL: (They're) having breakfast. etc.

  (f) Asking questions in pairs: What and Why.

  TEACHER: Ask me if father's reading his newspaper.
  PUPIL: Is father reading his newspaper?
  TEACHER: What . . .
  PUPIL: What is father reading? etc.

- **Acting the Scene**

  Invite four pupils to come to the front of the class to act the scene. The Narrator's part (frame 1) should be omitted. Prompt the children as often as is necessary while they are acting their parts, though they should feel free to add words and phrases of their own if they wish to.

- **Unprepared Reading**

  Professor Boffin's Umbrella, page 31, captions 1 and 2.

- **Activity**

  Song: Sally in our alley. See page 253 for music. Teach the final verse and repeat the song from the beginning. Explain that the references to 'master' and 'seven long years' indicate that the boy is an apprentice.

- **Writing**

  Workbook 3a, Lesson 59.
  Guided Composition. The correct answer reads: Father didn't eat his breakfast this morning. He read his newspaper. Mother wanted to give him some toast and tea. Father didn't pay any attention to her. Mother was cross. She gave the children some toast, butter and marmalade. They enjoyed their breakfast. Then father wanted to have his breakfast. "There's none left," mother said.   55 Words

Lesson 60

- **Spelling Drill:** Books shut.

  Oral and Written
  pipe/tube; puppet/rubber; nippy/robber, back/
  packet.
  Ask individual pupils to spell these words
  orally. As soon as a word has been spelt correctly, write it on the blackboard. When all the
  words have been written, erase them. Then
  dictate them to the class.

- **Phonic Practice:** Sounds and Spellings: Books
  open.

  The letters f [f] and v [v]
  Chorus and Group Repetition
  Ask the pupils to repeat after you the words at
  the top of page 60 of the Pupils' Book.

- **Repetition Drill:** Books open.

  Chorus and Group Repetition

  TEACHER: *The 41st picture.*
  Would you like any soup? *All
  together!*
  Yes, please. I'd love some. *All
  together!*

  Practise these patterns with the items shown.

- **Pattern Drill:** Books open.

  Illustrate each exercise first by providing the
  stimulus and the response. Make sure the pupils
  really understand how they must respond.
  Then conduct the drills given below. If a child
  makes a mistake, correct him and ask him to
  repeat the right answer.

  (a) To elicit: I like (soup). Do you like (soup)?

     TEACHER: *The 41st picture.*
     PUPIL: I like soup. Do you like soup?
     etc.

  (b) To elicit: I want some (soup). Do you want
      any?

     TEACHER: *The 41st picture.*
     PUPIL: I want some soup. Do you want
     any? etc.

  (c) To elicit: I'd like some soup. Would you like
      any?

     Point out that these patterns mean exactly
     the same as those practised in (b) above
     with *want,* except that they are more polite.
     Illustrate on the blackboard the relationship
     between unelided and elided forms: I
     would = I'd.

     TEACHER: *The 41st picture.*
     PUPIL: I'd like some soup. Would you
     like any? etc.

  (d) To elicit: Would you like any (soup)? Yes,
      please. I'd love some.

     TEACHER: *The 41st picture.*
     1st PUPIL: Would you like any soup,
     (Bob)?
     2nd PUPIL: Yes, please. I'd love some. etc.

  (e) To elicit:
     Yes, there is/are some left.
     No, there is/are none left.
     Provide cues by nodding or shaking the
     head.

     TEACHER: *The 41st picture.*
     Is there any soup left? *(Nodding)*
     PUPIL: Yes, there's some left.
     TEACHER: *The 42nd picture.*
     Is there any rice left? *(Shaking
     head)*
     PUPIL: No, there's none left. etc.

  (f) To elicit: I'd love to have some soup. Is/are
      there any left?

     TEACHER: *The 41st picture.*
     PUPIL: I'd love to have some soup. Is
     there any left? etc.

- **Unprepared Reading**

  Professor Boffin's Umbrella, page 31, final
  caption.

- **Activity**

  It's time for a story: Timmy, page 262.

  Write the following words on the blackboard
  and explain them: *boiled* (egg), *burst, full*
  (replete), *fetched, tummy, pants, elastic.* Now
  read the story to the class.

- **Writing**

  Workbook 3a, Lesson 60.

Lesson 60 Would you like any . . . ? I'd love some.
Is there/Are there any left?
I'd love to have some . . .

| knife | knives | wife | wives | loaf | loaves | thief | thieves |

41st

soup

42nd

rice

43rd

JAM

jam

44th

MARMALADE

marmalade

45th

steak

46th

chicken

47th

gravy

48th

toast

49th

beans

50th

carrots

51st

lemons

52nd

pears

53rd

lollipops

54th

vegetables

55th

flowers

56th

eggs

Mid-Year Tests

General Remarks

The Attainment Test at the end of Workbook 3a may now be set. The test below may be given *instead of* or *in addition to* the test in the Workbook. Mark scales for the written tests appear on page 249.

Alternative or Supplementary Test

Guided Composition: Father helps mother

Read the story, then answer the questions:

Mother got up late yesterday. She washed and dressed. Then she went into the kitchen quickly. She was in a hurry. "It's late," she said. "Jim must go to work and the children must go to school. I must hurry."
   Then father came into the kitchen. He had his newspaper in his hand. "Don't hurry, Betty," he said. "I'll help you with the breakfast."
5   "Thanks, Jim," mother said. "You can make the toast."
   Father put two slices of bread in the toaster and switched it on. Then he began to read his newspaper. Soon the kitchen was full of smoke, but father didn't notice a thing!

Questions

Answer these questions in one paragraph. Do not use more than 60 words.

1   Did mother get up early or late yesterday?
2   Did she want to make breakfast for the family, or not?
3   Was she in a hurry, or not?
4   Who came into the kitchen then?
5   Did he say, "I'll help you" or "I can't help you"?
6   Did mother say, "You can make the tea" or "You can make the toast"?
7   Did father put some bread in the toaster, or not?
8   Did he begin to read his newspaper, or not?
9   What did he burn?
10   Did he notice anything, or not?

Multiple Choice Questions

Only *one* answer is right in each exercise. Put a circle round the correct letter: A, B, C, or D.

1   Father read his newspaper and
   A   didn't burn the toast.
   B   switched off the toaster.
   C   forgot about the toast.
   D   looked at the toaster.
2   I'll help you with the breakfast.
   . . . . help you with the breakfast?
   A   Do you want to   B   Do you want me to   C   I want you to   D   Do you want
3   The kitchen was full of smoke.
   There was . . . . smoke in the kitchen.
   A   no   B   a little   C   some   D   a lot of

Language Questions

A Look at this example. Then do the same.

> I want you to burn all this rubbish.
> *Would you burn all this rubbish for me please?*

1 I want you to start the engine.

....

2 I want you to mind the children.

....

3 I want you to clear the table.

....

B Look at these examples. Then do the same.

> The sentence is very easy. (copy)
> *That's why I was able to copy it.*
> The sentence is too difficult. (copy)
> *That's why I wasn't able to copy it.*

1 English is very easy. (learn)

....

2 The poem is too difficult. (remember)

....

3 This piece of music is too difficult. (practise)

....

4 This song is very easy. (sing)

....

C Look at this example. Then do the same.

> He couldn't lift the weight. (weak)
> *He was too weak to lift it. He wasn't able to lift it.*

1 He couldn't buy the car. (poor)

....

2 She couldn't win the prize. (ugly)

....

3 He couldn't play in the match. (ill)

....

4 She couldn't pass the test. (stupid)

....

D Look at these examples. Then do the same.

> Sue dug very fast. (Sandy)
> *Yes, but Sandy dug faster than Sue.*
> *He dug very much faster.*
> Lillie danced very beautifully. (Sue)
> *Yes, but Sue danced more beautifully than Lillie.*
> *She danced very much more beautifully.*

1 The glider flew very high. (The plane)

....

....

2 Billy spoke very politely. (Sandy)

....

....

3 Billy climbed very far. (Tom)

....

....

4 Sandy played very well. (Sue)

....

....

5 Sandy wrote very carefully. (Sue)

....

....

6 Sandy studied very hard. (Sue)

....

....

E Look at these examples. Then do the same.

> I haven't got enough butter.   *I've got too little.*
> I haven't got enough toys.   *I've got too few.*

1 I haven't got enough sugar. ....

2 I haven't got enough chocolate. ....

3 I haven't got enough chocolates. ....

4 I haven't got enough sweets. ....

F Look at these examples. Then do the same.

| Those holes are deep. (same) | They're the same depth. |
| Those holes are deep. (different) | They're different in depth. |

1 Those drawers are wide. (same) ....
2 Those towers are high. (different) ....
3 Those boys are heavy. (same) ....
4 Those pools are long. (different) ....
5 Those sheds are square. (same) ....

G Put in *something, anything* or *nothing*:

1 Did you buy any new clothes? No, I bought ....
2 You mustn't eat .... before lunch.
3 Did you lend him ....? No, I didn't.
4 There's .... in this drawer. It looks like a pencil.
5 I didn't find anything. I found ....

H Look at these examples. Then do the same.

| I'd love some soup. | There's none left. |
| I'd love some beans. | There are none left. |

1 I'd love some gravy. ....
2 I'd love some chicken. ....
3 I'd love some vegetables. ....
4 I'd love some carrots. ....
5 I'd love some jam. ....

I Look at this example. Then do the same.

lollipops/1 penny each/very cheap indeed
How much do those lollipops cost?
They cost 1 penny each. They're very cheap indeed.

1 house/$25,000/very expensive indeed

....

....

2 model cars/25 pence each/cheap

....

....

Lesson 61 Don't show off!

Narrator:	Sándy and Súe have néw róller-skátes, but they cán't skáte yét.
Sandy:	Lóok óut, Súe!
Sue:	Lóok óut, Sándy!
Both:	Óuch!

Sue:	Lóok! Hére cómes Álan Bláke! He's shówing óff as úsual.

Alan:	Há! Há! Cán't you skáte yét?
Sandy:	Nó, we cán't. Can yóu?
Alan:	Of cóurse, I cán. It's éasy!

Sue:	Wóuld you líke to bórrow my skátes?
Alan:	I'd lóve to.

Alan:	Now wátch mé. You must skáte like thís.

Alan:	Óuch!
Sue:	It sérves you ríght!
Sandy:	Shów-off!

I had a little nut-tree

I had a little nut-tree and nothing would it bear,
Except a silver nutmeg and a golden pear.
The King of Spain's daughter came to visit me,
And all for the sake of my little nut-tree;
I skipped over the water, I danced over the sea,
And all the birds in the air couldn't catch me.

Content and Basic Aims

PATTERNS AND STRUCTURAL WORDS	VOCABULARY		
	Nouns	*Expressions*	*Verbs*
Would you like to (win a prize)? *I'd like/love to (win a prize).* *I'd like (her) to (win a prize).* *Tell (her) not to (lose her handbag).* *I wouldn't like (her) to (lose her handbag).*	roller-skate(s) show off	as usual Ha! Ha! Here comes (Alan). show off (vb. & noun)	borrow show off skate

● **General Remarks**

Polite invitations involving the use of the infinitive after *would like* and *would love* are introduced here. Related patterns introduced earlier (Book 2, TU 59) are repeated.

Note that two new ancillary books will be commenced in this Unit: Link Reader 3, *Marley Castle*, and *Workbook 3b*.

● **Aural/Oral Procedure**

As for Lesson 59.

● **Graded Comprehension Questions**

(a) Yes/No Tag Answers: have/can/is/would/ must/does/did.

> TEACHER: Have Sandy and Sue got new bicycles?
> PUPIL: No, they haven't.
> TEACHER: Have they got new roller-skates?
> PUPIL: Yes, they have. etc.

(b) Tag Rejoinders.

> TEACHER: Sandy and Sue've got new roller-skates.
> PUPIL: They have, haven't they?
> TEACHER: They haven't got new bicycles.
> PUPIL: They haven't, have they? etc.

(c) Questions with Who: have/can't/is/would/ did.

> TEACHER: Who's got new roller-skates?
> PUPIL: Sandy and Sue have. etc.

(d) Double Questions.

> TEACHER: Have Sandy and Sue got new bicycles, or new roller-skates?
> PUPIL: They haven't got new bicycles. They've got new roller-skates.

(e) General Questions: What and Why.

> TEACHER: What've Sandy and Sue got?
> PUPIL: New roller-skates. etc.

(f) Asking questions in pairs: What and Why.

> TEACHER: Ask me if they've got new roller-skates.
> PUPIL: Have they got new roller-skates?
> TEACHER: What . . .
> PUPIL: What've they got? etc.

● **Acting the Scene**

Invite four pupils to come to the front of the class to act the scene. The Narrator's words (frame 1) should be omitted.

● **Unprepared Reading**

Link Reader 3: Marley Castle, page 1.

New Words: *exciting, adventures, notes* (= jottings), *cliffs, bay, steep, hotel, castle, iron, beginning.*
Write the new words on the blackboard and explain them. Ask one or two pupils to read.

● **Activity**

Song: I had a little nut-tree. See page 253 for music. Ask the pupils to repeat the new song several times after you in chorus.

● **Writing**

Workbook 3b, Lesson 61.

Workbook 3b contains thirty guided composition exercises which will train the pupils to write *compound* and *complex* sentences. Lessons 61–89 deal with compound sentences; Lessons 91–119 with *complex* sentences.

The pupils will work as before. They will again answer each question with a *complete sentence* and write their answers consecutively to make a *complete paragraph.* Now, however, they will often be required to answer two or three questions *in a single sentence* using the conjunction(s) given in brackets at the end of each series of questions.

The correct answer reads:

Sandy and Sue have got new roller-skates, *but* they can't skate yet. They tried to skate yesterday, *but* they both fell down. Alan Blake saw them *and* laughed. "I can skate. It's easy," he said. He borrowed Sue's skates *and* put them on. He couldn't skate *so* he fell down.

"It serves you right," Sue said.

"Show-off!" Sandy said.

60 Words

Lesson 62

- **Spelling Drill:** Books shut.

  Oral and Written
  to/do/dirty; try/dry/tidy; tap/dad/today; wet/ red/date.

- **Phonic Practice:** Sounds and Spellings: Books open.

  The letters v [v] and f [f]
  Chorus and Group Repetition

- **Reading and Repetition Drill:** Books open.

  Chorus and Group Repetition
  Pictures A–H only.

  TEACHER: *Picture A.*
  Would you like to win a prize? *All together!*
  I'd like to win a prize. *All together!*
  I'd love to win a prize. *All together!*
  etc.

- **Pattern Drill:** Books open.

  Pictures A–H only.

  (a) To elicit: I want to (win a prize). Would you like to (win a prize)?

  TEACHER: *Picture A.*
  PUPIL: I want to win a prize. Would you like to win a prize? etc.

  (b) To elicit: I'd like to (win a prize). Would you like to (win a prize)?

  Remind the pupils of the relationship between unelided and elided forms: I would = I'd.

  TEACHER: *Picture A.*
  PUPIL: I'd like to win a prize. Would you like to win a prize? etc.

  (c) To elicit: I'd love to (win a prize). Would you like to (win a prize)?

  Point out that we do not say 'Would you love to . . . ?'

  TEACHER: *Picture A.*
  PUPIL: I'd love to win a prize. Would you like to win a prize? etc.

  (d) To elicit: I'd like (her) to (win a prize). Would you like (her) to (win a prize)?

  TEACHER: *Picture A.*
  What would you like her to do?
  PUPIL: I'd like her to win a prize. Would you like her to win a prize? etc.

  Use object pronouns as indicated by pictures.

- **Reading and Repetition Drill:** Books open.

  Pictures I–P only.

TEACHER: *Picture I.*
Tell her not to lose her handbag.
I wouldn't like her to lose her handbag. etc.

Use object pronouns as indicated by pictures.

- **Pattern Drill:** Books open.

  Pictures I–P only.

  (a) To elicit: Tell (her) not to (lose her handbag). I don't want (her) to (lose her handbag).

  TEACHER: *Picture I.*
  PUPIL: Tell her not to lose her handbag. I don't want her to lose her handbag. etc.

  (b) To elicit: Tell (her) not to (lose her handbag). I wouldn't like (her) to (lose her handbag).

  TEACHER: *Picture I.*
  PUPIL: Tell her not to lose her handbag. I wouldn't like her to lose her handbag. etc.

  (c) To elicit: I don't want you to (lose your handbag).

  TEACHER: *Picture I.*
  PUPIL: I don't want you to lose your handbag. etc.

  (d) To elicit: I wouldn't like you to (lose your handbag).

  TEACHER: *Picture I.*
  PUPIL: I wouldn't like you to lose your handbag. etc.

- **Unprepared Reading**

  Marley Castle, page 2.

  New Words and Expressions: *reception* (desk), *parents, manager* (hotel), *choose, on display, plain and coloured* (cards).

- **Activity**

  A Guessing Game: I spy with my little eye.
  Play this game in the way suggested in Lesson 56.

- **Writing**

  Workbook 3b, Lesson 62.

Lesson **62** Like to

mo<u>ve</u> <u>far</u>   dri<u>ve</u> <u>fast</u>   lea<u>ve</u> <u>flat</u>   ha<u>ve</u> <u>fun</u>

Would you like to . . . ? I'd like to . . . I'd love to . . .

A
win a prize

B
burn this rubbish

C
mind the baby

D
become a doctor

E
receive lots of
presents on your
birthday

F
appear on TV

G
sit in the sun

H
sail round the
world

Tell (her) not to . . .   I don't want/wouldn't like (her) to . . .

I
lose her handbag

J
worry about it

K
drop the dishes

L
hide in the shed

M

lie on the wet
grass

N

whisper during
the lesson

O

forget his
umbrella

P

hurt himself

Lesson 63 The Customs

Narrator:	Mŕ Bláke has béen abróad. He has júst retúrned. He's góing thróugh the Cústoms.	1 
Customs Officer: *Mr Blake:*	Háve you got ánything to decláre, sír? Nó, I've got nóthing to decláre.	2 
Customs Officer: *Mr Blake:*	Wóuld you ópen this súitcase pléase, sír? Cértainly.	3 
Mr Blake: *Customs Officer:*	I've got some smáll présents for my chíldren and sómething for my wífe. Í sée.	4 
Customs Officer: *Mr Blake:* *Customs Officer:* *Mr Blake:*	You háven't gót a néw wátch or a néw cámera? Nó. Whát about thís cámera? It bélonged to my grándfather!	5 
Mr Blake: *Customs Officer:*	Máy I gó nów? Yés, of cóurse, sír. Thánk you véry múch.	6 

Content and Basic Aims

PATTERNS AND STRUCTURAL WORDS	VOCABULARY		
I've got nothing to (read)/(play) with. I want something to (read)/(play) with. Have you got (a book) (for me) to (read)? I want/I'd like (a book) to (read). I haven't got anything to (read). Have you got anything to (read)? I've got (a book) to (read). I don't know what to (read).	*Nouns*	*Verbs*	*Expression*
	bike brush cloth comb (the) customs customs officer job sand suitcase watch	declare dry return	I see (= I understand)
		Adv.	
		abroad certainly	

● **General Remarks**

Patterns involving the use of some/any/no compounds and the infinitive after *want, like* and *have got* will be practised here. Note the use of *with* after certain verbs.

● **Aural/Oral Procedure**

(a) Listening (Books shut)
(b) Listening and Understanding (Books open; pictures only)
(c) Listening (Books shut)
(d) Listening and Chorus Repetition (Books shut)
(e) Listening and Group Repetition (Books shut)
(f) Reading Aloud: Chorus and Individual (Books open)

● **Graded Comprehension Questions**

(a) Yes/No Tag Answers: has/is/will/did/may.

TEACHER: Has Mr Blake been to London?
PUPIL: No, he hasn't.
TEACHER: Has he been abroad?
PUPIL: Yes, he has. etc.

(b) Tag Rejoinders.

TEACHER: Mr Blake has been abroad.
PUPIL: He has, hasn't he?
TEACHER: He hasn't been to London.
PUPIL: He hasn't, has he? etc.

(c) Questions with Who: has/hasn't/is/will/ may.

TEACHER: Who has been abroad?
PUPIL: Mr Blake has. etc.

(d) Double Questions.

TEACHER: Has Mr Blake been to London or has he been abroad?
PUPIL: He hasn't been to London. He's been abroad. etc.

(e) General Questions: Where, What, Whose.

TEACHER: Where has Mr Blake been?
PUPIL: Abroad. etc.

(f) Asking questions in pairs: Where, What and Which.

TEACHER: Ask me if he's been abroad.
PUPIL: Has he been abroad?
TEACHER: Where . . .
PUPIL: Where has he been? etc.

● **Acting the Scene**

Invite two pupils to come to the front of the class to act the scene. The Narrator's part (frame 1) should be omitted. A case or a large bag would be a useful prop.

● **Unprepared Reading**

Marley Castle, page 3.
New Word: *life.*

● **Activity**

Repeat the following songs:

(a) I had a little nut tree. Lesson 61.
(b) Sally in our alley. Lessons 55–59.

● **Writing**

Workbook 3b, Lesson 63.

Guided Composition. The correct answer reads: Mr Blake came home from abroad *and* went through the Customs. He didn't have anything to declare, *but* he opened one of his cases for the Customs Officer. Mr Blake had some small presents, *but* he didn't have a new watch or a new camera. He had a very old camera, *so* he didn't pay any money to the Customs.
   "May I go now?" he asked.
   "Yes, of course, sir," the Customs Officer said.

74 Words

Lesson 64

- **Spelling Drill:** Books shut.

Oral and Written
counted; posted; visited; waited; folded; tasted; painted.

- **Phonic Practice:** Sounds and Spellings: Books open.

The letters v [v] and w [w]
Chorus and Group Repetition

- **Reading and Repetition Drill:** Books open.

Chorus and Group Repetition

TEACHER: *Picture G.*
  I've got nothing to read. *All together!*
  I want something to read. *All together!*
  Have you got a book for me to read? *All together!*

Practise these patterns with the items given.

- **Pattern Drill:** Books open.

(a) To elicit: No, I've got nothing to (read). I want something to (read).

  TEACHER: *Picture G.*
    Have you got anything to read?
  PUPIL: No, I've got nothing to read. I want something to read. etc.

(b) To elicit: No, I haven't. Have you got (a book) for me to (read)?

  TEACHER: *Picture G.*
    Have you got anything to read?
  PUPIL: No, I haven't. Have you got a book for me to read? etc.

(c) To elicit: I want (a book to read).

  TEACHER: *Picture G.*
    What do you want?
  PUPIL: I want a book to read. etc.

(d) To elicit: I'd like (a book to read).

  TEACHER: *Picture G.*
    What would you like?
  PUPIL: I'd like a book to read. etc.

(e) To elicit: I haven't got anything (to read). Have you got anything to (read)? Yes, I've got (a book to read).

  TEACHER: *Picture G.*
  1st PUPIL: I haven't got anything to read. Have you got anything to read?
  2nd PUPIL: Yes, I've got a book to read. etc.

(f) To elicit: I don't know what to (read).

  TEACHER: *Picture G.*
    What's the matter with you?
  PUPIL: I don't know what to read. etc.

- **Unprepared Reading**

Marley Castle, page 4.
New Words: *present, sold, all alone, haunted.*

- **Dictation**

Dictate the following passage:

  "I'm góing to sét the táble," móther sáid./
  "Wóuld you líke to hélp me pléase, Súe?/
  "Yés, múm," Súe sáid./
  "Bréakfast's réady," móther cálled./Sándy came in quíckly./He had some tóast and mármalade./Fáther came in láte./"I'd líke some tóast," he sáid./
  "There's nóne léft,"/móther ánswered./

- **Writing**

Workbook 3b, Lesson 64.

Lesson 64

I've got nothing to (read).
I want something to (read).
Have you got (a book) for me to (read)?

move w<u>o</u>man   dr<u>i</u>ve w<u>i</u>fe   lea<u>ve</u> week   sha<u>ve</u> way

G
book
to read

H
jobs
to do

I
milk
to drink

J
food
to eat

K
bike
to ride

L
pictures
to look at

M
money
to spend

N
dress
to wear

O
sand
to play with

P
pencil
to draw with

Q
fork
to eat with

R
comb
to comb my hair
with

S
cloth
to wash with

T
skipping-rope
to skip with

U
spade
to dig with

V
key
to unlock the door
with

W
knife
to cut with

X
pen
to write with

Y
brush
to paint with

Z
cloth
to dry the dishes
with

132

Lesson **65**   Television Day: Mozart

TV Commentary:

Would you like to be able to play a musical instrument really well? Who wouldn't! Perhaps you are learning to play an instrument now. Perhaps your mother tells you to practise— and perhaps you don't enjoy it! We'd all like to play easily and well. Mozart could. His parents never told him to practise. They couldn't stop him! Wolfgang Amadeus Mozart was born in 1756. He learnt to play the violin at the age of four. In his short life he wrote a tremendous amount of music. Everybody praised Mozart for his wonderful music, but nobody paid him any money. He got poorer and poorer and couldn't pay his bills. In the end he became ill and died. He was only 35 years old. He is one of the greatest musicians of all time.

Oh, dear! What can the matter be?

Oh, dear! What can the matter be?
Dear, dear! What can the matter be?
Oh, dear! What can the matter be?
Johnny's so long at the fair.

Lesson 65

Content and Basic Aims

PATTERNS AND STRUCTURAL WORDS	VOCABULARY			
	Nouns	*dj.*	*Verbs*	*Expressions*
He was born in (1756). *What (would you like) to do?* *(I)'d like/(I) want/hope/wish/need/* *(I) must remember/will try/began/* *learnt/forgot to (return by train).* *That's just what (I'd like) to do.*	amount astronaut life musician parent(s) sandcastle	tremendous	die get (= become) hope praise	in the end of all time Who wouldn't!

- **General Remarks**

The use of the infinitive after certain (mainly familiar) verbs will be practised here. This Unit amplifies the use of *like/love to* (TU's 31 and 32). Compare Book 1, TU 49.

- **Aural/Oral Procedure**

(a) Listening (Books shut)
(b) Intensive Reading (Books open)
The passage should be played or read to the class in small units. During each pause, explain unfamiliar words. Rather than give direct explanations, try to elicit as much information as possible from the pupils.
(c) Listening (Books shut)
(d) Reading Aloud: Individual (Books open)

- **Graded Comprehension Questions**

(a) Yes/No Tag Answers: would/am/does/do/could/did/was/is.

TEACHER: Would you like to be able to play a musical instrument really well?
PUPIL: (Yes, I would.) etc.

(b) Tag Rejoinders.

TEACHER: You'd like to play the piano.
PUPIL: I would, wouldn't I?
TEACHER: You wouldn't like to play the violin.
PUPIL: I wouldn't, would I? etc.

(c) General Questions: What, Why, When, How.

TEACHER: What are you learning to play?
PUPIL: (A musical instrument.) etc.

(d) Asking questions in pairs: What, Why, When.

TEACHER: Ask me if I would like to play a musical instrument.
PUPIL: Would you like to play a musical instrument?
TEACHER: What . . .
PUPIL: What would you like to play? etc.

- **Oral Composition**

Write the following notes on the blackboard:

Like to play?
Perhaps you are learning.
Practice: don't enjoy it.
Mozart: couldn't stop him.
Born 1756.
Learnt to play violin—age of 4.
Wrote a lot of music.
Everybody praised him—no money.
Poor—ill.
Died, 35 years old.

Now ask one or two pupils to reconstruct the passage by referring to the notes.

- **Unprepared Reading**

Marley Castle, page 5.

- New Words and Expressions: *ghost, marry, mysteriously, visitor, sign, Private! Keep Out!*

- **Activity**

Song: Oh, dear! What can the matter be? See page 253 for music. Ask the pupils to repeat the first verse several times after you in chorus.

- **Writing**

Workbook 3b, Lesson 65.

Guided Composition. The correct answer reads: Wolfgang Amadeus Mozart was born in 1756 *and* he learnt to play the violin at the age of four. He wrote a lot of music in his short life. He became very famous, *but* he didn't get much money. He got poorer and poorer *so* he couldn't pay his bills. In the end he became ill *and* died at the age of 35. He is one of the greatest musicians of all time.

73 Words

Lesson 66

- **Spelling Drill:** Books shut.

  Oral and Written
  listened; opened; cleaned; played; filled; shared; turned; answered; pulled; remembered; enjoyed.

- **Phonic Practice:** Sounds and Spellings: Book open.

  The letters v [v], f [f] and w [w]
  Chorus and Group Repetition

- **Reading and Repetition Drill:** Books open.

  Chorus and Group Repetition

  TEACHER: *Picture a.*
  What would you like to do? *All together!*
  I'd like to return home by train. *All together!*
  Picture b.
  What would you like to do? *All together!*
  I'd like to be an actor. *All together!*
  Picture c.
  What do you want to do?
  I want to see a film. *All together!*

  Vary the form of the questions to suit the tenses given.

- **Pattern Drill:** Books open.

  (a) To elicit:
  What (would you like) to do?
  I('d like) to (return home by train).

  TEACHER: *Picture a.*
  1st PUPIL: What would you like to do?
  2nd PUPIL: I'd like to return home by train. etc.

  (b) To elicit:
  What (would Sandy like) to do?
  (He'd like) to (return home by train).

  TEACHER: *Picture a.*
  1st PUPIL: What would Sandy like to do?
  2nd PUPIL: He'd like to return home by train. etc.

  (c) To elicit: That's just what I('d like) to do.

  TEACHER: *Picture a.*
  You'd like to return home by train, I suppose.
  PUPIL: That's just what I'd like to do. etc.

  (d) To elicit: That's just what (he'd like) to do.

  TEACHER: *Picture a.*
  Sandy would like to return by train, I suppose.
  PUPIL: That's just what he'd like to do. etc.

- **Unprepared Reading**

  Marley Castle, page 6.
  New Words: *wave* (vb.), *air.*

- **Activity**

  It's time for a story: New Roller-skates, page 263.

  Write the following words on the blackboard and explain them: *crash, no hands* (cycling), *tied.* Now read the story to the class.

- **Writing**

  Workbook 3b, Lesson 66.

Lesson 66 What (would you like) to do?

| <u>v</u>ery | <u>f</u>at | <u>wo</u>man | | <u>v</u>oice | <u>f</u>ood | <u>w</u>ood | | <u>v</u>illage | <u>f</u>ill | <u>w</u>ill |

Sandy: I'd like to . . .

a

return home
by train

b

be
an actor

Billy: I want to . . .

c

see
a film

d

buy
a new bike

Tom: I hope to . . .

e

collect
some coins

f

become
an astronaut

Sandy: I wish to . . .

g

earn
some money

h

see
your camera

Sandy: I need to . . .

i

have
a haircut

j

comb
my hair

Mr Blake: I must remember to . . .

k

declare
this watch

l

wake up
early

Sandy: I'll try to . . .

m

mend
this clock

n

build
a sandcastle

Mother: I began to . . .

o

sweep
the floor

p

dry
the dishes

Sue: I learnt to . . .

q

speak
German

r

play
the flute

Mother: I forgot to . . .

s

turn off
the tap

t

turn off
the electricity

Lesson **67** Green stripes

Narrator:	Sándy, Súe and Álan are góing to the párk.	1 
Sue: *Alan:*	Lét's pláy on the gráss. We're nót allówed to, Súe. Lóok at that sígn. It sáys: KÉEP ÓFF!	2 
Sandy: *Sue:*	Lét's féed the dúcks. We're nót allówed to. Lóok at that sígn. It sáys: DÓN'T FÉED THE DÚCKS!	3 
Alan: *Sandy:*	Lét's sít hére. We're nót allówed to. Lóok at that sígn. It sáys: WÉT PÁINT.	4 
Man in white suit:	Dón't sit thére, chíldren. Í sat thére a móment agó. I dídn't sée the sígn.	5 
Man in white suit:	And nów I've gót gréen strípes on my súit!	6 

He promised to buy me a bunch of blue ribbons,
He promised to buy me a bunch of blue ribbons,
He promised to buy me a bunch of blue ribbons,
To tie up my pretty brown hair. And it's
Oh, dear! What can the matter be? etc.

Content and Basic Aims

PATTERNS AND STRUCTURAL WORDS	VOCABULARY			
(I am) sure/certain/ready/afraid/glad/ happy/pleased/sorry/allowed/surprised to . . .	*Nouns*	*Adj.*	*Verb*	*Expressions*
	duck ice paint sign stripe(s)	allowed certain pleased sure surprised	feed	keep off (the grass) stay up (not go to bed) wet paint
			Prep.	
			till	

- **General Remarks**

The use of the infinitive after certain adjectives and adjectival past participles will be practised here. This is a further extension of the verbal pattern introduced in the previous Unit. Compare, also, the use of *able/unable* to in TU's 14 and 15.

- **Aural/Oral Procedure**

(a) Listening (Books shut)
(b) Listening and Understanding (Books open; pictures only)
(c) Listening (Books shut)
(d) Listening and Chorus Repetition (Books shut)
(e) Listening and Group Repetition (Books shut)
(f) Reading Aloud: Chorus and Individual (Books open)

- **Graded Comprehension Questions**

(a) Yes/No Tag Answers: are/does/did/has.

TEACHER: Are the children going to school?
PUPIL: No, they aren't.
TEACHER: Are the children going to the park?
PUPIL: Yes, they are. etc.

(b) Tag Rejoinders.

TEACHER: The children are going to the park.
PUPIL: They are, aren't they?
TEACHER: They aren't going to school.
PUPIL: They aren't, are they? etc.

(c) Questions with Who: are/do/mustn't/did/ didn't/has.

TEACHER: Who's going to the park.
PUPIL: The children *are*. etc.

(d) Double Questions.

TEACHER: Are the children going to school, or to the park?
PUPIL: They aren't going to school. They're going to the park. etc.

(e) General Questions: Where, Why, When and What.

TEACHER: Where are the children going?
PUPIL: To the park. etc.

(f) Asking questions in pairs: Where, Why, What and When.

TEACHER: Ask me if the children are going to the park.
PUPIL: Are the children going to the park?
TEACHER: Where . . .
PUPIL: Where are the children going? etc.

- **Acting the Scene**

Invite four pupils to come to the front of the class to act the scene. The Narrator's part (frame 1) should be omitted. The children could be asked to make some signs like those in the dialogue.

- **Unprepared Reading**

Marley Castle, page 7.

- **Activity**

Song: Oh, dear! What can the matter be? See page 253 for music. Teach the last verse.

- **Writing**

Workbook 3b, Lesson 67.

Guided Composition. The correct answer reads: Sandy, Sue and Alan went to the park yesterday, *but* they weren't allowed to play on the grass *or* feed the ducks. They wanted to sit on a seat, *but* they couldn't. A sign on the seat said: WET PAINT. A man in a white suit told the children not to sit on the seat. "I sat there a moment ago," he said. He had green stripes on his suit.

70 Words

Lesson 68

- **Spelling Drill:** Books shut.

  Oral and Written
  carried; hurried; tried; cried; copied; studied; dried; worried.

  Point out to the pupils that 'y' is preceded by a consonant and is therefore dropped and replaced by '-ied' in the past.

- **Phonic Practice:** Sounds and Spellings: Books open.

  The letters f [f] and p [p]
  Chorus and Group Repetition

- **Reading and Repetition Drill:** Books open.

  Chorus and Group Repetition

  TEACHER: *Picture g.*
         I'm sure to reach the bird's nest. *All together!*
        Picture h.
        I'm sure to fall. *All together!* etc.

- **Pattern Drill:** Books open.

  (a) To elicit: I'm (sure) to (reach the bird's nest).

      TEACHER: *Picture g.*
      PUPIL: I'm sure to reach the bird's nest. etc.

  (b) To elicit: I was (sure) to (reach the bird's nest).

      TEACHER: *Picture g.*
      PUPIL: I was sure to reach the bird's nest. etc.

  (c) To elicit: He is (sure) to (reach the bird's nest).

      TEACHER: *Picture g.*
               Tell me about Sandy.
      PUPIL: He is sure to reach the bird's nest. etc.

  (d) To elicit: He was (sure) to (reach the bird's nest).

      TEACHER: *Picture g.*
               Tell me about Sandy.
      PUPIL: He was sure to reach the bird's nest. etc.

  (e) To elicit: Is he (sure) to (reach the bird's nest)?

      TEACHER: *Picture g.*
      PUPIL: Is he sure to reach the bird's nest? etc.

  (f) To elicit: Was he (sure) to (reach the bird's nest)?

      TEACHER: *Picture g.*

PUPIL: Was he sure to reach the bird's nest? etc.

- **Unprepared Reading**

  Marley Castle, page 8.
  New Word: *inside*.

- **Activity**

  A Competition
  Class groups or teams will compete against each other. The teacher will give each group an *adjective + to* (any of those in Lesson 68). The groups will be given three minutes to compile a list of suitable verbs which can follow the adjective given to them. The pupils in each group may consult each other and make suggestions to the group leader who will write out the list. The group with the longest list of suitable verbs is the winner.

- **Writing**

  Workbook 3b, Lesson 68.

Lesson **68** I'm sure to/certain to/ready to . . .

<u>foo</u>t <u>pu</u>t	<u>fu</u>ll <u>pu</u>ll	ski<u>p</u> <u>fa</u>st	ca<u>p</u> <u>fi</u>ve

Sandy: I'm sure to . . .

g

reach
the bird's nest

h

fall

Alan: I'm certain to . . .

i

win
the raffle

j

miss
the bus

Sue: I'm ready to . . .

k

dive
into the water

l

leave

Sandy: I'm afraid to . . .

m

skate
on thin ice

n

climb
the fireman's
ladder

Father: I'm glad to . . .

o

hear it

p

meet you

Sandy: I'm happy to . . .

q

do
a job for you

r

run
an errand for you

Father: I'm pleased to . . .

s

meet you

t

be here

Sue: I'm sorry to . . .

u

disturb you

v

make
a noise

Sue: I'm allowed to . . .

w

stay up
till 9.0 o'clock

x

use
the telephone

Mother: I'm surprised to . . .

y

see you

z

hear it

Lesson 69 Wrong number

Sue:	Pút a cóin in the slót, Sándy, and díal our númber.	1
Sandy (dialling):	Áll ríght, Súe.	

Sandy:	Máy I spéak to Mŕs Clárk pléase?	2
Voice:	Mŕs Whó?	
Sandy:	Mŕs Clárk.	
Voice:	You've díalled the wróng númber.	

Sue:	Is thát múm, Sándy?	3
Sandy (hand over mouthpiece):	Nó, it's a lády. She sáys that I've díalled the wróng númber. She sóunds ráther cróss.	
Sue:	Sáy that you're sórry.	
Sandy:	I'm sórry.	

Sue:	Trý agáin and bé cáreful!	4
Sandy:	All right.	

Sandy:	Máy I spéak to Mŕs Clárk pléase?	5
Voice (crossly):	It's yóu again, ís it? You've dialled the wróng númber agáin!	
Sandy:	Sórry.	

Sue:	Whích númber did you díal, Sándy?	6
Sandy:	434–0278.	
Sue:	Dón't you knów that óur númber is 435–0278?	

Content and Basic Aims

PATTERNS AND STRUCTURAL WORDS	VOCABULARY		
	Noun	*Verbs*	*Expressions*
(Father) (thinks/has told me) that (he) is/has/can/must will . . . *I know/I don't know what (father) (thinks/has told you).*	mouthpiece (telephone)	believe dial (a number) lock promise	(Mrs) Who? telephone numbers: e.g. 435–0278 the wrong number

● **General Remarks**

Noun clauses in which no tense change is involved are introduced here; *that* is not omitted. Some of the verbs previously practised with the infinitive construction (TU 33) are reintroduced. Indirect questions after *know* (+what) are practised briefly. (Compare TU 32.)

● **Aural/Oral Procedure**

(a) Listening (Books shut)
(b) Listening and Understanding (Books open; pictures only)
(c) Listening (Books shut)
(d) Listening and Chorus Repetition (Books shut)
(e) Listening and Group Repetition (Books shut)
(f) Reading Aloud: Chorus and Individual (Books open)

● **Graded Comprehension Questions**

(a) Yes/No Tag Answers: is/will/has/does.

> TEACHER: Is Sue going to put a coin in the slot?
> PUPIL: No, she isn't.
> TEACHER: Is Sandy going to put a coin in the slot?
> PUPIL: Yes, she is. etc.

(b) Tag Rejoinders.

> TEACHER: Sandy is going to dial a number.
> PUPIL: He is, isn't he?
> TEACHER: Sue isn't going to dial a number.
> PUPIL: She isn't, is she? etc.

(c) Questions with Who: is/will/has/does.

> TEACHER: Who is going to put a coin in the slot?
> PUPIL: Sandy is. etc.

(d) Double Questions.

> TEACHER: Is Sue going to dial a number or is Sandy?
> PUPIL: Sue isn't going to dial a number. Sandy is. etc.

(e) General Questions: What, Who . . . to, Why, Which.

> TEACHER: What is Sandy going to put in the slot?
> PUPIL: A coin. etc.

(f) Asking questions in pairs: What, Who . . . to, Why, Which.

> TEACHER: Ask me if Sandy is going to put a coin in the slot.
> PUPIL: Is Sandy going to put a coin in the slot?
> TEACHER: What . . .
> PUPIL: What is Sandy going to put in the slot? etc.

● **Acting the Scene**

Invite three pupils to come to the front of the class to act the scene. Two toy telephones would be very useful props.

● **Unprepared Reading**

Marley Castle, page 9.

● **Activity**

Repeat:

(a) Oh, dear! What can the matter be? (Lessons 65 and 67).
(b) I had a little nut-tree. (Lesson 61).

● **Writing**

Workbook 3b, Lesson 69.

Guided Composition. The correct answer reads: Sandy and Sue wanted to telephone mother from a telephone-box. Sandy dialled a number *and* a lady answered the phone. It was the wrong number *and* Sandy said, "I'm sorry." Sandy dialled the wrong number again *and* the lady was very cross.
"Which number did you dial, Sandy?" Sue asked.
Sandy dialled 434–0278, *but* the right number is 435–0278.

59 Words

Lesson 70

- **Spelling Drill:** Books shut.

Oral and Written
looked; walked; knocked; washed; touched;
stopped; jumped; mixed; watched; worked.

Draw the pupils' attention to the difference
between pronunciation and spelling in these
past forms.

- **Phonic Practice:** Sounds and Spellings: Books
open.

The letters f [f] and ph [f]
Chorus and Group Repetition

- **Reading and Repetition Drill:** Books open.

Chorus and Group Repetition

TEACHER: *Picture 1.*
What does father think? *All together!*
He thinks that the food tastes awful.
All together!
Picture 3.
What has Sandy told you? *All
together!*
He has told me that he'll be able to
skate soon. *All together!* etc.

- **Pattern Drill:** Books open.

(a) To elicit: (Father thinks) that (the food
tastes awful).

TEACHER: *Picture 1.*
What does father think?
PUPIL: Father thinks that the food
tastes awful. etc.

(b) To elicit: I (think) that (the food tastes
awful). Elicit first person responses throughout.

TEACHER: *Picture 1.*
What do you think?
PUPIL: I think that the food tastes
awful. etc.

(c) To elicit: That (the food tastes awful).

TEACHER: *Picture 1.*
What does father think?
PUPIL: That the food tastes awful. etc.

(d) To elicit: I know what (father thinks).

TEACHER: *Picture 1.*
What does father think?
PUPIL: I know what father thinks. etc.

(e) To elicit: I don't know what (father thinks).

TEACHER: *Picture 1.*
What does father think?
PUPIL: I don't know what father thinks.
etc.

- **Unprepared Reading**

Marley Castle, page 10.
New Words and Expressions: *seized, arms*
(limbs), *screamed, gardener, rough, shook,
frightened, towards, shook his fist, once.*

- **Activity**

Dictation

Dictate the following passage:
"Whát will you trý to dó, Sándy?"/Súe
ásked.
"I'll trý to búild a sándcastle,"/Sándy
ánswered.
"Áre you allówed to pláy in the sánd?"/
"Yés, I ám."
"Háve you gót a spáde to díg with?"
"Yés, I háve."
Sándy búilt a lóvely cástle./Thén móther
sáid,/"Cóme in for téa now, Sándy,/and dón't
forgét to wásh your hánds."

- **Writing**

Workbook 3b, Lesson 70.

Lesson 70   He thinks that/He has told me that . . .

fine   photograph   traffic   telephone   finish   alphabet

Father thinks that . . .

1

the food tastes
awful

2

the music sounds
terrible

Sandy has told me that . . .

3

he'll be able
to skate soon

4

he'll put a coin in
the slot

Sue knows that . . .

5

she can take a
photo

6

she can lift this
suitcase

Mother has said that . . .

7

she has combed
her hair

8

she has fed
the ducks

Billy feels that

9

he has caught a
cold

10

he has got a
temperature

Alan has promised that

11

he won't show
off

12

he won't play
on the grass

Mrs Blake believes that

13

it's going to
rain

14

there's someone
at the door

Father has remembered that

15

his shirts are
at the cleaner's

16

it's his wife's
birthday

Mother hopes that

17

she hasn't lost
her handbag

18

father has taken
his umbrella

Father has forgotten that

19

he must lock
his car

20

he must get up
at 7.0 o'clock

144

Lesson 71 The ticket machine

Narrator: Sándy and Súe are at a ráilway-státion.
They wánt to búy their tíckets
from a tícket machíne.

Sandy: Whát must we dó, Súe?
Sue: We must put twó cóins in the slót.
Sandy: I'm glád
that I've got some smáll chánge.

Sandy: Whát must we dó nów?
Sue: Nów we must préss this bútton.
Lóok: it says, PRÉSS.

Sandy: I've préssed it,
but nóthing's háppening.
I'm súre
that the machíne's émpty.

Sandy bangs the machine.
Porter: You mústn't báng that machíne.
I'm súre
that it's émpty.

Sue: Nó, it ísn't.
Lóok! It's gíving us lóts of tíckets!

145

Lesson 71

Content and Basic Aims

PATTERNS AND STRUCTURAL WORDS	VOCABULARY		
	Nouns	*Verbs*	*Expression*
(Sandy)'s (sure) that (he will become a scientist). *What's (Sandy) (sure of)?* *I know what (Sandy)'s (sure of).* *I know why (Sandy)'s (sure).*	button (pushbutton) porter railway-station	bang press	small change

● **General Remarks**

Noun clauses in which no tense change is involved will be practised again; *that* is not omitted. Some of the adjectives previously introduced with the infinitive construction (TU 34) are reintroduced. Indirect questions after *know* (+what/why) are practised briefly. Note also the use of prepositions after adjectives and adjectival past participles.

● **Aural/Oral Procedure**

(a) Listening (Books shut)
(b) Listening and Understanding (Books open; pictures only)
(c) Listening (Books shut)
(d) Listening and Chorus Repetition (Books shut)
(e) Listening and Group Repetition (Books shut)
(f) Reading Aloud: Chorus and Individual (Books open)

● **Graded Comprehension Questions**

(a) Yes/No Tag Answers: are/do/must/has/is.

> TEACHER: Are the children at a bus-stop?
> PUPIL: No, they aren't.
> TEACHER: Are they at a railway-station?
> PUPIL: Yes, they are. etc.

(b) Tag Rejoinders.

> TEACHER: The children are at a railway-station.
> PUPIL: They are, aren't they?
> TEACHER: They aren't at a bus-stop.
> PUPIL: They aren't are they? etc.

(c) Questions with Who: are/do/has.

> TEACHER: Who is at the railway-station?
> PUPIL: The children *are*. etc.

(d) Double Questions.

> TEACHER: Are the children at a bus-stop. or at a railway-station?
> PUPIL: They aren't at a bus-stop. They're at a railway-station. etc.

(e) General Questions: Where, What and Why.

> TEACHER: Where are the children?
> PUPIL: At a railway-station. etc.

(f) Asking questions in pairs: Where, What and Why.

> TEACHER: Ask me if the children are at a railway-station.
> PUPIL: Are the children at a railway-station?
> TEACHER: Where . . .
> PUPIL: Where are the children? etc.

● **Acting the Scene**

Invite three pupils to come to the front of the class to act the scene.

● **Unprepared Reading**

Marley Castle, page 11.
New Words and Expressions: *dark, corridor, darkness, suit of armour, knight.*

● **Activity**

Repeat:
(a) Sally in our alley. (Lessons 55–59).
(b) I love sixpence. (Lessons 41–47).

● **Writing**

Workbook 3b, Lesson 71.

Guided Composition. The correct answer reads: Sandy and Sue were going to travel by train. They wanted to buy their tickets from a ticket machine. Sandy put two coins into the machine *and* pressed the button, *but* nothing happened. Sandy banged the machine *and* a porter spoke to him.

"You mustn't bang that machine," the porter said. "I'm sure that it's empty."

He was wrong. Lots of tickets came out of the machine.

67 Words

Lesson 72

- **Spelling Drill:** Books shut.

  Oral and Written
  pumped; picked; asked; helped; fixed; smoked;
  parked; passed; kicked; noticed.

  Draw the pupils' attention to the difference
  between pronunciation and spelling in these past
  forms.

- **Phonic Practice:** Sounds and Spellings: Books
  open.

  The letters th [ð] and [θ]
  Chorus and Group Repetition

- **Reading and Repetition Drill:** Books open.

  Chorus and Group Repetition

  TEACHER: *Picture 1.*
      What's Sandy sure of? *All together!*
      He's sure that he will become a
      scientist. *All together!* etc.

  Note that 'Why' must be used in Frames 15
  and 16.

- **Pattern Drill:** Books open.

  (a) To elicit: (Sandy)'s (sure) that (he will
  become a scientist).

      TEACHER: *Picture 1.*
          What's Sandy sure of?
      PUPIL: Sandy's sure that he will become
          a scientist. etc.

      Use 'Why' in Frames 15 and 16.

  (b) To elicit: I am (sure) that (I'll become a
  scientist).

      Elicit first person responses throughout.

      TEACHER: *Picture 1.*
          What are you sure of?
      PUPIL: I'm sure that I'll become a
          scientist. etc.

      Use 'Why' in Frames 15 and 16.

  (c) To elicit: What's (Sandy sure of)?
  Omit Frames 15 and 16.

      TEACHER: *Picture 1.*
          Sandy's sure that he will become
          a scientist.
      PUPIL: What's Sandy sure of? etc.

  (d) To elicit: Why is (he sure)?
  Point out that 'What . . . (of)?' = 'Why . . .?'

      TEACHER: *Picture 1.*
          Sandy's sure that he will become
          a scientist.
      PUPIL: Why is he sure? etc.

  (e) To elicit: I know what (he's sure of).
  Omit Frames 15 and 16.

      TEACHER: *Picture 1.*
          Sandy will become a scientist.
          He's sure of it.
      PUPIL: I know what he's sure of. etc.

  (f) To elicit: I know why (he's sure).

      TEACHER: *Picture 1.*
          Sandy will become a scientist.
          He's sure of it.
      PUPIL: I know why he's sure. etc.

- **Unprepared Reading**

  Marley Castle, page 12.
  New Words: *hall, narrow, means that* . . .

- **Activity**

  It's time for a story. At the Park, page 263.
  New Word: *keeper.* Explain the new word,
  then read the story to the class.

- **Writing**

  Workbook 3b, Lesson 72.

Lesson 72 He's sure that/He's certain that . . .

<u>th</u>at <u>th</u>ank   <u>th</u>en <u>th</u>in   <u>th</u>is <u>th</u>ief   <u>th</u>ey <u>th</u>rew

[Of] Sandy's sure that . . .

1

he will become a scientist

2

he won't become a musician

[Of] Father's certain that . . .

3

he knows best

4

he drives well

[Of] Sandy's afraid that . . .

5

he will lose all his marbles

6

he will miss the train

[About] Sue's glad that . . .

7

she has seen the sign

8

she has bought a gramophone record

[About] Alan's sorry that . . .

9

he has broken the mirror

10

he has had an accident

[About] Sue's happy that . . .

11

she has got new roller-skates

12

she has got a new skipping-rope

[At] Father's surprised that . . .

13

there's a hole in his pocket

14

there's a nest in his chimney

[−] Sue's lucky that . . .

15

she can swim across the river

16

she can buy a ticket for the concert

[About] Mother's pleased that . . .

17

the sun is shining

18

the holidays are over and the house is quiet

[About] Sandy's unhappy that . . .

19

he must remain in bed

20

he must drink his medicine

148

Lesson 73 Guess what!

Sue: Lóok, Sándy!
Múm's looking óut of the kítchen wíndow.
She's crýing.

Sandy: Póor múm!
Whát's the mátter with her, Súe?
Sue: Í'll go in and ásk her, Sándy.
Yóu wáit hére.

Sandy: Díd you ásk her, Súe?
Sue: Yés, I díd.
Guéss what she sáys!

Sandy: She sáys she's cút her fínger.
Sue: Nó! You're wróng.

Sandy: She sáys she féels sád.
Sue: Nó! You're wróng.

Sandy: Óh, Í give up.
Whát does she sáy, then?
Sue: She sáys she's péeling ónions!

Some folk do

Some folk like to sigh, some folk do, some folk do;
Some folk long to die, but that's not me nor you.

Long live the merry, merry heart
That laughs by night and day,
Like the Queen of Mirth,
No matter what some folk say.

Content and Basic Aims

PATTERNS AND STRUCTURAL WORDS	VOCABULARY	
	Noun	*Verbs*
You wait here. *(Father) (thinks/is sure/has told me) (the food tastes awful).* Guess what *(father) (thinks).*	onion	give up (= surrender) peel

- **General Remarks**

  Noun clauses in which no tense change is involved will be practised again; *that* will be omitted. Patterns with verbs (TU 35) and adjectives (TU 36) will be reintroduced here. Indirect questions after *guess* (+what) will be practised briefly.

- **Aural/Oral Procedure**

  (a) Listening (Books shut)
  (b) Listening and Understanding (Books open; pictures only)
  (c) Listening (Books shut)
  (d) Listening and Chorus Repetition (Books shut)
  (e) Listening and Group Repetition (Books shut)
  (f) Reading Aloud: Chorus and Individual (Books open)

- **Graded Comprehension Questions**

  (a) Yes/No Tag Answers: is/will/did/does/has.

  TEACHER: Is mum looking out of the bedroom window?
  PUPIL: No, she isn't.
  TEACHER: Is she looking out of the kitchen window?
  PUPIL: Yes, she is. etc.

  (b) Tag Rejoinders.

  TEACHER: Mother is looking out of the kitchen window.
  PUPIL: She is, isn't she?
  TEACHER: She isn't looking out of the bedroom window.
  PUPIL: She isn't, is she? etc.

  (c) Questions with Who: is/will/did/does.

  TEACHER: Who's looking out of the kitchen window?
  PUPIL: Mother is. etc.

  (d) Double Questions.

  TEACHER: Is mother looking out of the bedroom or the kitchen window?
  PUPIL: She isn't looking out of the bedroom window. She's looking out of the kitchen window. etc.

  (e) General Questions: Where, What, Why.

  TEACHER: Where's mother?
  PUPIL: In the kitchen. etc.

  (f) Asking questions in pairs: Where, What and Why.

  TEACHER: Ask me if mother is in the kitchen.
  PUPIL: Is mother in the kitchen?
  TEACHER: Where . . .
  PUPIL: Where is mother? etc.

- **Acting the Scene**

  Invite three pupils to come to the front of the class to act the scene. A real onion would be a useful prop.

- **Unprepared Reading**

  Marley Castle, page 13.
  New Words: *bright, end* (side), *steep.*

- **Activity**

  Song: Some folk do. See page 254 for music. Ask the pupils to repeat the first verse and chorus several times after you.

- **Writing**

  Workbook 3b, Lesson 73.

  Guided Composition. The correct answer reads: Sandy and Sue were in the garden *and* they saw mother at the kitchen window. "Look!" Sue said. "Mother's crying." Sue went into the kitchen, *but* Sandy waited in the garden. Then Sue returned. "Guess what mother says!" Sue said to Sandy. Sandy tried to guess, *but* he couldn't, *so* Sue told him. "She says she's peeling onions," Sue said.

  60 Words

Lesson 74

- **Spelling Drill:** Books shut.

  Oral and Written
  listened/carried/looked; pumped/hurried/open-
  ed; copied/helped/cleaned; played/watched/
  studied.
  Remind the pupils of the spelling rules given in
  Lessons 68, 70 and 72.

- **Phonic Practice:** Sounds and Spellings: Books
  open.

  The letters th [θ] and [ð]
  Chorus and Group Repetition

- **Reading and Repetition Drill:** Books open.

  Chorus and Group Repetition

  TEACHER: *Picture 1.*
  What does father think? *All together!*
  He thinks the food tastes awful. *All together!*

  Picture 2.
  What's Sandy sure of? *All together!*
  He's sure he will become a scientist. *All together!*

  Use 'Why' in Frame 16.

- **Pattern Drill:** Books open.

  (a) To elicit: (He thinks) that (the food tastes awful).

  TEACHER: *Picture 1.*
  What does father think?
  PUPIL: He thinks that the food tastes awful. etc.

  Use 'Why' in Frame 16. Make sure the word *that* is included in all the responses.

  (b) To elicit: (He thinks the food tastes awful).

  TEACHER: *Picture 1.*
  What does father think?
  PUPIL: He thinks the food tastes awful. etc.

  Use 'Why' in Frame 16. Make sure the word *that* is omitted in all the responses; point out that we usually omit this word.

  (c) To elicit: (I think the food tastes awful.)
  Elicit first person responses throughout.

  TEACHER: *Picture 1.*
  What do you think?
  PUPIL: I think the food tastes awful. etc.

  Use 'Why' in Frame 16. Make sure the word *that* is omitted.

  (d) To elicit: That (the food tastes awful).

  TEACHER: *Picture 1.*
  Guess what father thinks!

  PUPIL: That the food tastes awful. etc.

  Use 'Why' in Frame 16. The word *that* must be included.

  (e) To elicit: Guess what (father thinks).
  (The food tastes awful).

  TEACHER: *Picture 1.*
  1st PUPIL: Guess what father thinks!
  2nd PUPIL: The food tastes awful. etc.

  Omit Frame 16. The word *that* must be omitted.
  The pupils may need help with prepositions after adjectives.

- **Unprepared Reading**

  Marley Castle, page 14.
  New Words: *jacket, sleeves.*

- **Activity**

  A Guessing Game: Guess What!

  Two pupils leave the room taking a copy of the Pupils' Book with them. While outside, they choose one of the statements in Lesson 74. When the two pupils return, members of the class must guess which statement they have chosen.

  1st PUPIL — *(indicating 2nd Pupil who remains silent throughout)*: Guess what he says.
  MEMBER OF CLASS: He says the sun is shining.
  1st PUPIL: No, he doesn't.
  MEMBER OF CLASS: He says he won't show off.
  1st PUPIL: Yes, he does.
  TEACHER: Good. Sit down A and B. Now you C and D.

  Members of class should use 'say' throughout.

- **Writing**

  Workbook 3b, Lesson 74.

Lesson 74   He thinks he . . .
He's sure he . . .
He's told me he . . .

He thinks	He's sure	He's told me	He's certain
1	2	3	4
the food tastes awful	he will become a scientist	he'll be able to skate soon	he drives well

She knows	He's afraid	She's said	She's glad
5	6	7	8
she can lift the suitcase	he'll lose his marbles	she's combed her hair	she's seen the sign

He feels	He's sorry	He's promised	She's happy
9	10	11	12
he's caught a cold	he's broken the mirror	he won't show off	she's got new roller-skates

She believes	He's surprised	He's remembered	She's lucky
13	14	15	16

it's going to rain	there's a hole in his pocket	it's his wife's birthday	she can swim across the river

She hopes	She's pleased	He's forgotten	He's unhappy
17	18	19	20

she hasn't lost her handbag	the sun's shining	he must lock his car	he must remain in bed

Lesson 75 Television Day: Don't complain about arithmetic!

TV Commentary:

I'm sure some of you like arithmetic very much. Perhaps it's your favourite subject. But I'm certain some of you don't like it at all. Perhaps you do sums because you *have to* do them! Can you add DCCLXVII and CCLVI? A Roman child couldn't do this sum. He had to use a counting-board. But it is a simple sum really.

Here it is in Roman numbers:

$$\begin{array}{r} \text{DCCLXVII} \\ + \ \text{CCLVI} \\ \hline \end{array}$$

Answer: MXXIII

And here it is in Arabic numbers:

$$\begin{array}{r} 767 \\ + \ 256 \\ \hline \end{array}$$

Answer: 1023

Easy, isn't it? Who says arithmetic is difficult? We don't have to use Roman numbers and we must thank the Arabs for this. They gave the world simple numbers. So don't complain about arithmetic!

Some folk fear to smile, some folk do, some folk do;
Others laugh through guile, but that's not me nor you.

Long live, etc.

Content and Basic Aims

PATTERNS AND STRUCTURAL WORDS	VOCABULARY		
I have to/I've got to/Do you (really) have to/Have you (really) got to/I'll have to/Did you have to/I had to (add these figures).	*Nouns*	*Adj.*	*Verbs*
	Arab arithmetic counting-board figure (number) play table-cloth	Arabic Roman simple	add complain thank

- **General Remarks**

Statements and questions involving the use of *have to* and have *got to* are introduced here. These forms are compared with *must* which was first introduced in Book 2, TU's 17 and 18.

- **Aural/Oral Procedure**

(a) Listening (Books shut)
(b) Intensive Reading (Books open)
   The passage should be played or read to the class in small units. During each pause, explain unfamiliar words. Rather than give direct explanations, try to elicit as much information as possible from the pupils.
(c) Listening (Books shut)
(d) Reading Aloud: Individual (Books open)

- **Graded Comprehension Questions**

(a) Yes/No Tag Answers: do/is/can/could/did/must.

   TEACHER: Do you like arithmetic?
   PUPIL: Yes, I do/No, I don't. etc.

(b) Tag Rejoinders.

   TEACHER: You like (arithmetic).
   PUPIL: I do, don't I?
   TEACHER: You don't like (arithmetic).
   PUPIL: I don't, do I? etc.

(c) Double Questions.

   TEACHER: Do you like (arithmetic) or (history)?
   PUPIL: I don't like (arithmetic). I like (history). etc.

(d) General Questions: Which, Why, What, How.

   TEACHER: Which is your favourite subject?
   PUPIL: (Arithmetic). etc.

(e) Asking questions in pairs: Which, Why, What, Why.

   TEACHER: Ask me if I like arithmetic.
   PUPIL: Do you like arithmetic?
   TEACHER: Which subject . . .

PUPIL: Which subject do you like? etc.

- **Oral Composition**

Write the following notes on the blackboard:

Some of you like arithmetic.
Perhaps—favourite subject.
Some don't.
You *have to* do it.
Add DCCLXVII and CCLVI?
Roman child—counting-board.
Simple really.
Roman and Arabic numbers.
We must thank the Arabs.

Now ask one or two pupils to reconstruct the passage by referring to the notes. They may do this at the front of the class, using the blackboard to illustrate the difference between Roman and Arabic numerals.

- **Unprepared Reading**

Marley Castle, page 15.

- **Activity**

Song: Some folk do. See page 254 for music. Teach the next verse.

- **Writing**

Workbook 3b, Lesson 75.
Guided Composition. The correct answer reads: Some children like arithmetic very much, *but* other children don't like it at all. A Roman child couldn't add DCCLXVII and CCLVI. He had to use a counting-board. This sum looks easy in Arabic numbers. It looks like this: $767 + 256 = 1023$. We don't use Roman numbers now *and* we must thank the Arabs for this.
56 Words

Lesson 76

- **Spelling Drill:** Books shut.

  Oral and Written
  baked/left; ticket/helped; spent/washed;/touched/sent; skipped/seat; watched/packet.

- **Phonic Practice:** Sounds and Spellings: Books open.

  The letters s [z] and th [ð]
  Chorus and Group Repetition

- **Reading and Repetition Drill:** Books open.

  Chorus and Group Repetition

  TEACHER: *Picture 1.*
  I must add these figures. *All together!*
  I have to add these figures. *All together!*
  I've got to add these figures. *All together!*

  Repeat these patterns with the items given. Point out that all three statements carry the same meaning.

- **Pattern Drill:** Books open.

  (a) To elicit: I have to (add these figures).

  TEACHER: *Picture 1.*
  What must you do?
  PUPIL: I have to add these figures. etc.

  (b) To elicit: I've got to (add these figures).

  TEACHER: *Picture 1.*
  What must you do?
  PUPIL: I've got to add these figures. etc.

  (c) To elicit: Do you really have to (add these figures).

  TEACHER: *Picture 1.*
  I have to add these figures.
  PUPIL: Do you really have to add these figures? etc.

  (d) To elicit: Have you really got to (add these figures)?

  TEACHER: *Picture 1.*
  I've got to add these figures.
  PUPIL: Have you really got to add these figures? etc.

  (e) To elicit: I'll have to (add these figures).

  TEACHER: *Picture 1.*
  What'll you have to do?
  PUPIL: I'll have to add these figures. etc.

  (f) To elicit:
  Did you have to (add these figures)?
  Yes, I had to (add these figures).

  TEACHER: *Picture 1.*
  1st PUPIL: Did you have to add these figures.

2nd PUPIL: Yes, I had to add these figures. etc.

- **Unprepared Reading**

  Marley Castle, page 16.
  New Words: *chase, rumbling, thunder, footsteps, bump into.*

- **Activity**

  Dictation

  Dictate the following passage:

  Sándy is íll./The dóctor sáys/he must remáin in béd./The dóctor thínks/Sándy has cáught a cóld./Póor Sándy!/It's his bírthday, tóo!/Fáther has prómised/he will búy Sándy/a níce présent./He's súre Sándy will líke it.

- **Writing**

  Workbook 3b, Lesson 76.

Lesson 76

I must/have to/have got to/
will have to/had to . . .
Do you have to/Did you have to/
Have you got to . . . ?

---

lo<u>s</u>e   <u>th</u>ose   ri<u>s</u>e   <u>th</u>en   cars   <u>th</u>ese   ha<u>s</u>   <u>th</u>at

---

1

add these figures

2

dial 0240 again

3

peel these onions

4

guess the right answer

5

share these sweets

6

fold the table-cloth

7

lock the door

8

appear in a play

9

promise to be good

10

stop the traffic

11

buy a ball of string

12

get a hammer and some nails

13

have a meal at a restaurant

14

complain about the food

15

plant some flowers

Lesson 77 No litter!

Narrator:	Sándy and Súe are at the zóo. They are with their párents. They have júst had a pícnic lúnch.

Sandy: I dón't wánt to fínish this sándwich.
I'm fúll.
(He throws the sandwich away.)
Mother: You mústn't thrów it thére, Sándy!

Sue: You're nót allówed to
thrów lítter on the gráss.
Lóok at thát sígn.
It says, NÓ LÍTTER! PLÉASE BÉ TÍDY!

Mother: Pút it in that lítter-básket.
Sandy: It's tóo fár awáy, múm.
Mother: Lázybones!

Sue: It's áll ríght, Sándy.
You dón't háve to wálk
to the lítter-básket.
It isn't nécessary.

Sue: You néedn't thrów the sándwich awáy.
Gíve it to Júmbo, the élephant.
He lóves sándwiches!

Some folk fret and scold, some folk do, some folk do;
They'll soon be dead and cold, but that's not me nor you.

Long live, etc.

Content and Basic Aims

PATTERNS AND STRUCTURAL WORDS	VOCABULARY	
Don't/you mustn't/you're not allowed to (park here) because (it says 'No Parking'). Don't/you needn't/you don't have to/it isn't necessary to (take a taxi) because (a bus is coming).	*Nouns*	*Adj.*
	drum	necessary
	elephant	
	litter	*Expressions*
	litter-basket	
	picnic lunch	a long time
	taxi	I'm full (= I've had
	zoo	enough to eat)

● **General Remarks**

The use of *needn't/don't have to* indicating absence of necessity will be practised here. These forms are compared and contrasted with *mustn't* (it is forbidden) which was first introduced in Book 2, TU 18. The adjective + infinitive construction introduced previously (TU 34) will be practised again with *necessary* and *allowed.*

● **Aural/Oral Procedure**

(a) Listening (Books shut)
(b) Listening and Understanding (Books open; pictures only)
(c) Listening (Books shut)
(d) Listening and Chorus Repetition (Books shut)
(e) Listening and Group Repetition (Books shut)
(f) Reading Aloud: Chorus and Individual (Books open)

● **Graded Comprehension Questions**

(a) Yes/No Tag Answers: are/have/does/is/can/ will/need.

TEACHER: Are Sandy and Sue at the sea-side?
PUPIL: No, they aren't.
TEACHER: Are they at the zoo?
PUPIL: Yes, they are. etc.

(b) Tag Rejoinders.

TEACHER: Sandy and Sue are at the zoo.
PUPIL: They are, aren't they?
TEACHER: They aren't at the seaside.
PUPIL: They aren't, are they? etc.

(c) Questions with Who: are/have/doesn't/ mustn't/needn't/does.

TEACHER: Who's at the zoo?
PUPIL: Sandy and Sue *are.* etc.

(d) Double Questions.

TEACHER: Are Sandy and Sue at the seaside or at the zoo?

PUPIL: They aren't at the seaside. They're at the zoo. etc.

(e) General Questions: Where, Who . . . with, What, Why.

TEACHER: Where are Sandy and Sue?
PUPIL: At the zoo. etc.

(f) Asking questions in pairs: Where, Who, What and Why.

TEACHER: Ask me if they are at the zoo.
PUPIL: Are they at the zoo?
TEACHER: Where . . .
PUPIL: Where are they? etc.

● **Acting the Scene**

Invite five pupils to come to the front of the class to act the scene. One of them should take the part of the elephant.

● **Unprepared Reading**

Marley Castle, page 17.

● **Activity**

Song: Some folk do. See page 254 for music.

Teach the final verse of this song.

● **Writing**

Workbook 3b, Lesson 77.

Guided Composition. The correct answer reads: Sandy and Sue are at the zoo with their parents. Sandy is eating a sandwich, *but* he doesn't want to finish it, *so* he throws it away. His mother says he mustn't throw litter on the grass, *so* he picks it up, *but* he's too lazy to walk to the basket. Then an elephant appears *and* Sue tells Sandy he needn't throw the sandwich away. She tells him to give it to Jumbo. Jumbo loves sandwiches.

76 Words

Lesson 78

- **Spelling Drill:** Books shut.

  Oral and Written
  tin/drink/think; tree/draw/three; seat/loud/
  south; boat/need/teeth.

- **Phonic Practice:** Sounds and Spellings: Books open.

  The letters s [z] and th]θ]
  Chorus and Group Repetition

- **Reading and Repetition Drill:** Books open.

  Chorus and Group Repetition
  Pictures 1–6 only.

  TEACHER: *Picture 1.*
  Don't park here. *All together!*
  You mustn't park here. *All together!*
  You're not allowed to park here, *All together!*
  because it says 'No Parking'. *All together!* etc.

- **Pattern Drill:** Books open.

  Only Pictures 1–6 should be drilled.

  (a) To elicit: Don't (park here). You mustn't.

  TEACHER: *Picture 1.*
  PUPIL: Don't park here. You mustn't. etc.

  (b) To elicit: You mustn't (park here) because (it says 'No Parking').

  TEACHER: *Picture 1.*
  Why mustn't I park here?
  PUPIL: You mustn't park here because it says 'No Parking'. etc.

  (c) To elicit: You're not allowed to (park here) because (it says 'No Parking').

  TEACHER: *Picture 1.*
  Why aren't I allowed to park here?
  PUPIL: You're not allowed to park here because it says 'No Parking'. etc.

- **Reading and Repetition Drill**

  Pictures 7–12 only.

  TEACHER: *Picture 7.*
  Don't take a taxi. *All together!*
  You needn't take a taxi. *All together!*
  You don't have to take a taxi. *All together!*
  It isn't necessary to take a taxi, *All together!*
  because a bus is coming. *All together!* etc.

  Point out the difference between *mustn't* (you aren't allowed to) and *needn't* (it isn't necessary to).

- **Pattern Drill**

  Only Pictures 7–12 should be drilled.

  (a) To elicit: No, you needn't. It isn't necessary.

  TEACHER: *Picture 7.*
  Must I take a taxi?
  PUPIL: No, you needn't. It isn't necessary. etc.

  (b) To elicit: No, you don't have to. It isn't necessary.

  Conduct the drill in the way shown in (a) above.

  (c) To elicit: You needn't (take a taxi) because (a bus is coming).

  TEACHER: *Picture 7.*
  Why don't I have to take a taxi?
  PUPIL: You needn't take a taxi, because a bus is coming. etc.

  (d) To clicit: You don't have to (take a taxi) because (a bus is coming.)

  Conduct the drill in the way shown in (c) above.

  (e) To elicit: It isn't necessary to (take a taxi) because (a bus is coming).

  Conduct the drill in the way shown in (c) above.

- **Unprepared Reading**

  Marley Castle, page 18.
  New Words and Expressions: *spoke to himself, tapped (knocked), breath, accidentally, pushed over, crash.*

- **Activity**

  It's time for a story: The Pot of Stew, page 264. New Words: *look after, themselves, do the shopping, prepare, lines* (punishment), *stew, salt, tray, delicious, recipe.* Write the new words on the blackboard and explain them. Now read the story to the class.

- **Writing**

  Workbook 3b, Lesson 78.

Lesson **78** Mustn't and Needn't

Don't/You mustn't/You're not allowed to/because . . .

1	2	3

park here It says 'No Parking'.	play with matches They're dangerous.	bang that drum The baby's asleep.

4	5	6

talk in the library It says 'Silence'.	drink this medicine It says 'Poison'.	smoke here It says 'No Smoking'.

Don't/You needn't/You don't have to . . .
It isn't necessary to/because . . .

7	8	9

take a taxi A bus is coming.	buy a newspaper I've already bought one.	look for your pen I've already found it.

10	11	12

press the button I've already pressed it.	do the exercise again You haven't made any mistakes.	wait for me I'll be a long time.

Lesson 79   Mrs Dumpling's on a diet!

Narrator: Mrs Dúmpling
is Mrs Bláke's fríend.
She's háving téa with the Blákes.
Mrs Dúmpling's on a díet,
but she's véry fát.

Mrs Blake: Háve anóther sándwich,
Mrs Dúmpling.
Mrs Dumpling: Wéll, I shóuldn't réally.
I'm on a díet, you knów.
Óh, áll ríght, then.

Mrs Blake: Háve anóther bíscuit,
Mrs Dúmpling.
Mrs Dumpling: Wéll, I óughtn't to,
but I'll júst háve a líttle one.

Mrs Blake: Háve anóther slíce of cáke.
Mrs Dumpling: Nó, thánk you.
I shóuldn't.

Mrs Blake: Áre you súre?
Mrs Dumpling: Wéll, I'll júst háve a smáll slíce.
I óughtn't to, réally.
I've álready hád twó slíces.

Timmy: Nó, you háven't.
You've álready hád fíve.
I've cóunted them.
Mrs Blake: Tímmy!

Content and Basic Aims

PATTERNS AND STRUCTURAL WORDS	VOCABULARY		
	Noun	*Verbs*	*Expressions*
Yes, (he) should/ought to. *No, (he) shouldn't/oughtn't to.* *(I) should/ought to (clean my car),* *but (I) don't feel like it.* *Should (he) . . .? Ought (he) to . . .?* *What should (he)/ought (he) to do?*	diet	dust tidy empty mark (correct) repair	I don't feel like it. (I'm not in the mood for . . .) on a diet

● **General Remarks**

Should and *ought to* to express obligation and the failure to meet obligation are introduced here. They are contrasted briefly with *must/have to/have got to.* (TU 38)

● **Aural/Oral Procedure**

(a) Listening (Books shut)
(b) Listening and Understanding (Books open; pictures only)
(c) Listening (Books shut)
(d) Listening and Chorus Repetition (Books shut)
(e) Listening and Group Repetition (Books shut)
(f) Reading Aloud: Chorus and Individual (Books open)

● **Graded Comprehension Questions**

(a) Yes/No Tag Answers: is/should/ought/will/has.

To elicit a subject followed by an auxiliary verb. Elicit only negative answers with *should* and *ought to.*

TEACHER: Is Mrs Dumpling Mr Clark's friend?
PUPIL: No, she isn't.
TEACHER: Is she Mrs Blake's friend?
PUPIL: Yes, she is. etc.

(b) Tag Rejoinders.

Make affirmative and negative statements to elicit tag rejoinders.

TEACHER: Mrs Dumpling is Mrs Blake's friend.
PUPIL: She is, isn't she?
TEACHER: She isn't Mrs Clark's friend.
PUPIL: She isn't, is she? etc.

(c) Questions with Who: is/shouldn't/oughtn't to/will/has.
To elicit a subject followed by an auxiliary verb.

TEACHER: Who is Mrs Blake's friend?
PUPIL: Mrs Dumpling is. etc.

(d) Double Questions.

To elicit negative and affirmative statements.

TEACHER: Is Mrs Dumpling Mrs Clark's, or Mrs Blake's friend?
PUPIL: She isn't Mrs Clark's friend. She's Mrs Blake's friend. etc.

(e) General Questions: Whose, Why, What, How many.

TEACHER: Whose friend is Mrs Dumpling?
PUPIL: Mrs Blake's. etc.

(f) Asking questions in pairs: Who, Why, How many.

TEACHER: Ask me if she is Mrs Blake's friend.
PUPIL: Is she Mrs Blake's friend?
TEACHER: Who . . .
PUPIL: Who is Mrs Blake's friend? etc.

● **Acting the Scene**

Invite a few pupils to come to the front of the class to act the scene. The Narrator's part (frame 1) should be omitted.

● **Unprepared Reading**

Marley Castle, page 19.
New Words and Expressions: *in our way* (obstacle), *get away* (escape), *except.*

● **Activity**

Repeat:
(a) Some folk do. (Lessons 73–77.)
(b) The more we are together. (Lesson 35.)

● **Writing**

Workbook 3b, Lesson 79.

Guided Composition. The correct answer reads: Mrs Dumpling had tea with the Blakes yesterday. She's on a diet *but* she likes food *and* she's very fat. Mrs Dumpling had some sandwiches, some biscuits and some cake for tea. Then Mrs Blake said, "Have another slice of cake."

"No, thank you. I shouldn't." Mrs Dumpling answered. "I've already had two slices."

"No, you haven't!" Timmy said. "You've already had five. I've counted them."

66 Words

Lesson 80

- **Spelling Drill:** Books shut.

  Oral and Written
  cake; make; take; lake; wake; bake; break;
  steak; look; like.

  Ask individual pupils to spell these words
  orally. As soon as a word has been spelt
  correctly, write it on the blackboard. When all
  the words have been written, erase them. Then
  dictate them to the class.

- **Phonic Practice:** Sounds and Spellings: Books
  open.

  The letters th [ð] s [z] and th [θ]
  Chorus and Group Repetition
  Ask the pupils to repeat after you the words
  at the top of page 80 of the Pupils' Book.

- **Reading and Repetition Drill:** Books open.

  Chorus and Group Repetition

  TEACHER: *Picture 1.*
  I should clean my teeth, but I don't
  feel like it. *All together!*
  I ought to clean my teeth, but I
  don't feel like it. *All together!*

  Practise these patterns with each frame. Point
  out that *should* and *ought to* have the same
  meaning; *must/have to/have got to* are stronger
  than *should* and *ought.*

- **Pattern Drill:** Books open.

  Illustrate each exercise first by providing the
  stimulus and the response. Make sure the pupils
  really understand how they must respond.
  Then conduct the drills given below. If a child
  makes a mistake, correct him and ask him to
  repeat the right answer.

  (a) To elicit: Yes, he should. No, he isn't. He
  doesn't feel like it.

  TEACHER: *Picture 1.*
  Should he clean his teeth?
  PUPIL: Yes, he should.
  TEACHER: Is he going to clean his teeth?
  PUPIL: No, he isn't. He doesn't feel like
  it. etc.

  (b) To elicit: Yes, he ought to. No, he isn't.
  He doesn't feel like it.

  Conduct the drill in the way shown in (a) above.

  (c) To elicit: Yes, he's got to (clean his teeth)
  and he's going to do it now.

  TEACHER: *Picture 1.*
  Must he clean his teeth?
  PUPIL: Yes, he's got to clean his teeth
  and he's going to do it now. etc.

  (d) To elicit: I should (clean my teeth), but I
  don't feel like it.

  TEACHER: *Picture 1.*
  Clean your teeth! Don't be so
  lazy!
  PUPIL: I should clean my teeth, but I
  don't feel like it. etc.

  (e) To elicit: I ought to (clean my teeth), but
  I don't feel like it.

  Conduct the drill in the way shown in (d) above.

  (f) Asking questions in pairs: What.

  TEACHER: Ask me if he should clean his
  teeth.
  PUPIL: Should he clean his teeth?
  TEACHER: What . . .
  PUPIL: What should he do? etc.

- **Unprepared Reading**

  Marley Castle, page 20.
  New Word: *escape.*

- **Activity**

  A Guessing Game
  The teacher invites a pupil to the front of the
  class and hands him a piece of paper with a
  statement written on it. (Any of those in Lesson
  80 may be given.) Members of the class must
  guess the correct statement.

  MEMBER OF CLASS: Why don't you clean your
  teeth?
  PUPIL: I should, but I don't feel
  like it.
  MEMBER OF CLASS: Why don't you post these
  letters.
  PUPIL: I'm going to post them. I've
  got to post them.
  TEACHER: Good! Sit down A. Now
  you B.

- **Writing**

  Workbook 3b, Lesson 80.

Lesson **80** I should/I ought to/but I don't feel like it.

that lose thank then rise thin this sees thief

1

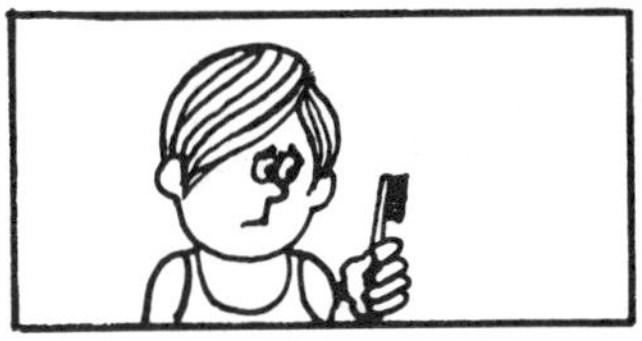

clean my teeth

2

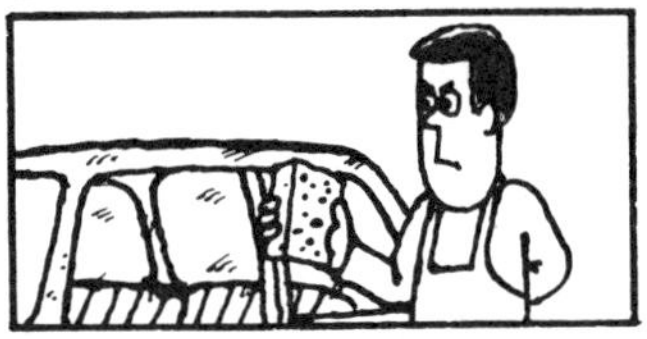

wash the car

3

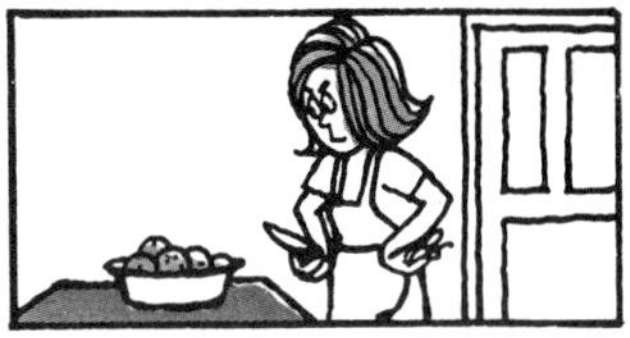

peel the potatoes

4

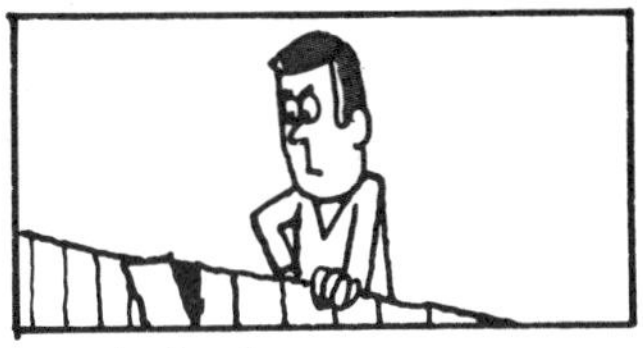

repair the fence

5

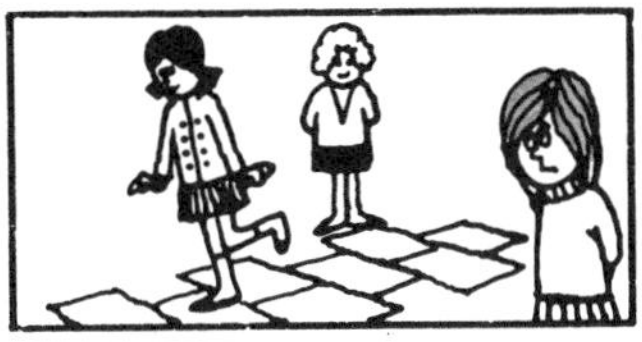

play a game

6

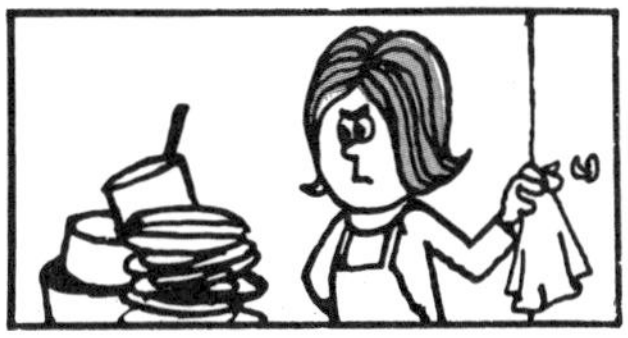

dry the dishes

7

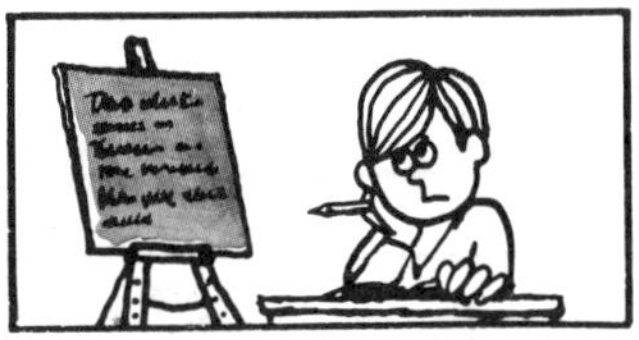

copy these sentences

8

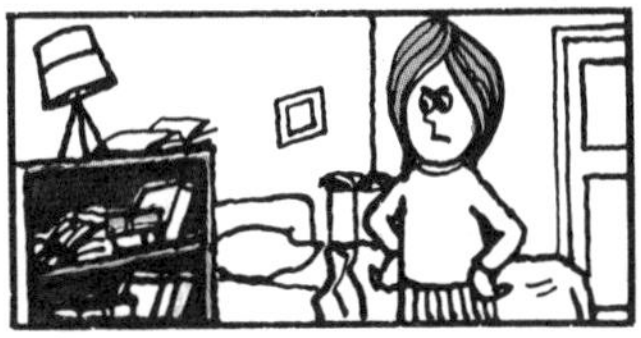

tidy my room

9

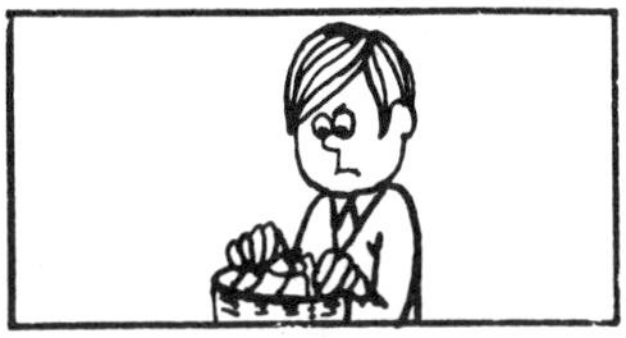

empty the waste-paper basket

10

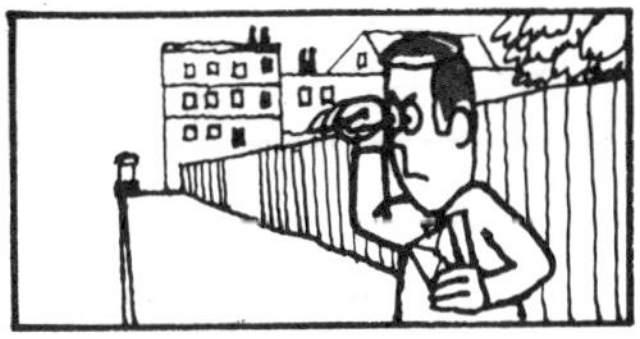

post these letters

11

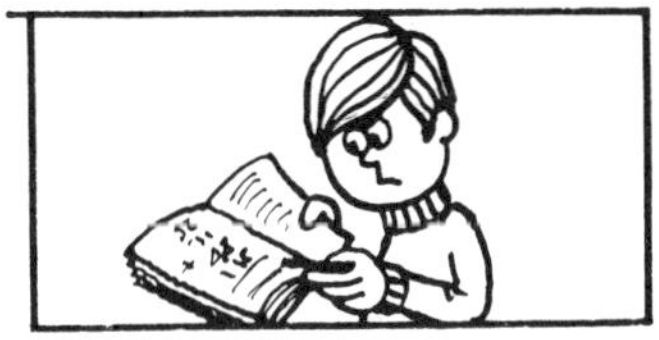

add these figures

12

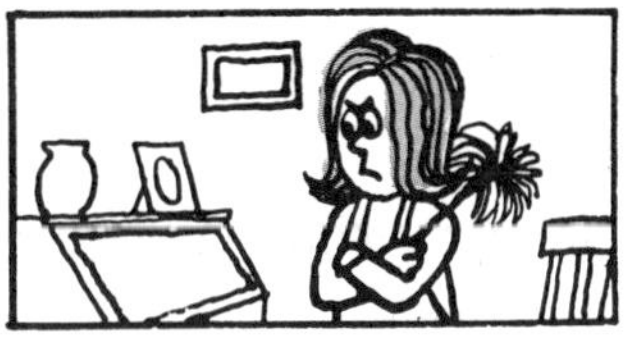

dust the furniture

13

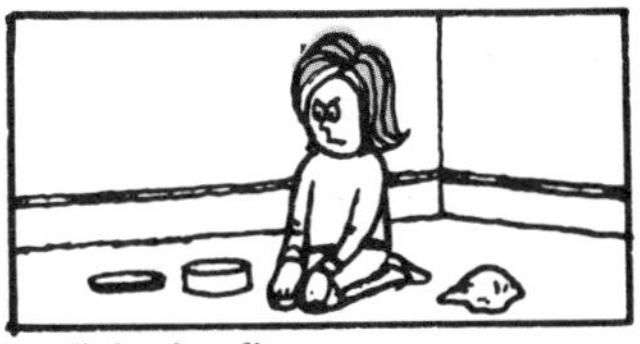

polish the floor

14

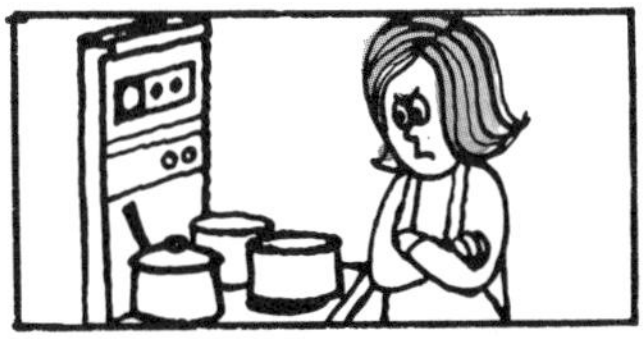

cook a meal

15

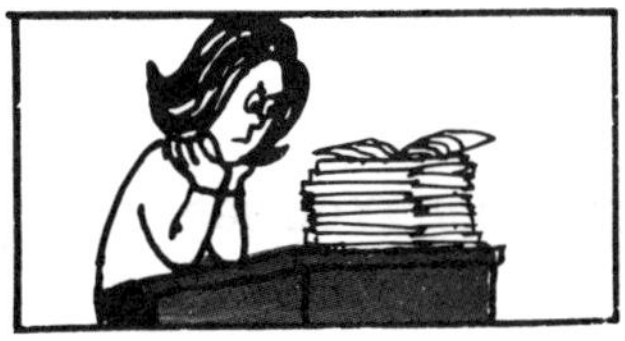

mark these exercise-books

Lesson **81** Service with a smile!

Mother: Yóu look búsy, Jím.   1
Father: Yés, I've júst wátered the gárden.
Mother: You néedn't have.
        The chíldren wátered it this mórning.
Father: Réally? Then I wátered it for nóthing.

Father: I'm góing to cléan the cár nów.   2
Mother: Áll ríght, Jím.

Mother: Thát was quíck, Jím.   3
        Háve you cléaned the cár alréady?
Father: Nó, I dídn't háve to.
        The chíldren are cléaning it fór me.

Father: They're véry búsy todáy.   4
        Whát's the mátter with them?
Mother: They wánt to éarn some
        éxtra pócket-móney.

Sandy: Your cár's réady, dád.   5

Mother: You sée, Jím.   6
        Sérvice with a smíle!

Content and Basic Aims

PATTERNS AND STRUCTURAL WORDS	VOCABULARY	
	Nouns	*Expressions*
Yes, but (I) needn't have.		
No, (I) didn't have to.	service	Really? (Is that so?)
(I) needn't've (watered the garden) because	smile	Service with a smile!
(it rained).	vase	for nothing (to no
(I watered it) for nothing.		purpose)
(I) didn't have to (water the garden).	*Verbs*	
(It rained) so (I) didn't have to (water it).		
Did he have to . . .? Yes,, he had to, because . . .	expect	
Question Tags.	water	

- **General Remarks**

Needn't have (it was a waste of time, effort etc.)
and *didn't have to* (it didn't prove necessary) are
contrasted. (Compare TU 39.)

Note that Question Tags will now replace
Tag Rejoinders in the Graded Comprehension
Questions.

- **Aural/Oral Procedure**

(a) Listening (Books shut)
(b) Listening and Understanding (Books open;
pictures only)
(c) Listening (Books shut)
(d) Listening and Chorus Repetition (Books
shut)
(e) Listening and Group Repetition (Books
shut)
(f) Reading Aloud: Chorus and Individual
(Books open)

- **Graded Comprehension Questions**

(a) Yes/No Tag Answers: has/did/is/do.

TEACHER: Has father just cut the grass?
PUPIL:　No, he hasn't.
TEACHER: Has he just watered the garden?
PUPIL:　Yes, he has. etc.

(b) Question Tags.

Make affirmative and negative statements
to elicit question tags.

TEACHER: Father looks busy.
PUPIL:　Father looks busy, doesn't he?
TEACHER: Father doesn't look tired.
PUPIL:　Father doesn't look tired, does
he? etc.

(c) Questions with Who: does/has/needn't have/
did/is/do.

TEACHER: Who looks busy?
PUPIL:　Father does. etc.

(d) Double Questions.

TEACHER: Has father just cut the grass or
watered the garden?
PUPIL:　He hasn't cut the grass. He's
just watered the garden. etc.

(e) General Questions: Why, What.

TEACHER: Why does father look busy?
PUPIL:　Because he's just watered the
garden. etc.

(f) Asking questions in pairs: Why, What.

TEACHER: Ask me if father looks busy.
PUPIL:　Does father look busy?
TEACHER: Why . . .
PUPIL:　Why does father look busy? etc.

- **Acting the Scene**

Invite four children to come to the front of the
class to act the scene.

- **Unprepared Reading**

Marley Castle, page 21.
New Words and Expressions: *fool* (noun), *went
on* (continued), *click* (sound), *gun, one more
chance.*

- **Activity**

Repeat the following:
(a) Solomon Grundy (Lesson 39).
(b) Ducks and drakes (Lesson 49).
(c) A lame tame crane (Lesson 51).

- **Writing**

Workbook 3b, Lesson 81.

Guided Composition. The correct answer reads:
Father watered the garden, *but* it wasn't
necessary. The children watered it this morning,
but father didn't know this. Then father wanted
to clean the car, *but* he didn't have to. The
children cleaned it for him. They wanted to
earn some extra pocket-money, *so* they did some
jobs for father.

51 Words

Lesson 82

- **Spelling Drill:** Books shut.

Oral and Written
clock; shock; locker; kick; stick; pick; thick; trick; ticket; quick.
Point out that 'ck' must be used after a short vowel.

- **Phonic Practice:** Sounds and Spellings: Books open.

The letters s [s] and s [z]
Chorus and Group Repetition

- **Reading and Repetition Drill:** Books open.

Chorus and Group Repetition

TEACHER: *Picture 1.*
I needn't have watered the garden because it rained. *All together!*
I didn't have to water the garden because it rained. *All together!*

Point out the difference between *needn't have* (I did something for nothing) and *didn't have to* (I didn't do anything because it wasn't necessary).

- **Pattern Drill:** Books open.

(a) To elicit: Yes, but I needn't have. It wasn't necessary because (it rained).

TEACHER: *Picture 1.*
Did you water the garden?
PUPIL: Yes, but I needn't have. It wasn't necessary because it rained. etc.

(b) To elicit: No, I didn't have to. It wasn't necessary because (it rained).

TEACHER: *Picture 1.*
Did you water the garden?
PUPIL: No, I didn't have to. It wasn't necessary because it rained. etc.

(c) To elicit: Yes. I needn't have (watered) the garden because (it rained). I (watered it) for nothing.

TEACHER: *Picture 1.*
Did you water the garden?
PUPIL: Yes, I needn't have watered the garden because it rained. I watered it for nothing. etc.

(d) To elicit: No. He didn't have to (water the garden). (It rained) so (he) didn't have to (water it).

TEACHER: *Picture 1.*
Did he water the garden?
PUPIL: No. He didn't have to water the garden. It rained so he didn't have to water it. etc.

(e) To elicit:
Did he have to (water the garden)?
Yes, he had to because (it didn't rain).

TEACHER: *Picture 1.*
1st PUPIL: Did he have to water the garden?
2nd PUPIL: Yes, he had to because it didn't rain. etc.

Note that all the second responses are negative with the exception of Number 5.

- **Unprepared Reading**

Marley Castle, page 22.
New Word: *below*.

- **Activity**

Dictation

Dictate the following passage:

"You should repáir that fénce,"/móther sáid. "You óught to dó it nów."/
"I cán't dó it nów," fáther ánswered./"I háve to/repáir the gáte fírst."/
Fáther wórked hárd/and repáired the gáte and the fénce./Móther was pléased./"It's níce now,"/shé sáid./
"I'm glád you líke it,"/fáther sáid.

- **Writing**

Workbook 3b, Lesson 82.

Lesson 82 I needn't have/I did it for nothing.
I didn't have to/It wasn't necessary to.

clock<u>s</u> dog<u>s</u>   hat<u>s</u> head<u>s</u>   cake<u>s</u> game<u>s</u>   pipe<u>s</u> pencil<u>s</u>

1

water(ed) the garden
It rained.

2

knock(ed) at the door
She saw me through the
window.

3

dust(ed) the furniture
It was clean.

4

pick(ed) any flowers
There were some in
the vase.

5

return(ed) home early
My parents didn't
expect me.

6

pump(ed) up the tyres
They were OK.

7

shout(ed) to her
She could hear me.

8

wash(ed) the clothes
They were clean.

9

look(ed) for my pen
It was in my pocket.

10

bak(ed) any cakes
Mother made some.

11

polish(ed) the floor
It was clean.

12

call(ed) the doctor
He was all right.

Lesson 83 Something's burning!

Father: Yóu look tíred, déar.
Mother: Yés. I had to íron thése clóthes.

Mother: Hére are your shírts, Jím.
Father: Thánk you, Bétty.
Whére's my néw blúe shírt?
Mother: I háven't íroned it yét.

Father: Bétty!
Sómething's búrning!
Can you sméll it?
Mother: You're ríght.

Father: Lóok!
The íron's stíll ón!

Mother: I shóuld have túrned it óff,
but I forgót.
I'll túrn it off nów.

Father: Lóok at my níce blúe shírt!
There's a bíg hóle in it!
Mother: I'm sórry, Jím.
Father: Néver mínd, déar.

Sandy Macnab

There was an old fellow named Sandy Macnab,
Who had for his supper a very fine crab,
And had to be taken home in a cab.

Content and Basic Aims

PATTERNS AND STRUCTURAL WORDS	VOCABULARY	
Yes, (he) should have. (He) should have/ought to have . . . but (he) didn't feel like it/(he) forgot. (What) did you have to (do)? (What) should you have (done)?	*Noun* iron (electric appliance)	*Expression* The (iron)'s on.
	Verb	
	iron	

● **General Remarks**

Had to (necessity) is contrasted with *should have/ought to have* (failure to meet past obligation). (Compare TU 40.)

● **Aural/Oral Procedure**

(a) Listening (Books shut)
(b) Listening and Understanding (Books open; pictures only)
(c) Listening (Books shut)
(d) Listening and Chorus Repetition (Books shut)
(e) Listening and Group Repetition (Books shut)
(f) Reading Aloud: Chorus and Individual (Books open)

● **Graded Comprehension Questions**

(a) Yes/No Tag Answers: does/did/has/can/ is/should/will.

TEACHER: Does mother look well?
PUPIL: No, she doesn't.
TEACHER: Does she look tired?
PUPIL: Yes, she does. etc.

(b) Question Tags.

Make affirmative and negative statements to elicit question tags.

TEACHER: Mother looks tired.
PUPIL: Mother looks tired, doesn't she?
TEACHER: Mother doesn't look well.
PUPIL: Mother doesn't look well, does she? etc.

(c) Questions with Who: does/did/hasn't/can/ should have/will/is.

TEACHER: Who looks tired?
PUPIL: Mother does. etc.

(d) Double Questions.

TEACHER: Does mother look well or tired?
PUPIL: She doesn't look well. She looks tired. etc.

(e) General Questions: How, Why, What.

TEACHER: How does mother look?
PUPIL: Tired. etc.

(f) Asking questions in pairs: How, Why, What.

TEACHER: Ask me if mother looks tired.
PUPIL: Does mother look tired?
TEACHER: How . . .
PUPIL: How does mother look? etc.

● **Acting the Scene**

Invite two children to come to the front of the class to act the scene. A toy iron would be a useful prop.

● **Unprepared Reading**

Marley Castle, page 23.
New Words and Expressions: *pleasantly, scar, corner* (of his eye), *carpet.*

● **Activity**

Song: Sandy Macnab. See page 254 for music. This song should be taught as a three-part round.

● **Writing**

Workbook 3b, Lesson 83.

Guided Composition. The correct answer reads: Mother had to iron a lot of clothes yesterday, *so* she look tired. Father came into the kitchen *and* asked for his new blue shirt, *but* it wasn't ready. Suddenly, he cried, "Something's burning!" Mother should have turned off the iron, *but* she forgot. She turned it off *and* father noticed a hole in his nice blue shirt. Mother felt sorry, *but* father said, "Never mind!"

66 Words

Lesson **84**

- **Spelling Drill:** Books shut.

  Oral and Written
  cake/clock; make/shock; stick/take; thick/
  wake; break/trick; quick/look.
  Point out that 'k' is used after a long vowel
  and 'ck' after a short one.

- **Phonic Practice:** Sounds and Spellings: Books
  open.

  The letters s [z] and s [s]
  Chorus and Group Repetition

- **Reading and Repetition Drill:** Books open.

  Chorus and Group Repetition

  TEACHER: *Picture 1.*
      He had to clean his teeth and he did.
      All together!
      He should have cleaned his teeth, but
      he didn't feel like it. *All together!*
      He ought to have cleaned his teeth,
      but he forgot. *All together!*

  Practise these patterns with each frame. Point
  out that *should have* and *ought to have* carry the
  same meaning; *had to* is stronger than either
  of the modal verbs.

- **Pattern Drill:** Books open.

  (a) To elicit: Yes, (he) should have. No, he
  didn't.

  TEACHER: *Picture 1.*
      Should Sandy have cleaned his
      teeth?
  PUPIL: Yes, he should have.
  TEACHER: Did he clean his teeth?
  PUPIL: No, he didn't.

  (b) To elicit: (He) had to (clean his teeth). Yes,
  he did.

  TEACHER: *Picture 1.*
      What did Sandy have to do?
  PUPIL: He had to clean his teeth.
  TEACHER: Did he clean his teeth?
  PUPIL: Yes, he did. etc.

  (c) To elicit: I don't know. I should have
  (cleaned my teeth), but I didn't feel like it.

  TEACHER: *Picture 1.*
      Why didn't you clean your teeth?
  PUPIL: I don't know. I should have
      cleaned my teeth, but I didn't
      feel like it. etc.

  (d) To elicit: No, I haven't. I ought to have
  (cleaned my teeth), but I forgot.

  TEACHER: *Picture 1.*
      Haven't you cleaned your teeth
      yet?

PUPIL: No, I haven't.
TEACHER: You ought to have.
PUPIL: I ought to have cleaned my
    teeth, but I forgot. etc.

(e) Asking questions in pairs: What . . . do.

TEACHER: Ask me if I had to clean my
    teeth.
PUPIL: Did you have to clean your
    teeth?
TEACHER: What . . .
PUPIL: What did you have to do? etc.

(f) Asking questions in pairs: What . . . do.

TEACHER: Ask me if I should have cleaned
    my teeth.
PUPIL: Should you have cleaned your
    teeth?
TEACHER: What . . .
PUPIL: What should you have done? etc.

- **Unprepared Reading**

  Marley Castle, page 24.
  New Word: *secret.*

- **Activity**

  It's time for a story: Just One of Those Days!
  page 265.
  New Words and Expressions: *Just one of those
  days, bad-tempered, mess.* Write the new words
  and expressions on the blackboard and explain
  them. Now read the story to the class.

- **Writing**

  Workbook 3b, Lesson 84.

Lesson 84 I had to ... and I did!
I should have ... but I didn't feel like it!
I ought to have ... but I forgot!

tomatoe<u>s</u>   <u>s</u>oap   glasse<u>s</u>   <u>s</u>top   matche<u>s</u>   <u>s</u>mile   boxe<u>s</u>   soft

1

clean(ed) my teeth

2

close(d) the window

3

peel(ed) the potatoes

4

repair(ed) the fence

5

play(ed) a game

6

dry(-ied) the dishes

7

copy(-ied) the sentence

8

tidy(-ied) my room

9

empty(-ied) the basket

10

post(ed) that letter

11

add(ed) these figures

12

dust(ed) the furniture

13

polish(ed) the floor

14

cook(ed) a meal

15

mark(ed) these exercise-books

Lesson 85 Television Day: The Lascaux Cave

TV Commentary:

Have you heard of the Lascaux Cave and the famous pictures there? In 1941, a French schoolboy, Marcel Ravidat, and three of his friends explored a hill near the village of Montignac. Suddenly, Marcel's dog disappeared down a hole in the rocks. The hole was dark. Perhaps it was dangerous down there. Marcel shouldn't have gone into it alone, but he did. He rescued the dog. Marcel and his friends decided to go down the hole together the next day. The boys returned the next morning with ropes and candles. They climbed into the hole and came to a big cave. They accidentally made a great discovery. They found pictures of animals on the walls. Prehistoric men painted these pictures more than 20,000 years ago. The Lascaux Cave has been famous ever since—just because of four boys and a dog!

Lesson 85

Content and Basic Aims

PATTERNS AND STRUCTURAL WORDS	VOCABULARY			
(He) mustn't (park here) and (he) isn't going to.	*Nouns*	*Adj.*	*Verbs*	*Adv.*
(He) shouldn't/oughtn't to (park here), but (he's) going to. *(He) shouldn't have/oughtn't to have (parked here), but (he) did.* *(He) shouldn't/shouldn't have (park (ed) here) because (it says 'No Parking'.)*	cave discovery rock rope	dark prehistoric	decide disappear explore hear of rescue	accidentally (by chance) alone because of

- **General Remarks**

Shouldn't/oughtn't to and *shouldn't have/oughtn't to have* are contrasted with *mustn't*. (Compare TU's 39 and 40.)

- **Aural/Oral Procedure**

  (a) Listening (Books shut)
  (b) Intensive Reading (Books open)
  The passage should be played or read to the class in small units. During each pause, explain unfamiliar words. Rather than give direct explanations, try to elicit as much information as possible from the pupils.
  (c) Listening (Books shut)
  (d) Reading Aloud: Individual (Books open)

- **Graded Comprehension Questions**

  (a) Yes/No Tag Answers: have/did/was/should/ has.

    TEACHER: Have you heard of the Lascaux Cave?
    PUPIL: Yes, I have/No, I haven't. etc.

  (b) Question Tags.
  Make affirmative and negative statements to elicit question tags.

    TEACHER: You've heard of the Lascaux Cave.
    PUPIL: You've heard of the Lascaux Cave, haven't you?
    TEACHER: You haven't heard of the Lascaux Cave.
    PUPIL: You haven't heard of the Lascaux Cave, have you? etc.

  (c) Double Questions.

    TEACHER: Did the boy explore the hill in 1931, or 1941?
    PUPIL: He didn't explore it in 1931. He explored it in 1941. etc.

  (d) General Questions: Why, When, Where and How.

    TEACHER: Why is the Lascaux Cave famous?

    PUPIL: Because there are famous pictures there. etc.

  (e) Asking questions in pairs: Why, When, Where and How.

    TEACHER: Ask me if the Lascaux Cave is famous. etc.

- **Oral Composition**

  Write the following notes on the blackboard:

  Lascaux—famous pictures.
  Marcel and three friends.
  Dog disappeared.
  Marcel rescued it.
  Next day—decided to go down.
  Returned—ropes, candles.
  Big cave—great discovery—pictures.
  Prehistoric men—20,000 years ago.
  All because of four boys and a dog.

  Now ask one or two pupils to reconstruct the passage by referring to the notes.

- **Unprepared Reading**

  Marley Castle, page 25.
  New Words: *slide/slid, steps, close* (near).

- **Activity**

  Repeat:
  (a) Sandy Macnab (Lesson 83).
  (b) There's a hole in my bucket (Lessons 21–29).

- **Writing**

  Workbook 3b, Lesson 85.

  Guided Composition. The correct answer reads: In 1941, Marcel Ravidat and three of his friends explored a hill near the village of Montignac. Marcel's dog disappeared down a hole *and* Marcel followed it. He and his friends returned the next morning *and* explored the hole. They found pictures of animals on the walls. Prehistoric men painted these pictures more than 20,000 years ago.

  57 Words

Lesson 86

- **Spelling Drill:** Books shut.

  Oral and Written
  big/kitchen; dog/key; leg/kite; bag/bake; wake/
  game; stick/garden; make/glue.

- **Phonic Practice:** Sounds and Spellings: Books
  open.
  The letters s [s] and sh [ʃ]
  Chorus and Group Repetition

- **Reading and Repetition Drill:** Books open.

  Chorus and Group Repetition

  TEACHER: *Picture 1.*
  He mustn't park here and he isn't
  going to. *All together!*
  He shouldn't park here but he's
  going to. *All together!*
  He oughtn't to park here but he's
  going to. *All together!*
  He shouldn't have parked here but
  he did. *All together!*
  He oughtn't to have parked here but
  he did. *All together!*

  Point out that *mustn't* is stronger than *shouldn't*
  and *oughtn't to.*

- **Pattern Drill:** Books open.

  (a) To elicit: He mustn't (park here). (It says
  'No Parking').

  TEACHER: *Picture 1.*
  Why isn't father going to park
  here?
  PUPIL: He mustn't park here. It says
  'No Parking'. etc.

  (b) To elicit: (Father) shouldn't (park here)
  but (he's) going to.

  TEACHER: *Picture 1.*
  It says 'No Parking'.
  PUPIL: Father shouldn't park here but
  he's going to. etc.

  (c) To elicit: (Father) oughtn't to (park here)
  but (he's) going to.

  Conduct the drill in the way shown in (b)
  above.

  (d) To elicit: (Father) shouldn't have (parked
  here) but (he) did.

  TEACHER: *Picture 1.*
  It says 'No Parking'.
  PUPIL: Father shouldn't have parked
  here but he did. etc.

  (e) To elicit: (Father) oughtn't to have (parked
  here) but (he) did.

  TEACHER: *Picture 1.*
  It says 'No Parking'.
  PUPIL: Father oughtn't to have parked
  here but he did. etc.

  (f) To elicit: (He) mustn't (park here) because
  (it says 'No Parking').

  TEACHER: *Picture 1.*
  Why mustn't father park here?
  PUPIL: He mustn't park here because
  it says 'No Parking'. etc.

  (g) To elicit: (He's) going to (park here). (He)
  shouldn't (park here) because (it says 'No
  Parking').

  TEACHER: *Picture 1.*
  What's father going to do?
  PUPIL: He's going to park here. He
  shouldn't park here because it
  says 'No Parking'. etc.

  (h) To elicit: (He parked here). (He) shouldn't
  have (parked here) because (it says 'No
  Parking').

  TEACHER: *Picture 1.*
  What did father do?
  PUPIL: He parked here. He shouldn't
  have parked here because it says
  'No Parking'. etc.

- **Unprepared Reading**

  Marley Castle, page 26.
  New Words and Expressions: *search* (noun),
  police station, it's already long past your bedtime.

- **Activity**

  An Elimination Game
  Pupils should make statements involving the
  use of *shouldn't.* Any pupil who fails to respond
  when the teacher points at him is eliminated.

  TEACHER *(pointing at a pupil):* What shouldn't
  you do?
  PUPIL: (I shouldn't eat in class.)
  TEACHER: *(pointing at another pupil):* What
  shouldn't you do?
  PUPIL: (I shouldn't talk during the lesson.)
  TEACHER *(pointing at another pupil):* What
  shouldn't you do?
  PUPIL *(hesitating):* I . . .
  TEACHER: You are out. etc.

- **Writing**

  Workbook 3b, Lesson 86.

Lesson 86

He mustn't . . . and he isn't going to
He shouldn't . . . but he's going to
He oughtn't to . . . but he's going to
He shouldn't have . . . but he did
He oughtn't to have . . . but he did

<u>Su</u>e <u>sh</u>oes <u>s</u>eat <u>sh</u>eet <u>s</u>afe <u>sh</u>ave <u>s</u>ign <u>sh</u>ine

---

Father

1

park/parked here
It says 'No Parking'.

The children

3

sail/sailed on the lake
It says 'No Sailing'.

The children

5

feed/fed the animals
It says 'Do not feed the animals'.

Sandy

7

bang/banged his drum
The baby's asleep.

Sue

9

ride/ridden this bicycle
The tyres are flat.

The children

2

swim/swum in the river
It says 'No Swimming'.

Sandy

4

walk/walked on the grass
It says 'Keep Off'.

The children

6

talk/talked in the library
It says 'Silence'.

Mrs Dumpling

8

eat/eaten those cakes
She's on a diet.

The baby

10

play/played with matches
They're dangerous

Lesson **87** Don't waste electricity and water!

Narrator:	Fáther's góing into the báthroom. He's góing to háve a sháve.

1

Father:	Whó left the líght on?
Sue:	Í did, dád.

2

Father:	You mústn't wáste electrícity, Súe. You must álways túrn the líght off.
Sue:	Yés, dád.

3

Sue:	I shóuld turn it óff, but I óften forgét. Sháll I túrn it off nów, dád?
Father:	Nó, I'm góing to háve a sháve.

4

Sandy:	Háve you fínished, dád? I wánt to háve a wásh.
Father:	Yés, cóme ín, Sándy.

5

Sandy:	Whó left the táp on?
Father:	Ér . . . Í did, Sándy.
Sandy:	You mústn't wáste wáter, dád. You must álways túrn the táp off.

6

Tongue-twister: Peter Piper

Peter Piper picked a peck of pickled pepper,
A peck of pickled pepper Peter Piper picked.
If Peter Piper picked a peck of pickled pepper,
Where's the peck of pickled pepper Peter Piper picked?

Content and Basic Aims

PATTERNS AND STRUCTURAL WORDS	VOCABULARY
Revision: *must/have to/have got to/mustn't/not allowed to/needn't/don't have to/it isn't necessary to/should/ought to . . . but/shouldn't/oughtn't to . . . but.*	*Expression* Who left (the light) on?

● **General Remarks**

Patterns introduced in Teaching Units 38, 39, 40 and 43 are brought together and revised in this Unit.

● **Aural/Oral Procedure**

(a) Listening (Books shut)
(b) Listening and Understanding (Books open; pictures only)
(c) Listening (Books shut)
(d) Listening and Chorus Repetition (Books shut)
(e) Listening and Group Repetition (Books shut
(f) Reading Aloud: Chorus and Individual (Books open)

● **Graded Comprehension Questions**

(a) Yes/No Tag Answers: is/did/must/should/will/has/does.

TEACHER: Is Father going into the living-room?
PUPIL: No, he isn't.
TEACHER: Is he going into the bathroom?
PUPIL: Yes, he is. etc.

(b) Question Tags.

Make affirmative and negative statements to elicit question tags.

TEACHER: Father's going into the bathroom.
PUPIL: Father's going into the bathroom, isn't he?
TEACHER: He isn't going into the living-room.
PUPIL: He isn't going into the living-room, is he? etc.

(c) Questions with Who: is/did/mustn't/must/should/has/does.

TEACHER: Who's going into the bathroom?
PUPIL: Father is. etc.

(d) Double Questions.

TEACHER: Is father going into the living-room or the bathroom?
PUPIL: He isn't going into the living-room. He's going into the bathroom, etc.

(e) General Questions: Where, Why and What.

TEACHER: Where's father going?
PUPIL: Into the bathroom. etc.

(f) Asking questions in pairs: Where, Why and What.

TEACHER: Ask me if father's going into the bathroom.
PUPIL: Is father going into the bathroom?
TEACHER: Where . . .
PUPIL: Where's father going? etc.

● **Acting the Scene**

Invite three children to come to the front of the class to act the scene.

● **Unprepared Reading**

Marley Castle, page 27.
New Expression: *round the back.*

● **Activity**

Teach the new tongue-twister, 'Peter Piper'.

● **Writing**

Workbook 3b, Lesson 87.
Guided Composition. The correct answer reads: Sue left the light on in the bathroom *and* father noticed it. "You mustn't waste electricity, Sue," father said. Father had a shave *and* left the bathroom, *but* he didn't turn the tap off. Sandy noticed it *and* said, "You mustn't waste water, dad." Both Sandy and father smiled.

49 Words

Lesson 88

- **Spelling Drill:** Books shut.

  Oral and Written
  key/coat/goal; kite/class/glass; kind/came/
  game; kitchen/coin/glider.

- **Phonic Practice:** Sounds and Spellings: Books open.

  The letters ss [s] and sh [ʃ]
  Chorus and Group Repetition

- **Reading and Repetition Drill:** Books open.

  Pictures 1–3 only.

  TEACHER: *Picture 1.*
  I must take a taxi because there isn't
  a bus. *All together!*
  I have to take a taxi because there
  isn't a bus. *All together!*
  I've got to take a taxi because there
  isn't a bus. *All together!*

- **Pattern Drill:** Books open.

  Pictures 1–3 only.

  (a) To elicit: I must (take a taxi). Because (there isn't a bus).

  TEACHER: *Picture 1.*
  What must you do?
  PUPIL: I must take a taxi.
  TEACHER: Why?
  PUPIL: Because there isn't a bus. etc.

  Repeat this exchange to elicit *have to* and *have got to.*

- **Reading and Repetition Drill**

  Pictures 4–6 only.
  Ask the pupils to repeat the following:
  I mustn't park here because it says 'No Parking'.
  I'm not allowed to park here because it says 'No Parking'.

- **Pattern Drill**

  (b) To elicit: I mustn't (park here). Because (it says 'No Parking').

  TEACHER: *Picture 4.*
  What mustn't you do?
  PUPIL: I mustn't park here.
  TEACHER: Why?
  PUPIL: Because it says 'No Parking'.
  etc.

  Repeat this exchange to elicit *I'm not allowed to.*

- **Reading and Repetition Drill**

  Pictures 7–9 only.

  Repeat the patterns indicated in the Pupils' Book with *needn't, don't have to* and *isn't necessary to.*

Point out that *must = have to,* but *mustn't* is not the same as *don't have to.*

- **Pattern Drill**

  (c) To elicit: I needn't (take a taxi). Because (a bus is coming).

  TEACHER: *Picture 7.*
  Why don't you take a taxi?
  PUPIL: I needn't take a taxi.
  TEACHER: Why?
  PUPIL: Because a bus is coming. etc.

  Repeat this exchange to elicit *don't have to/ isn't necessary to.*

- **Reading and Repetition Drill:** Pictures 10–12 only.

- **Pattern Drill**

  (d) To elicit: I should (tidy my room) because (it's untidy). No, I don't feel like it.

  TEACHER: *Picture 10.*
  What should you do?
  PUPIL: I should tidy my room because it's untidy.
  TEACHER: Are you going to?
  PUPIL: No, I don't feel like it. etc.

  Repeat this exchange to elicit *ought to.*

- **Reading and Repetition Drill:** Pictures 13–15 only.

- **Pattern Drill**

  (e) To elicit: I shouldn't (eat any cakes) because (I'm on a diet). Yes, I'm going to.

  TEACHER: *Picture 13.*
  Why shouldn't you eat any cakes?
  PUPIL: I shouldn't eat any cakes because I'm on a diet.
  TEACHER: Are you going to?
  PUPIL: Yes, I'm going to. etc.

  Repeat this exchange to elicit *oughtn't to.*

- **Unprepared Reading**
  Marley Castle, page 28.

- **Activity**
  Dictation
  Dictate the following passage:

  "Háve a cáke, Mŕs Dúmpling,"/móther sáid./
  "I shóuldn't," Mŕs Dúmpling ánswered,/
  "but I'll júst háve a líttle óne."/Póor Mŕs
  Dúmpling!/Lífe's véry,hárd./She lóves cákes and
  swéets./She's ón a díet/and she óughtn't to éat
  them/but she álways dóes!

- **Writing**
  Workbook 3b, Lesson 88.

Lesson 88 Revision: must, mustn't, needn't, should, shouldn't, etc.

glass <u>sh</u>are   pa<u>ss</u> <u>sh</u>ow   mi<u>ss</u> <u>sh</u>ave   dre<u>ss</u> <u>sh</u>out

I must/I have to/I've got to . . .

1

take a taxi
because there isn't
a bus

2

buy a newspaper
because you haven't
bought one

3

press the button
because you haven't
pressed it

I mustn't/I'm not allowed to . . .

4

park here
because it says 'No
Parking'

5

play with matches
because they're
dangerous

6

talk in the library
because it says
'Silence'

I needn't/I don't have to/It isn't necessary to . . .

7

take a taxi
because a bus is
coming

8

buy a newspaper
because you've already
bought one

9

press the button
because you've already
pressed it

I should/I ought to/but I don't feel like it.

10

tidy my room
because it's untidy

11

empty the basket
because it's full

12

dust the furniture
because it's dirty

I shouldn't/I oughtn't to/but I'm going to.

13

eat any cakes
because I'm on a diet

14

walk on the grass
because it says 'Keep Off'

15

swim in the river
because it says 'No
Swimming'

Lesson 89 A very kind waiter

Narrator: Lást wéek
fáther tóok the fámily to a réstaurant
as a spécial tréat.

Father: Máy we sée the ménu pléase?
Waiter: Of cóurse, sír.

Father: Would you áll líke to begín with sóup?
All: Yés, pléase.
Father: Fóur sóups pléase.
Waiter: Véry góod, sír.

Mother: Sándy! Whát are you dóing?
Sandy: I'm pútting some sált in my sóup.

Sandy: Úgh! It tástes sálty!
Mother: You shóuldn't have pút any sált in it.
You shóuld have tásted it fírst.

Waiter: Néver mínd.
I'll bríng anóther pláte of sóup.
Father: That's véry kínd of you.

Lesson 89

Content and Basic Aims

PATTERNS AND STRUCTURAL WORDS	VOCABULARY	
Revision: *had to/it was necessary to/needn't have . . . (I) did it for nothing/didn't have to/it wasn't necessary to/should have/ought to have . . . but/shouldn't have/oughtn't to have . . . but.*	*Nouns*	*Verb*
	menu salt waiter	begin with
	Adj.	*Expressions*
	salty special	That's very kind of you. Very good. (= All right.)

• General Remarks

Patterns introduced in Teaching Units 38, 41, 42 and 43 are brought together and revised in this Unit.

• Aural/Oral Procedure

(a) Listening (Books shut)
(b) Listening and Understanding (Books open; pictures only)
(c) Listening (Books shut)
(d) Listening and Chorus Repetition (Books shut)
(e) Listening and Group Repetition (Books shut)
(f) Reading Aloud: Chorus and Individual (Books open)

• Graded Comprehension Questions

(a) Yes/No Tag Answers: did/may/would/is/does/should have/will.

TEACHER: Did father take the family to a cinema?
PUPIL: No, he didn't.
TEACHER: Did he take them to a restaurant?
PUPIL: Yes, he did. etc.

(b) Question Tags.

Make affirmative and negative statements to elicit question tags.

TEACHER: Father took them to a restaurant.
PUPIL: Father took them to a restaurant, didn't he?
TEACHER: He didn't take them to a cinema.
PUPIL: He didn't take them to a cinema, did he? etc.

(c) Questions with Who: did/would/is/shouldn't/should have/will.

TEACHER: Who took them to a restaurant?
PUPIL: Father did. etc.

(d) Double Questions.

TEACHER: Did father take them to a cinema or a restaurant?
PUPIL: He didn't take them to a cinema. He took them to a restaurant. etc.

(e) General Questions: Where, What, How many, Why.

TEACHER: Where did father take them?
PUPIL: To a restaurant. etc.

(f) Asking questions in pairs: Where, What, How many, Why.

TEACHER: Ask me if father took them to a restaurant.
PUPIL: Did father take them to a restaurant?
TEACHER: Where . . .
PUPIL: Where did father take them? etc.

• Acting the Scene

Invite five children to come to the front of the class to act the scene. An exercise-book may be used to represent a 'menu'.
The Narrator's part, frame 1, should be omitted.

• Unprepared Reading

Marley Castle, page 29.

• Activity

Repeat the tongue-twister, 'Peter Piper' introduced in Lesson 87.

• Writing

Workbook 3b, Lesson 89.
Guided Composition. The correct answer reads: They all went to a restaurant last week. They sat down at a table *and* father read the menu. Then he asked the waiter to bring four plates of soup. Sandy put a lot of salt in his soup *so* it didn't taste nice. He should have tasted it first, *but* it didn't matter. The kind waiter brought Sandy another plate of soup.

63 Words

Lesson 90

- **Spelling Drill:** Books shut.

  Oral and Written
  cinema; bicycle; concert; face; fence; cement;
  city; race; piece; electricity.

- **Phonic Practice:** Sounds and Spellings: Books
  open.

  The letters sh [ʃ] and t [ʃ]
  Chorus and Group Repetition

- **Reading and Repetition Drill:** Books open.

  Pictures 1–3 only.
  Ask the pupils to repeat the following:
  I had to dial 0240 because I wanted to speak to
  mum. It was necessary to dial 0240 because I
  wanted to speak to mum. etc.

- **Pattern Drill:** Books open.

  Pictures 1–3 only.

  (a) To elicit: I had to (dial 0240). Because (I
  wanted to speak to mum).

TEACHER:	*Picture 1.*
	What did you have to do?
PUPIL:	I had to dial 0240.
TEACHER:	Why?
PUPIL:	Because I wanted to speak to mum. etc.

  Repeat this exchange to elicit: *It was necessary to.*

- **Reading and Repetition Drill**

  Pictures 4–6 only.

  Ask the pupils to repeat the following:
  I needn't have watered the garden because it
  rained. I did it for nothing. etc.

- **Pattern Drill**

  (b) To elicit: Yes. I needn't have (watered the
  garden). Because (it rained). I did it for
  nothing.

TEACHER:	*Picture 4.*
	You watered the garden, didn't you?
PUPIL:	Yes, I needn't have watered the garden.
TEACHER:	Why?
PUPIL:	Because it rained. I did it for nothing. etc.

- **Reading and Repetition Drill**

  Pictures 7–9 only.

  Ask the pupils to repeat the following:
  I didn't have to dust the furniture because it was
  clean.
  It wasn't necessary to dust the furniture because
  it was clean. etc.

Point out the contrast between *didn't have to*
and *needn't have.*

- **Pattern Drill**

  (c) To elicit: No. I didn't have to dust the
  furniture. Because it was clean.

TEACHER:	*Picture 7.*
	Did you dust the furniture?
PUPIL:	No. I didn't have to dust the furniture.
TEACHER:	Why?
PUPIL:	Because it was clean. etc.

  Repeat this exchange to elicit *It wasn't necessary
  to.*

- **Reading and Repetition Drill:** Pictures 10–12
  only.

  Repeat the patterns indicated in the Pupils'
  Book with *should have* and *ought to have.*

- **Pattern Drill**

  (d) To elicit: I should have (dried the dishes)
  because (they were wet). No. I didn't feel
  like it.

TEACHER:	*Picture 10.*
	What should you have done?
PUPIL:	I should have dried the dishes because they were wet.
TEACHER:	Did you?
PUPIL:	No, I didn't feel like it. etc.

  Repeat this exchange with *ought to have.*

- **Reading and Repetition Drill:** Pictures 13–15
  only.

  Repeat the patterns indicated in the Pupils'
  Book with *shouldn't have* and *oughtn't to have.*

- **Pattern Drill**

  (e) To elicit: Yes, I shouldn't have (ridden it)
  because (the tyres are flat).

TEACHER:	*Picture 13.*
	You rode this bike, didn't you?
PUPIL:	Yes, I shouldn't have ridden it because the tyres are flat. etc.

  Repeat this exchange to elicit *oughtn't to have.*

- **Unprepared Reading**
  Marley Castle, page 30.

- **Activity**

  It's time for a story: Father and Sandy Go
  Fishing, page 265.
  New Words: *fishing-lines, pier, bait, hooks,
  silver, excited, fresh.*

- **Writing**
  Workbook 3b, Lesson 90.

  Explain the words *expressions and column;*
  make sure the pupils understand the instructions.

Lesson 90 Revision: had to, needn't have, didn't have to, etc.

wa<u>sh</u>   sta<u>ti</u>on   fi<u>sh</u>   na<u>ti</u>on   pu<u>sh</u>   collec<u>ti</u>on   ru<u>sh</u>   produc<u>ti</u>on

I had to/It was necessary to . . .

1

dial 0240
because I wanted to
speak to mum

2

add these figures
because I wanted to
do this sum

3

peel some onions
because I wanted to
make some soup

I needn't have/I did it for nothing.

4

watered the garden
because it rained

5

returned home early
because my parents
didn't expect me

6

picked any flowers
because there were some
in the vase

I didn't have to/It wasn't necessary to . . .

7

dust the furniture
because it was clean

8

pump up these tyres
because they were OK

9

call the doctor
because he was all right

I should have/I ought to have/but I didn't feel like it.

10

dried the dishes
because they were wet

11

tidied my room
because mother wanted me to

12

emptied the basket
because mother wanted
me to

I shouldn't have/I oughtn't to have/but I did.

13

ridden this bike
because the tyres are flat

14

swum in the river
because it says 'No Swimming'

15

walked on the grass
because it says 'Keep Off'

Lesson 91 Make up your mind!

Narrator: Móther and fáther
are at a depártment-stóre.
They're in the hát depártment.
Móther is búying a hát.

Mother: I líke this whíte hát véry múch.
I máy buy it, but I'm nót súre.

Mother: I líke this bláck óne, tóo.
Father: Wíll you búy it, déar?
Mother: I dón't knów. I míght.

Mother: Whích one do yóu líke, Jím?
Father: I dón't knów.
They bóth súit you.

Mother: I líke this whíte hát véry múch.
Father: Máke up your mínd pléase, Bétty!
Áre you góing to búy it, or nót?
Mother: Perháps I sháll, perháps I shán't.

Mother: Í've just hád a góod idéa, Jím!
Father: Whát?
Mother: I'm góing to búy *bóth* of them.
Father: Óh!

Lesson 91

Content and Basic Aims

PATTERNS AND STRUCTURAL WORDS	VOCABULARY	
	Nouns	Expression
(I) may/might (iron these trousers). *I'm not sure.* *(I) may/might not.* *Perhaps (she will) . . . Perhaps (she won't).*	department-store (hat) department	Make up your mind.

● **General Remarks**

Patterns involving the use of *may/might* to express uncertainty will be practised here. Compare requests for permission involving the use of *may* introduced in TU 9.

● **Aural/Oral Procedure**

(a) Listening (Books shut)
(b) Listening and Understanding (Books open; pictures only)
(c) Listening (Books shut)
(d) Listening and Chorus Repetition (Books shut)
(e) Listening and Group Repetition (Books shut)
(f) Reading Aloud: Chorus and Individual (Books open)

● **Graded Comprehension Questions**

(a) Yes/No Tag Answers: are/is/does/may/will/do/has.

TEACHER: Are mother and father at the grocer's?
PUPIL: No, they aren't.
TEACHER: Are they at a department-store?
PUPIL: Yes, they are. etc.

(b) Question Tags.

TEACHER: They're at a department-store.
PUPIL: They're at a department-store, aren't they?
TEACHER: They aren't at the grocer's.
PUPIL: They aren't at the grocer's, are they? etc.

(c) Questions with Who: are/is/does/may/will/has.

TEACHER: Who's in the hat department?
PUPIL: Mother and father *are*. etc.

(d) Double Questions.

TEACHER: Are they at the grocer's or at a department-store?
PUPIL: They aren't at the grocer's. They're at a department-store. etc.

(e) General Questions: Where, What, Which and Why.

TEACHER: Where are mother and father?
PUPIL: At a department-store. etc.

(f) Asking questions in pairs: Where, What, Which and Why.

TEACHER: Ask me if they are at a department-store.
PUPIL: Are they at a department-store?
TEACHER: Where . . .
PUPIL: Where are they? etc.

● **Acting the Scene**

Invite three children to come to the front of the class to act the scene. Black and white hats would be useful props. The Narrator's part, frame 1, should be omitted.

● **Unprepared Reading**

Marley Castle, page 31.
New Words and Expressions: *prisoners, earth* (soil), *fell asleep, plan.*

● **Activity**

Repeat:
(a) Peter Piper, Lesson 87.
(b) Sandy Macnab, Lesson 83.
(c) Some folk do, Lessons 73–77.

● **Writing**

Workbook 3b, Lesson 91.
From this point on the pupils will practise writing *complex* as well as *simple* and *compound* sentences. They will gradually be introduced to a variety of conjunctions, as and when they occur in the main structures. These will always be given in brackets as before.
Guided Composition. The correct answer reads: Mother and father went to the hat department *because* mother wanted to buy a hat. She tried on two hats *and* she liked them both very much. Father liked them both, too, *and* mother couldn't make up her mind. Then she smiled *because* she had a good idea. "I'm going to buy both of them," she said. She felt very pleased, but father didn't.

64 Words

Lesson 92

● **Spelling Drill:** Books shut.

Oral and Written
cold/cinema/smile; cool/city/say; bake/cement/
stone; cap/bicycle/stop.

● **Phonic Practice:** Sounds and Spellings: Books open.

The letters ss [s] and ch [tʃ]
Chorus and Group Repetition

● **Reading and Repetition Drill:** Books open.

Chorus and Group Repetition

TEACHER: *Picture 1.*
    I may iron these trousers. I'm not
    sure. *All together!*
    I might iron these trousers. I'm not
    sure. *All together!*

Practise these patterns with the items given.
Point out that *may* and *might* carry the same
meaning.

● **Pattern Drill:** Books open.

(a) To elicit: I may (iron these trousers). I'm
not sure.

TEACHER: *Picture 1.*
    What are you going to do?
PUPIL: I may iron these trousers. I'm
    not sure. etc.

(b) To elicit: I might (iron these trousers). I'm
not sure.

TEACHER: *Picture 1.*
    What are you going to do?
PUPIL: I might iron these trousers. I'm
    not sure.

(c) To elicit: I don't know. I may not.

TEACHER: *Picture 1.*
    Will you iron these trousers?
PUPIL: I don't know. I may not. etc.

(d) To elicit: I might not. I can't make up my
mind.

TEACHER: *Picture 1.*
    Will you iron these trousers?
PUPIL: I might not. I can't make up my
    mind. etc.

(e) To elicit: What do you think (she)'ll do?
(She) may (iron these trousers). She isn't
sure.

TEACHER: *Picture 1.*
1st PUPIL: What do you think she'll do?
2nd PUPIL: She may iron these trousers.
    She isn't sure. etc.

(f) To elicit: What do you think (she)'ll do?
(She) might (iron these trousers). She isn't
sure.

TEACHER: *Picture 1.*
1st PUPIL: What do you think she'll do?
2nd PUPIL: She might iron these trousers.
    She isn't sure. etc.

(g) To elicit: Perhaps (she) will. Perhaps (she)
won't.

TEACHER: *Picture 1.*
    Will she iron these trousers, do
    you think?
PUPIL: Perhaps she will. Perhaps she
    won't. etc.

● **Unprepared Reading**

Marley Castle, page 32.
New Words and Expressions: *breathe, right-
hand pocket, key-ring, frighten, gently.*

● **Activity**

A Game: Lucky Dip.
The teacher writes a number of imperative
statements on individual pieces of paper. (Any
of those given in Lesson 92.) The pieces of
paper are placed in a hat or bag and pupils
are invited to come up one at a time to choose
a piece of paper.

TEACHER: What are you going to do?
PUPIL   *(examining statement on piece of
    paper):* I may (play football). I'm
    not sure.

● **Writing**

Workbook 3b, Lesson 92.

Lesson 92 I may . . . /I might . . . /I'm not sure
Perhaps she will . . . /
Perhaps she won't . . .

gla<u>ss</u>   <u>ch</u>air   pa<u>ss</u>   <u>ch</u>urch   mi<u>ss</u>   <u>ch</u>ief   profe<u>ss</u>or   <u>ch</u>ild

1 iron these trousers

2 borrow some money

3 ask for a porter

4 build a sandcastle

5 have a slice of toast

6 have some marmalade

7 go on a picnic

8 play football

9 look at the window-display

10 become an astronaut

11 ask for the menu

12 learn a foreign language

13 buy a torch

14 visit Texas

15 go abroad

Lesson **93** Too good to be true!

Mother:	How múch is thát hándbag, Súe? I cán't sée the príce.	1
Sue:	I'm nót súre. It máy be 50 pénce.	

Mother:	50 pénce! It cán't be! Súrely it ísn't!	2
Sue:	Lét's gó ín and ásk.	

Mother:	How múch is thát hándbag?	3
Assistant:	Whích óne?	
Mother:	The óne in the wíndow.	

Assistant *(holding bag):*	50 pénce! It cán't be! It's máde of léather, nót plástic. Thís must be a mistáke. I'll ásk the mánager.	4

Assistant:	How múch is thís hándbag?	5
Manager:	It's £5, nót 50 pénce. Thís is a mistáke.	

Assistant:	I'm sórry mádam.	6
Mother:	I knéw it!	
Sue:	It was tóo góod to be trúe!	

Content and Basic Aims

PATTERNS AND STRUCTURAL WORDS	VOCABULARY	
(It) may be/can't be/must be (£5/22nd May/ grey/English/size 30/square/tired/7 years old/a butcher/reading). *Surely (it isn't)!*	*Nouns*	*Adv.*
	leather manager (of a store)	surely
		Expression
	Adj.	Too good to be true!
	round true	

● **General Remarks**

Patterns involving the use of *may be* (I'm not sure), *can't be* (in my opinion (it) isn't), and *must be* (in my opinion (it) is) are practised here. Compare TU 25.

● **Aural/Oral Procedure**

(a) Listening (Books shut)
(b) Listening and Understanding (Books open; pictures only)
(c) Listening (Books shut)
(d) Listening and Chorus Repetition (Books shut)
(e) Listening and Group Repetition (Books shut)
(f) Reading Aloud: Chorus and Individual (Books open)

● **Graded Comprehension Questions**

(a) Yes/No Tag Answers: is/can/will/did/was.

TEACHER: Is the handbag 50 pence?
PUPIL: No, it isn't.
TEACHER: Is it £5?
PUPIL: Yes, it is. etc.

(b) Question Tags.

TEACHER: The handbag costs £5.
PUPIL: The handbag costs £5, doesn't it?
TEACHER: It doesn't cost 50 pence.
PUPIL: It doesn't cost 50 pence, does it? etc.

(c) Questions with Who: can't/isn't/is/did.

TEACHER: Who can't see the price?
PUPIL: Mother can't. etc.

(d) Double Questions.

TEACHER: Does the handbag cost 50 pence or £5?
PUPIL: It doesn't cost 50 pence. It costs £5. etc.

(e) General Questions: How much, Where, What and Who.

TEACHER: How much is the handbag in the window?
PUPIL: £5. etc.

(f) Asking questions in pairs: How much, Where, What and Who.

TEACHER: Ask me if the handbag is £5.
PUPIL: Is the handbag £5?
TEACHER: How much . . .
PUPIL: How much is the handbag? etc.

● **Acting the Scene**

Invite four children to come to the front of the class to act the scene. A schoolbag could serve as a handbag; a price tag for 50 pence may be made and attached to it.

● **Unprepared Reading**

Marley Castle, page 33.

● **Activity**

Repeat:
(a) Some folk do, Lessons 73–77.
(b) Oh, dear! What can the matter be? Lessons 65–67.
(c) I had a little nut-tree, Lesson 61.

● **Writing**

Workbook 3b, Lesson 93.
Guided Composition. The correct answer reads: Mother and Sue looked at a handbag in a shop window, *but* they weren't sure of the price, *so* they both went into the shop *and* asked the assistant. The assistant took the handbag from the window and looked at the price. It was 50 pence. She couldn't believe it was so cheap *because* it was a leather handbag, *so* she called the manager. Mother and Sue were sorry to hear that the price was wrong. The handbag cost £5. "It was too good to be true!" Sue said.

89 Words

Lesson 94

- **Spelling Drill:** Books shut.

  Oral and Written
  knife/knives; wife/wives; loaf/loaves; thief/
  thieves; shelf/shelves; life/lives.
  Point out that nouns ending in 'f' or 'fe'
  usually take '-ves' in the plural. There are
  exceptions: e.g. chief/chiefs.

- **Phonic Practice:** Sounds and Spellings: Books
  open.

  The letters ch [tʃ] and tch [tʃ]
  Chorus and Group Repetition

- **Reading and Repetition Drill:** Books open.

  Chorus and Group Repetition
  TEACHER: *Picture 1.*
  How much is that handbag? *All together!*
  It may be £5. I'm not sure. *All together!*
  It can't be £5. Surely it isn't £5. *All together!*
  It must be £5. I'm sure it's £5. *All together!*

  Practise these patterns with each of the items
  shown.

- **Pattern Drill:** Books open.

  (a) To elicit: (It) may be (£5). I'm not sure.

  TEACHER: *Picture 1.*
  How much is that handbag?
  PUPIL: It may be £5. I'm not sure. etc.

  (b) To elicit: (It) can't be (£5). Surely (it) isn't
  (£5).

  TEACHER: *Picture 1.*
  Is that handbag £5?
  PUPIL: It can't be £5. Surely it isn't £5. etc.

  (c) To elicit: (It) must be (£5). I'm sure it's (£5).

  TEACHER: *Picture 1.*
  How much is that handbag?
  PUPIL: It must be £5. I'm sure it's £5. etc.

  (d) To elicit: (It) can't be (£5). (It) must be
  ($5).
  Pictures should be referred to in pairs.

  TEACHER: *Pictures 1 and 2.*
  Is that handbag £5 or $5?
  PUPIL: It can't be £5. It must be $5. etc.

  (e) To elicit: Surely (it) isn't (£5). (It) must be
  ($5). Pictures should be referred to in pairs.

  TEACHER: *Pictures 1 and 2.*
  Guess how much that handbag
  is!

  PUPIL: Surely it isn't £5. It must be $5.
  etc.

  (f) To elicit: I don't believe (it)'s (£5). (It) must
  be ($5).
  Pictures should be referred to in pairs.

  TEACHER: *Pictures 1 and 2.*
  I think that handbag is £5.
  PUPIL: I don't believe it's £5. It must be
  $5. etc.

- **Unprepared Reading**

  Marley Castle, page 34.
  New Words: *beach, tide.*

- **Activity**

  Dictation

  Dictate the following passage:

  "Whát are you góing to dó this mórning,
  Sándy?"/móther ásked./
  "I máy pláy with Bílly./I'm nót súre,"/Sándy
  sáid.
  Sándy wént to Bílly's hóuse./He tóok his
  fóotball with him.
  "You néedn't have bróught your báll, Sándy,"
  Billy sáid./"I háve a báll./Yóu should have léft
  yóurs at hóme."

- **Writing**

  Workbook 3b, Lesson 94.

Lesson 94

(It) may be/I'm not sure.
(It) can't be/Surely (it) isn't . . .
(It) must be/I'm sure (it) . . .

1

2

How much is that handbag?
£5 $5

3

4

What's the date today?
22nd May   23rd May

5

6

What colour's that hat?
grey   black

7

8

What shape's that building?
square   round

9

10

What size are those shoes?
size 30   size 40

11

12

What nationality is he?
English   American

13

14

How is he?
tired   ill

15

16

How old is she?
7   10

17

18

What's his job?
a butcher   a farmer

19

20

What's he doing?
reading   sleeping

Lesson 95 Television Day: "General Sherman"

TV Commentary:

You are looking at the biggest tree in the world. Its name is "General Sherman". General Sherman is growing on the slopes of the Rocky Mountains in the United States. General Sherman is about 11 metres across and about 35 metres round. During playtime join hands with 25 of your friends and make a circle. This will give you an idea of General Sherman's size. General Sherman is also very tall. It is over 80 metres high. It began as a tiny seed many years ago. Imagine! It has been growing since about 2000 B.C. It has been growing for almost 4000 years and it is still growing! General Sherman is as old as the Pyramids. It may live for another 2000 years. What will the world be like in 4000 A.D.? General Sherman will know!

Billy Boy

Where have you been all the day, Billy boy, Billy boy?
Where have you been all the day, my Billy boy?
I've been walking all the day
With my charming Nancy Grey
And my Nancy tickled my fancy,
Oh my charming Billy boy.

Content and Basic Aims

PATTERNS AND STRUCTURAL WORDS	VOCABULARY		
How long/Since when (have you) been (correct)ing (exercise-books)?	*Nouns*	*Expression*	*Verbs*
(I've(been (correct)ing (exercise-books) since (yesterday) for (two days) . . . and (I'm) still (correcting . . .).	circle general (military) Pyramid	join hands	imagine join
	Rocky Mountains seed	*Adj.*	*Adv.*
	slope time(s) (period) United States	tiny	also A.D. B.C.

● **General Remarks**

Patterns involving the use of the present perfect continuous with *since* and *for* are introduced here. Compare Book 2, TU's 45 and 46.

● **Aural/Oral Procedure**

(a) Listening (Books shut)
(b) Intensive Reading (Books open)
The passage should be played or read to the class in small units. During each pause, explain unfamiliar words. Rather than give direct explanations, try to elicit as much information as possible from the pupils.
(c) Listening (Books shut)
(d) Reading Aloud: Individual (Books open)

● **Graded Comprehension Questions**

(a) Yes/No Tag Answers: am/is/will/did/has/may.

TEACHER: Are you looking at the smallest tree in the world?
PUPIL: No, I'm not.
TEACHER: Are you looking at the biggest tree in the world?
PUPIL: Yes, I am. etc.

(b) Question Tags.

TEACHER: I am looking at the biggest tree in the world.
PUPIL: I am looking at the biggest tree in the world, *aren't I?* (N.B.)
TEACHER: I'm not looking at the smallest tree.
PUPIL: I'm not looking at the smallest tree, am I?

(c) Double Questions.

TEACHER: Are you looking at the smallest or the biggest tree in the world?
PUPIL: I'm not looking at the smallest tree in the world. I'm looking at the biggest one. etc.

(d) General Questions: What, Which, Where, When, How.

TEACHER: What are you looking at?
PUPIL: The biggest tree in the world. etc.

(e) Asking questions in pairs: What, Which, Where, When, How.

TEACHER: Ask me if I'm looking at the biggest tree in the world. etc.

● **Oral Composition**

Write the following notes on the blackboard:
Biggest tree in the world: General Sherman.
Growing—slopes—Rocky Mountains—U.S.A.
11 metres across; 35 metres round.
Playtime—join hands: 25 friends.
Very tall—80 metres high.
Began as a seed.
Growing since 2000 B.C.
Growing for 4000 years.
Old as the Pyramids.
May live another 2000 years—4000 A.D.

Now ask one or two pupils to reconstruct the passage by referring to the notes.

● **Unprepared Reading**

Marley Castle, page 35.
New Words: *singing, crack* (nouns).

● **Activity**

Song: Billy Boy. See page 254 for music.
Teach the first verse of this song.

● **Writing**

Workbook 3b, Lesson 95.
Guided Composition. The correct answer reads:
The biggest tree in the world, General Sherman, has been growing on the slopes of the Rocky Mountains in the United States *since* about 2000 B.C. It measures about 11 metres across, about 35 metres round *and* it's about 80 metres tall. It has been growing for almost 4000 years *and* it hasn't stopped yet. It may live till 4000 A.D.
61 Words

Lesson 96

● **Spelling Drill:** Books shut.

Oral and Written
move; far; drive; fast; leave; flat; have; fun;
village; wood; voice; food.

● **Phonic Practice:** Sounds and Spellings: Books open.

The letters ts [ts] and ch [tʃ]
Chorus and Group Repetition

● **Reading and Repetition Drill:** Books open.

Chorus and Group Repetition

TEACHER: *Picture 1.*
How long has Mrs Hart been correcting exercise-books? *All together!*
She's been correcting exercise-books since yesterday. *All together!*
She's been correcting exercise-books for two days. *All together!*

Practise these patterns with the items given.

● **Pattern Drill:** Books open.

(a) To elicit: How long has (Mrs Hart) been (correcting exercise-books)?
(She)'s been (correcting exercise-books) since (yesterday).

TEACHER: *Picture 1.*
1st PUPIL: How long has Mrs Hart been correcting exercise-books?
2nd PUPIL: She's been correcting exercise-books since yesterday. etc.

(b) To elicit: How long has (Mrs Hart) been (correcting exercise-books)?
(She)'s been (correcting exercise-books) for (two days).

TEACHER: *Picture 1.*
1st PUPIL: How long has Mrs Hart been correcting exercise-books?
2nd PUPIL: She's been correcting exercise-books for two days. etc.

(c) To elicit: How long have you been (correcting exercise-books)?
I've been (correcting exercise-books) since (yesterday). Omit No. 3.

TEACHER: *Picture 1.*
1st PUPIL: How long have you been correcting exercise-books?
2nd PUPIL: I've been correcting exercise-books since yesterday. etc.

(d) To elicit: How long have you been (correcting exercise-books)?
I've been (correcting exercise-books) for (two days). Omit No. 3.

TEACHER: *Picture 1.*
1st PUPIL: How long have you been correcting exercise-books?
2nd PUPIL: I've been correcting exercise-books for two days. etc.

(e) To elicit: Since when has (she) been (correcting exercise-books)?
(She)'s been (correcting exercise-books) since (yesterday) and (she)'s still (correcting them). Omit Nos. 9 and 10.

TEACHER: *Picture 1.*
1st PUPIL: Since when has she been correcting exercise-books?
2nd PUPIL: She's been correcting exercise-books since yesterday and she's still correcting them. etc.

(f) To elicit: Since when has (she) been (correcting exercise-books)?
(She)'s been (correcting exercise-books) for (two days) and (she)'s still (correcting them). Omit Nos. 9 and 10.

TEACHER: *Picture 1.*
1st PUPIL: Since when has she been correcting exercise-books?
2nd PUPIL: She's been correcting exercise-books for two days and she's still correcting them. etc.

● **Unprepared Reading**

Marley Castle, page 36.
New Words and Expressions: *strongroom, bars* (of e.g. a prison), *load* (vb.), *high tide.*

● **Activity**

It's time for a story: The Remarkable Rooster, page 266.
New Words and Expressions: *hen-run, hens, lay* (eggs), *rooster, crow* (vb.), *Cock-a-doodle-doo!* (sound imitation), *laid an egg, remarkable, vet.* (animal doctor), *golden.*

● **Writing**

Workbook 3b, Lesson 96.

Lesson 96 How long have you been . . .
I've been . . . since . . . for . . .

hat<u>s</u>   <u>ch</u>eer   ca<u>ts</u>   <u>ch</u>ur<u>ch</u>   put<u>s</u>   <u>ch</u>ange   si<u>ts</u>   <u>ch</u>imney

1

(Mrs Hart) correcting exercise-books
since yesterday
for two days

2

(The baby) crying
since one o'clock
for three hours

3

(That tree) growing
since 1932
for many years

4

(Mother) ironing clothes
since this morning
for three hours

5

(The men) exploring the cave
since April
for two months

6

(Sue) combing her hair
since eight o'clock
for three minutes

7

(Mother) dialling that number
since lunch-time
for a long time

8

(The workmen) digging that hole
since April 14th
for two weeks

9

(Sue) skating
since she was six
for quite a while

10

(Father) travelling abroad
since he was a boy
for many years

Lesson 97 "A bank robbery"

Whén Sándy and Súe were cóming hóme from schóol yésterday áfternóon,
they sáw a crówd of péople near a bánk.

Sándy and Súe jóined the crówd.
They were surprísed to see
twó thíeves in the stréet.

The thíeves were rúnning óut of the bánk.
They were hólding bágs full of móney.
The bánk mánager was rúnning áfter them.

A policeman was stánding amóng the crówd,
but he dídn't dó ánything!
"Quíck!" Sándy shóuted to the policeman.
"Cán't you sée those thíeves?"

The policeman smíled.
He póinted at a bíg cámera.
"We're máking a fílm," he sáid.

"Thóse mén aren't réal thíeves.
They're áctors.
And Í'm not a réal policeman, éither.
Í'm an áctor, tóo!"

Is she fit to be your wife, Billy boy, Billy boy?
Is she fit to be your wife, my Billy boy?
She's as fit to be my wife
As the fork is to the knife,
And my Nancy, etc.

Content and Basic Aims

PATTERNS AND STRUCTURAL WORDS	VOCABULARY			
When/Just as/While (Sue) was (dry)ing (the dishes she dropped a plate and broke it). *(Mother saw a nice hat) when/just as/while (she) was (walk)ing (through the Hat Department).* *While (Sandy) was (play)ing (the piano, Sue) was (play)ing (the flute).*	*Nouns*	*Prep.*	*Verb*	*Expression*
	bag bank (money) bank manager	among	point (at)	They joined the crowd.

● **General Remarks**

The past continuous as used to express continuous, interrupted and parallel actions is introduced here. It will be practised in connection with *when, while* and *just as*.

● **Aural/Oral Procedure**

(a) Listening (Books shut)
(b) Listening and Understanding (Books open; pictures only)
(c) Listening (Books shut)
(d) Listening and Chorus Repetition (Books shut)
(e) Listening and Group Repetition (Books shut)
(f) Reading Aloud: Chorus and Individual (Books open)

● **Graded Comprehension Questions**

(a) Yes/No Tag Answers: were/did/was/can/are/is.

TEACHER: Were Sandy and Sue going to school?
PUPIL: No, they weren't.
TEACHER: Were they coming home from school?
PUPIL: Yes, they were. etc.

(b) Question Tags.

TEACHER: They were coming home from school.
PUPIL: They were coming home from school, weren't they?
TEACHER: They weren't going to school.
PUPIL: They weren't going to school, were they? etc.

(c) Questions with Who: were/did/was/didn't.

TEACHER: Who was coming home from school?
PUPIL: Sandy and Sue *were*. etc.

(d) Double Questions.

TEACHER: Were Sandy and Sue going to school, or were they coming home from school?
PUPIL: They weren't going to school. They were coming home from school. etc.

(e) General Questions: Where, Why, What.

TEACHER: Where did they see the crowd of people?
PUPIL: Near a bank. etc.

(f) Asking questions in pairs: When, Where, Why and What.

TEACHER: Ask me if they saw a crowd of people.
PUPIL: Did they see a crowd of people?
TEACHER: When . . .
PUPIL: When did they see a crowd of people? etc.

● **Telling the Story**

Ask one or two pupils to reconstruct the story by referring only to the pictures. The pupils should remain seated during this exercise.

● **Unprepared Reading**

Marley Castle, page 37.
New Word: *lever*.

● **Activity**

Song: Billy Boy. See page 254 for music.
Teach the second verse.

● **Writing**

Workbook 3b, Lesson 97.
Guided Composition. The correct answer reads: Sandy and Sue were coming home from school yesterday afternoon *when* they saw a crowd of people near a bank. They were surprised *because* they saw two thieves. The thieves were running away with some money *and* the bank manager was running after them. The policeman in the crowd didn't do anything about it *because* this wasn't a real robbery. Some men were making a film *and* the 'policeman' and the 'thieves' were actors.

75 Words

Lesson 98

- **Spelling Drill:** Books shut.

  Oral and Written
  fine/photograph; traffic/telephone; finish/alphabet; lift/elephant.

- **Phonic Practice:** Sounds and Spellings: Books open.

  The letters ds [dz] and ch [tʃ]
  Chorus and Group Repetition

- **Reading and Repetition Drill:** Books open.

  Chorus and Group Repetition
  Ask the pupils to repeat the statements in Lesson 98 of the Pupils' Book.

- **Pattern Drill:** Books open or shut.

  (a) To elicit: (I was having a bath) when he arrived.

  > TEACHER: What were you doing when he arrived? . . . having a bath.
  > PUPIL: I was having a bath when he arrived.

  Substitute the following:
  sweeping the floor; burning the rubbish; building a sandcastle; feeding the ducks; dialling the number; serving the food; hiding behind a tree; lying in bed; diving into the pool; practising the piano; clearing the table; correcting my homework; mending my bicycle; unlocking the door; planting those flowers; minding the baby; digging the garden.

  (b) To elicit: When he arrived (I was having a bath).
  Conduct the drill in the way shown in (a) above substituting the same statements.

  (c) To elicit: He arrived just as (I was leaving).

  > TEACHER: When did he arrive? . . . leaving.
  > PUPIL: He arrived just as I was leaving.

  Substitute the following:
  combing my hair; drying the dishes; returning home from school; peeling these onions; measuring the room; pressing the button; skating across the lake; adding these figures; dusting the furniture; repairing this toy; ironing the clothes.

  (d) To elicit: He arrived while (I was having a bath).

  > TEACHER: When did he arrive? . . . having a bath.
  > PUPIL: He arrived while I was having a bath.

  Substitute the expressions given under (a) above.

  (e) To elicit: While I was cooking the dinner, he (was working in the garden).

  > TEACHER: What was he doing while you were cooking the dinner? . . . working in the garden.
  > PUPIL: While I was cooking the dinner, he was working in the garden.

  Substitute the following:
  having a wash; watching television; cleaning his shoes; listening to the radio; making the tea; changing his suit; sitting in the kitchen; reading the paper; playing hide-and-seek.

  (f) To elicit: I was cooking the dinner while he (was working in the garden).

  > TEACHER: What was he doing while you were cooking the dinner? . . . working in the garden.
  > PUPIL: I was cooking the dinner while he was working in the garden.

  Substitute the expressions given under (e) above.

- **Unprepared Reading**

  Marley Castle, page 38.

- **Activity**

  A Guessing Game.
  The teacher writes a list of activities on the blackboard—e.g. any of the expressions given under (a) above. A pupil is asked to leave the room and the class selects one of the expressions on the board. The pupil is recalled and he must guess which expression was chosen. He may consult the board if he wishes to. He has three guesses. If he guesses correctly he gets another go.

  > TEACHER (*addressing pupil who has just been recalled*): What were they doing while you were out of the room?
  > PUPIL (*consulting blackboard*): They were sweeping the floor.
  > TEACHER: No, they weren't. etc.

- **Writing**

  Workbook 3b, Lesson 98.

Lesson **98** What were they doing?

1

When Sue was drying the dishes,
she dropped a plate and broke it.

2

Mother saw a nice hat when she
was walking through the Hat
Department.

3

Just as they were going to leave,
someone knocked at the door.

4

The postman arrived just as they
were leaving.

5

While they were watching
television, the telephone rang.

6

Father cut himself while he was
shaving.

7

While Sandy was playing the
piano, Sue was playing her
flute.

8

Mother was cooking a meal while
father was digging in the garden.

Lesson 99 Sandy reads a joke

Narrator: Sándy is réading a cómic.
"Lísten to this jóke, Súe," he sáys.
"I'll réad it to you."

Sandy: Twó explórers were cráwling
acróss the désert.
They were dýing of thírst.

Sandy: Súddenly, óne of them lóoked up and sáid,
"Lóok! Did yóu see thát?
It was an oásis!"

Sandy: "An oásis!" the óther mán críed.
"It cán't have been!
Súrely it wásn't!
It múst have been a miráge."

Sandy: The explórers cráwled towárds the "oásis"

Sandy: Súddenly they bánged their héads
into sómething.
It wásn't an oásis,
and it wásn't a miráge.
It was an óil-pípe!

Can she cook a bit of steak, Billy boy, Billy boy?
Can she cook a bit of steak, my Billy boy?
She can cook a bit of steak,
Ay, and make a girdle cake,
And my Nancy, etc.

Content and Basic Aims

PATTERNS AND STRUCTURAL WORDS	VOCABULARY		
	Nouns		*Expression*
(It) may have been/can't have been/must have been (£5/22nd May/grey/English/size 30/square/tired/7 years old/a butcher/ reading). *Surely (it wasn't)!*	comic (book) explorer joke	mirage thirst oasis oil-pipe	bang your head into something

● **General Remarks**

Patterns involving the use of *may have been, can't have been* (in my opinion (it) wasn't), and *must have been* (in my opinion (it) was) are practised here. Compare TU 47.

● **Aural/Oral Procedure**

(a) Listening (Books shut)
(b) Listening and Understanding (Books open; pictures only)
(c) Listening (Books shut)
(d) Listening and Chorus Repetition (Books shut)
(e) Listening and Group Repetition (Books shut)
(f) Reading Aloud: Chorus and Individual (Books open)

● **Graded Comprehension Questions**

(a) Yes/No Tag Answers: is/will/are/did/was.

To elicit a subject followed by an auxiliary verb.

TEACHER: Is Sandy reading a book?
PUPIL: No, he isn't.
TEACHER: Is Sandy reading a comic?
PUPIL: Yes, he is. etc.

(b) Question Tags.

Make affirmative and negative statements to elicit question tags.

TEACHER: Sandy is reading a comic.
PUPIL: Sandy is reading a comic, isn't he?
TEACHER: He isn't reading a book.
PUPIL: He isn't reading a book, is he? etc.

(c) Questions with Who: is/will/are/did.

To elicit a subject followed by an auxiliary verb.

TEACHER: Who is reading a comic?
PUPIL: Sandy is. etc.

(d) Double Questions.

To elicit negative and affirmative statements.

TEACHER: Is Sandy reading a book or a comic?
PUPIL: He isn't reading a book. He's reading a comic. etc.

(e) General Questions: What, Where, Why.

TEACHER: What's Sandy reading?
PUPIL: A comic. etc.

(f) Asking questions in pairs: What, Where, Why.

TEACHER: Ask me if Sandy's reading a comic.
PUPIL: Is Sandy reading a comic?
TEACHER: What . . .
PUPIL: What's Sandy reading? etc.

● **Telling the Story**

Ask one or two pupils to tell the story by referring only to the pictures. Pupils should remain seated. Prompt the children as often as is necessary, though they should feel free to add words and phrases of their own if they wish to.

● **Unprepared Reading**

Marley Castle, page 39.
Ask one or two pupils to read this page without any preparation.

● **Activity**

Song: Billy Boy. See page 254 for music.
Teach the third verse of this song. Explain 'girdle cake': a cake cooked on an iron plate which was hung over the fire.

● **Writing**

Workbook 3b, Lesson 99.
Guided Composition. The correct answer reads: Yesterday Sandy read a joke to Sue. Two explorers were dying of thirst in the desert. *While* they were crawling over the sand, one of them looked up *and* saw an oasis. He told the other explorer about it, *but* his friend did not believe him. "It must have been a mirage," the other man said. They crawled towards the 'oasis' *and* suddenly banged their heads into an oil-pipe!

69 Words

Lesson 100

- **Spelling Drill:** Books shut.

  Oral and Written
  that/thank; then/thin; this/thief; they/threw;
  teeth/mother; north/father; mouth/other.

  Ask individual pupils to spell these words
  orally. As soon as a word has been spelt correctly, write it on the blackboard. When all
  the words have been written, erase them. Then
  dictate them to the class.

- **Phonic Practice:** Sounds and Spellings: Books
  open.

  The letters ch [tʃ] and j [dʒ]
  Chorus and Group Repetition
  Ask the pupils to repeat after you the words at
  the top of page 80 of the Pupils' Book.

- **Reading and Repetition Drill:** Books open.

  Chorus and Group Repetition

  TEACHER: *Picture 1.*
  How much was that handbag? *All
  together!*
  It may have been £5. I'm not sure.
  All together!
  It can't have been £5. Sure it wasn't
  £5. *All together!*
  It must have been £5. I'm sure it
  was £5. *All together!*

  Practise these patterns with each of the items
  shown.

- **Pattern Drill:** Books open.

  Illustrate each exercise first by providing the
  stimulus and the response. Make sure the pupils
  really understand how they must respond. Then
  conduct the drills given below. If a child makes
  a mistake, correct him and ask him to repeat
  the right answer.

  (a) To elicit: (It) may have been (£5). I'm not
  sure.

  TEACHER: *Picture 1.*
  How much was that handbag?
  PUPIL: It may have been £5. I'm not sure.
  etc.

  (b) To elicit: (It) can't have been (£5). Surely
  (it) wasn't (£5).

  TEACHER: *Picture 1.*
  Was that handbag £5?
  PUPIL: It can't have been £5. Surely it
  wasn't £5. etc.

  (c) To elicit: (It) must have been (£5). I'm sure
  it was (£5).

  TEACHER: *Picture 1.*
  How much was that handbag?

PUPIL: It must have been £5. I'm sure it
was £5. etc.

(d) To elicit: (It) can't have been (£5). (It) must
have been ($5).
Pictures should be referred to in pairs.

TEACHER: *Pictures 1 and 2.*
Was that handbag £5 or $5?
PUPIL: It can't have been £5. It must
have been $5. etc.

(e) To elicit: Surely (it) wasn't (£5). (It) must
have been ($5).
Pictures should be referred to in pairs.

TEACHER: *Pictures 1 and 2.*
Guess how much that handbag
was!
PUPIL: Surely it wasn't £5. It must have
been $5. etc.

(f) To elicit: I don't believe (it) was (£5). (It)
must have been ($5).

TEACHER: *Pictures 1 and 2.*
I think that handbag was £5.
PUPIL: I don't believe it was £5. It must
have been $5. etc.

- **Unprepared Reading**

  Marley Castle, page 40.

- **Activity**

  Dictation
  For notes regarding correct delivery, consult
  Revision Lesson 4. Dictate the following
  passage:

  Móther and Súe/have béen in a shóe-shóp for
  twó hóurs./They have been lóoking/for a níce
  páir of shóes./"We cán't fínd ánything, Súe,"/
  móther sáid./"Lét's gó."/Júst as they were
  léaving/they saw a lóvely páir of shóes/in the
  window./"They cán't be mý síze," móther sáid./
  But they wére/and she bóught them.

- **Writing**

  Workbook 3b, Lesson 100.

Lesson **100**
(It) may have been/I'm not sure.
(It) can't have been/Surely (it) wasn't . . .
(It) must have been/I'm sure (it) . . .

<u>ch</u>air <u>j</u>ump   <u>church</u> June   <u>ch</u>ief <u>J</u>apan   <u>change j</u>ar

1	2	3	4

How much was that handbag?   What was the date yesterday?
£5 $5   22nd May   23rd May

5   6   7   8

What colour was that hat?   What shape was that building?
grey   black   square   round

9   10   11   12

What size were those shoes?   What nationality was he?
size 30   size 40   English   American

13   14   15   16

How was he?   How old was she?
tired   ill   7   10

17   18   19   20

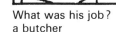
What was his job?   
a butcher   a farmer

What was he doing?
reading   sleeping

Lesson **101**   The sales

The sáles begán lást wéek.
Móther and Súe wént to the shóps.

1

They wálked dówn Óxford Stréet.
Súddenly, they mét Mŕs Dúmpling.
Mŕs Dúmpling was véry excíted.

2

"Óh, Mŕs Clárk," she sáid.
"Lóok at this béautiful fúr cóat.
I bóught it at the sáles for ónly £5!"

3

"£5!" móther críed.
"It cán't have cóst £5.
It múst have cóst móre than thát."
"It dídn't," Mŕs Dúmpling sáid.
"Lóok at the príce."

4

"Whére did you búy it?" móther ásked.
"In thát shóp," Mŕs Dúmpling sáid
and póinted dówn the stréet.

5

"We cán't get in thére!" Súe críed.
"It's líke a fóotball-mátch!"

6

Can she make a feather bed, Billy boy, Billy boy?
Can she make a feather bed, my Billy boy?
She can make a feather bed,
Fit for any sailor's head,
And my Nancy, etc.

Lesson **101**

Content and Basic Aims

PATTERNS AND STRUCTURAL WORDS	VOCABULARY	
(It) may/must/can't (cost £5). *(It) may have/must have/can't have* *(cost £5).*	*Noun*	*Adj.*
	sales	excited

- ### General Remarks

Patterns involving the use of *may/may have, can't/can't have* and *must/must have* are practised together with the verbs *cost, weigh,* etc., and with sense verbs. Compare TU's 47 and 50.

- ### Aural/Oral Procedure

(a) Listening (Books shut)
(b) Listening and Understanding (Books open; pictures only)
(c) Listening (Books shut)
(d) Listening and Chorus Repetition (Books shut)
(e) Listening and Group Repetition (Books shut)
(f) Reading Aloud: Chorus and Individual (Books open)

- ### Graded Comprehension Questions

(a) Yes/No Tag Answers: did/was/is.

TEACHER: Did the sales begin this week?
PUPIL: No, they didn't.
TEACHER: Did the sales begin last week?
PUPIL: Yes, they did. etc.

(b) Question Tags.

TEACHER: The sales began last week.
PUPIL: The sales began last week, didn't they?
TEACHER: They didn't begin this week.
PUPIL: They didn't begin this week, did they? etc.

(c) Questions with Who and What: did/was/can't have/must have.

TEACHER: Who went to the shops?
PUPIL: Mother and Sue did. etc.

(d) Double Questions.

TEACHER: Did the sales begin this week or last week?
PUPIL: They didn't begin this week. They began last week. etc.

(e) General Questions: When, Where, How much, Why.

TEACHER: When did the sales begin?
PUPIL: Last week. etc.

(f) Asking questions in pairs: When, Where, How much, Why.

TEACHER: Ask me if the sales began last week.
PUPIL: Did the sales begin last week?
TEACHER: When . . .
PUPIL: When did the sales begin? etc.

- ### Telling the Story

Ask one or two pupils to tell the story by referring only to the pictures. Pupils should remain seated.

- ### Unprepared Reading

Marley Castle, page 41.

- ### Activity

Song: Billy Boy. See page 254 for music.
Teach the final verse of this song.

- ### Writing

Workbook 3b, Lesson 101.
Guided Composition. The correct answer reads: The sales began last week, *so* mother and Sue went to the shops. *While* they were walking down Oxford Street, they met Mrs Dumpling. She was very excited *because* she bought a fur coat at the sales for only £5. Mother couldn't believe it, *but* Mrs Dumpling showed her the price. "Where did you buy it?" mother asked. Mrs Dumpling pointed down the street *and* mother and Sue went to the shop, *but* they couldn't get in *because* it was full of people.

83 Words

Lesson 102

- **Spelling Drill:** Books shut.

  Oral and Written
  lose/those; rise/them; cars/these; has/that; sees/there.

- **Phonic Practice:** Sounds and Spellings: Books open.

  The letters ch [tʃ] and j [dʒ]
  Chorus and Group Repetition

- **Reading and Repetition Drill:** Books open.

  Chorus and Group Repetition

  TEACHER: *Picture 1.*
  How much does that handbag cost? *All together!*
  It may cost £5. I'm not sure. *All together!*
  It can't cost £5. Surely it doesn't cost £5. *All together!*
  It must cost £5. I'm sure it does. *All together!*

  Practise these patterns with each of the items shown.

- **Pattern Drill:** Books open.

  (a) To elicit: (It) may (cost £5). I'm not sure.

  TEACHER: *Picture 1.*
  How much does that handbag cost?
  PUPIL: It may cost £5. I'm not sure. etc.

  (b) To elicit: (It) can't (cost £5). Surely it doesn't (cost £5).

  TEACHER: *Picture 1.*
  Does that handbag cost £5?
  PUPIL: It can't cost £5. Surely it doesn't cost £5. etc.

  (c) To elicit: (It) must (cost £5). I'm sure (it) does.

  TEACHER: *Picture 1.*
  How much does that handbag cost?
  PUPIL: It must cost £5. I'm sure it does. etc.

  (d) To elicit: (It) can't (cost £5). (It) must (cost $5).
  Pictures should be referred to in pairs.

  TEACHER: *Pictures 1 and 2.*
  Does that handbag cost £5 or $5?
  PUPIL: It can't cost £5. It must cost $5. etc.

- **Reading and Repetition Drill**

  Ask the pupils to repeat the following patterns:
  How much did that handbag cost?

It may have cost £5. I'm not sure.
It can't have cost £5. Surely it didn't cost £5.
It must have cost £5. I'm sure it did. etc.

- **Pattern Drill**

  (a) To elicit: (It) may have (cost £5). I'm not sure.

  TEACHER: *Picture 1.*
  How much did that handbag cost?
  PUPIL: It may have cost £5. I'm not sure. etc.

  (b) To elicit: (It) can't have (cost £5). Surely (it) didn't (cost £5).

  TEACHER: *Picture 1.*
  Did that handbag cost £5?
  PUPIL: It can't have cost £5. Surely it didn't cost £5. etc.

  (c) To elicit: (It) must have (cost £5). I'm sure (it) did.

  TEACHER: *Picture 1.*
  How much did that handbag cost?
  PUPIL: It must have cost £5. I'm sure it did. etc.

  (d) To elicit: (It) can't have (cost £5). (It) must have (cost $5).
  Pictures should be referred to in pairs.

  TEACHER: *Pictures 1 and 2.*
  Did that handbag cost £5 or $5?
  PUPIL: It can't have cost £5. It must have cost $5. etc.

- **Unprepared Reading**

  Marley Castle, page 42.
  New Expression: *swung on it.*

- **Activity**

  It's time for a story: The Ghost Story, page 267.
  New Words and Expressions: *exciting ghost story, the clock struck 12.0, haunted, kiss* (noun), *frightened.*

- **Writing**

  Workbook 3b, Lesson 102.

Lesson 102

(It) may (cost)/I'm not sure.
(It) can't (cost)/Surely (it) doesn't . . .
(It) must (cost)/I'm sure (it) does.
(It) may have (cost)/I'm not sure.
(It) can't have (cost)/Surely (it) didn't . . .
(It) must have (cost)/I'm sure (it) did.

---

rea<u>ch</u> <u>j</u>ar tea<u>ch</u> <u>j</u>am mu<u>ch</u> <u>j</u>ug pea<u>ch</u> <u>j</u>ust

---

1

2

How much (does/did) that handbag cost?
£5 $5

3

4

How much (does/did) that parcel weigh?
2 kilos   4 kilos

5

6

What (does/did) that pool measure?
48 metres   50 metres

7

8

How (does/did) Sandy feel?
ill   all right

9

10

What (does/did) that medicine taste like?
sweet   bitter

11

12

What (does/did) that music sound like?
nice   awful

13

14

What (does/did) that food smell like?
nice   nasty

15

16

What (does/did) that uniform look like?
smart   untidy

Lesson **103** Sandy takes some photos

Sándy hás a cámera.
Lást wéek he tóok some phótos
of Súe and Tímmy.

"Stánd thére pléase, Súe.
Stánd besíde her pléase, Tímmy," Sándy sáid.
"Now bóth smíle pléase.
Sáy, 'chéese'!"
Súe and Tímmy said "chéese" lóudly.

"Thát's the énd of the fílm," Sándy sáid.
"I múst háve it devéloped and prínted."

Sándy tóok his fílm to the chémist's.
"I wánt to háve it devéloped and prínted pléase,"
he sáid.

He collécted the négatives and prínts
a féw dáys láter.

He shówed the phótos to Súe.
Shé looked véry prétty.
But Tímmy lóoked fúnny.
He hásn't ány frónt téeth!

Lesson 103

Content and Basic Aims

PATTERNS AND STRUCTURAL WORDS	VOCABULARY	

PATTERNS AND STRUCTURAL WORDS	Nouns	Verbs
-self forms: (I didn't iron the dress) (myself).		
Someone else (ironed it for me).	negative (film)	develop (film)
I had (it) (ironed).	print (film)	print (film)
I shall have/must have (it) (ironed).		
Did (you) have (it) (ironed), or did (you)	*Adj.*	*Adv.*
(iron it) (yourself)?		
Where/When did (you) have (it) (ironed)?	front	else
	Expression	
	Say 'cheese' (= smile).	

● **General Remarks**

The causative use of *have* will be practised. Semantically related patterns involving the use of *else* and *-self* forms will also be introduced.

● **Aural/Oral Procedure**

(a) Listening (Books shut)
(b) Listening and Understanding (Books open; pictures only)
(c) Listening (Books shut)
(d) Listening and Chorus Repetition (Books shut)
(e) Listening and Group Repetition (Books shut)
(f) Reading Aloud: Chorus and Individual (Books open)

● **Graded Comprehension Questions**

(a) Yes/No Tag Answers: has/did/does/must.

TEACHER: Has Sandy got a radio?
PUPIL: No, he hasn't.
TEACHER: Has he got a camera?
PUPIL: Yes, he has. etc.

(b) Question Tags.

TEACHER: Sandy has a camera.
PUPIL: Sandy has a camera, hasn't he?
TEACHER: He hasn't got a radio.
PUPIL: He hasn't got a radio, has he? etc.

(c) Questions with Who: has/did/does/must.

TEACHER: Who has a camera?
PUPIL: Sandy has. etc.

(d) Double Questions.

TEACHER: Has Sandy a radio or a camera?
PUPIL: He hasn't a radio. He has a camera. etc.

(e) General Questions. What, When, Where, Why.

TEACHER: What's Sandy got?
PUPIL: A camera. etc.

(f) Asking questions in pairs: What, When, Where, Why.

TEACHER: Ask me if Sandy's got a camera.
PUPIL: Has Sandy got a camera?
TEACHER: What . . .
PUPIL: What's Sandy got? etc.

● **Telling the Story**

Ask one or two pupils to tell the story by referring only to the pictures. Pupils should remain seated.

● **Unprepared Reading**

Marley Castle, page 43.

● **Activity**

Repeat: Billy Boy, Lessons 95–101.

● **Writing**

Workbook 3b, Lesson 103.
Guided Composition. The correct answer reads: Last week Sandy took some photos of Sue and the boy next door. The boy's name is Timmy *and* he is only six years old. Timmy stood beside Sue *and* they both smiled *while* Sandy took some photos. Then Sandy took the film to the chemist's *because* he wanted to have it developed and printed. He collected the negatives and prints a few days later *and* showed the photos to Sue. Sue looked very pretty, *but* Timmy looked funny *because* he hasn't any front teeth!

85 Words

Lesson 104

- **Spelling Drill:** Books shut.

  Oral and Written
  books; cakes; clocks; desks; forks; trucks; parks; bricks; corks; tricks; lakes.
  Remind the pupils that we form plurals by adding 's' to the singular of nouns; after k/ke 's' is pronounced softly: [s].

- **Phonic Practice:** Sounds and Spellings: Books open.

  The letters ds [dz] and j [dʒ]
  Chorus and Group Repetition

- **Reading and Repetition Drill:** Books open.

  Chorus and Group Repetition

  TEACHER: *Picture 1.*
  I didn't iron the dress myself. *All together!*
  Someone else ironed it for me. *All together!*
  I had it ironed. *All together!*

  Repeat the captions beneath each picture.

- **Pattern Drill:** Books open.

  (a) To elicit: (I) didn't (iron the dress myself).
  (I) had (it) (ironed).

  TEACHER: *Picture 1.*
  Did you iron the dress yourself?
  PUPIL: I didn't iron the dress myself. I had it ironed. etc.

  (b) To elicit: (I) didn't (iron) (it) (myself).
  Someone else (ironed) (it) for (me).

  TEACHER: *Picture 1.*
  Did you iron the dress yourself?
  PUPIL: I didn't iron it myself. Someone else ironed it for me. etc.

  (c) To elicit: Did (you) have (it ironed), or did (you iron it) (yourself)?

  TEACHER: *Picture 1.*
  My dress looks nice.
  PUPIL: Did you have it ironed, or did you iron it yourself? etc.

  Use *look(s) nice* as a cue throughout.

  (d) To elicit: (I) didn't have (it ironed). (I) (ironed it) (myself).

  TEACHER: *Picture 1.*
  Did you have your dress ironed?
  PUPIL: I didn't have it ironed. I ironed it myself. etc.

  (e) To elicit: (I)'ll have (it ironed).

  TEACHER: *Picture 1.*
  What are you going to do about your dress?

  PUPIL: I'll have it ironed. etc.

  (f) To elicit: (I) must have (it ironed).

  TEACHER: *Picture 1.*
  What are you going to do about your dress?
  PUPIL: I must have it ironed. etc.

  (g) Asking questions in pairs: Where and When.

  TEACHER: *Picture 1.*
  Ask me if I had my dress ironed.
  PUPIL: Did you have your dress ironed?
  TEACHER: When . . .
  PUPIL: When did you have your dress ironed? etc.

- **Unprepared Reading**

  Marley Castle, page 44.
  New Words: *roared* (of the sea). *flashed* (a torch).

- **Activity**

  A Game: Lucky Dip.

  Write the following statements on individual pieces of paper: ironed my dress; washed my clothes; mended the clock; repaired the engine; built a house; cleaned the car; painted the fence; delivered the flowers; combed my hair; cut my hair; swept the floor; fed the ducks; developed the film; printed the film; made a puppet; baked a cake; sent the parcel. Put the pieces of paper in a hat or a bag. Pupils may then be invited to come to the front of the class and choose a piece of paper out of the hat.

  TEACHER: What did you do?
  PUPIL (*consulting piece of paper*): I swept the floor.
  TEACHER: Really? Did you sweep it yourself?
  PUPIL: No, I didn't sweep it myself. I had it swept.

- **Writing**

  Workbook 3b, Lesson 104.

Lesson **104**   I didn't do it myself.
Someone else did it for me.
I had it done.

hea<u>ds</u>	<u>j</u>ump	rea<u>ds</u>	<u>j</u>am	nee<u>ds</u>	<u>j</u>ug	she<u>ds</u>	<u>j</u>ust

1

I didn't iron the dress myself.
Someone else ironed it for me.
I had it ironed.

2

She didn't wash the clothes herself.
Someone else washed them for her.
She had them washed.

3

He didn't mend the clock himself.
Someone else mended it for him.
He had it mended.

4

You didn't repair the engine yourself.
Someone else repaired it for you.
You had it repaired.

5

We didn't build the house ourselves.
Someone else built it for us.
We had it built.

6

You didn't clean the car yourselves.
Someone else cleaned it for you.
You had it cleaned.

7

They didn't paint the fence themselves.
Someone else painted it for them.
They had it painted.

8

He didn't deliver the flowers himself.
Someone else delivered them for him.
He had them delivered.

9

I didn't comb my hair myself.
Someone else combed it for me.
I had it combed.

10

I didn't cut my hair myself.
Someone else cut it for me.
I had it cut.

Lesson **105** Television Day: . . . four, three, two, one, zero!

TV Commentary:

Ten, nine, eight, seven, six, five, four, three, two, one, zero! Whoosh! There is a great roar and a rocket starts its journey into space. Who was the first man to go up into space? Do you know? A Russian, Yuri Gagarin, was the first man who went up. That was on April 4th, 1961. He travelled once round the earth and his journey lasted 108 minutes. The next man that went up was an American, John Glenn. He went round the earth three times. That was on February 20th, 1962. His journey lasted 4 hours, 56 minutes. There have been many flights into space since 1961. Since that time astronauts have been to the moon. But we shall always remember the first men who went on this dangerous and exciting journey.

Lesson 105

Content and Basic Aims

PATTERNS AND STRUCTURAL WORDS	VOCABULARY		
	Nouns	*Expressions*	*Adj.*
The man/woman/men/women who/that (is/are coming out of the bank). *He's/she's/they're the man/woman/ men/women who(m) (I served).* *Who(m) did you (meet yesterday)?*	(an) American roar (the) earth rocket flight (a) Russian journey space (interstellar) moon zero	Whoosh!	exciting

● **General Remarks**

Patterns involving the use of the relative pronouns *who, who(m)*, and *that* are introduced here in connection with people (masculine, feminine: singular and plural).

● **Aural/Oral Procedure**

(a) Listening (Books shut)
(b) Intensive Reading (Books open)
    The passage should be played or read to the class in small units. During each pause, explain unfamiliar words. Rather than give direct explanations, try to elicit as much information as possible from the pupils.
(c) Listening (Books shut)
(d) Reading Aloud: Individual (Books open)

● **Graded Comprehension Questions**

(a) Yes/No Tag Answers: is/does/was/did/ have/will.

TEACHER: Was John Glenn the first man to go into space?
PUPIL: No he wasn't.
TEACHER: Was Yuri Gagarin the first man to go into space?
PUPIL: Yes, he was. etc.

(b) Question Tags.

TEACHER: Yuri Gagarin was the first man to go into space.
PUPIL: Yuri Gagarin was the first man to go into space, wasn't he?
TEACHER: John Glenn wasn't the first man to go into space.
PUPIL: John Glenn wasn't the first man to go into space, was he? etc.

(c) Double Questions.

TEACHER: Who was the first man to go into space: John Glenn, or Yuri Gagarin?
PUPIL: John Glenn wasn't the first man to go into space. Yuri Gagarin was. etc.

(d) General Questions: What, When, Where, How long, Why.

TEACHER: What do you hear when a rocket starts its journey?
PUPIL: A great roar. etc.

(e) Asking questions in pairs: When, What, Where, How long, Why.

● **Oral Composition**

Write the following notes on the blackboard:
Ten, nine, . . . zero.
Whoosh!—a rocket—journey—space.
Who was the first man?—A Russian.
Yuri Gagarin—April 4th, 1961.
Once round the earth—108 minutes.
Next man—an American.
John Glenn—Feb. 20th, 1962.
Three times round—4 hours 56 minutes.
Many flights since—moon.
Always remember the first men.
Now ask one or two pupils to reconstruct the passage by referring to the notes.

● **Unprepared Reading**

Marley Castle, page 45.
New Words and Expressions: *a police sergeant, motor-boat, thank goodness.*

● **Activity**

Repeat the following:
(a) I had a little nut-tree, Lesson 61.
(b) Sally in our alley, Lessons 55–59.

● **Writing**

Workbook 3b, Lesson 105.
Guided Composition. The correct answer reads:
On April 4th, 1961, Yuri Gagarin became the first man who went up into space. He travelled once round the earth *and* his journey lasted 108 minutes. The second flight into space was on February 20th, 1962. The astronaut, John Glenn, went round the earth three times *and* his journey took 4 hours, 56 minutes. Astronauts have been to the moon since that time, *but* we shall never forget the first men who went on this dangerous and exciting journey.

80 Words

Lesson 106

- **Spelling Drill:** Books shut.

  Oral and Written
  boats; coats; cats; hats; kites; robots; seats; cents; markets; tests; slots; puppets; elephants. Remind the pupils that we form plurals by adding 's' to the singular of nouns; after t/te 's' is pronounced softly: [s].

- **Phonic Practice:** Sounds and Spellings: Books open.

  The letters ds [dz], j [dʒ] and ch [tʃ]
  Chorus and Group Repetition

- **Reading and Repetition Drill:** Books open.

  Chorus and Group Repetition
  Ask the pupils to repeat the captions in Lesson 106.

- **Pattern Drill:** Books open or shut.

  (a) To elicit: Who (met him)?

  > TEACHER: She met him.
  > PUPIL: Who met him?

  Substitute the following:
  he sat there; they repaired it; she emptied it; he printed it; he developed it; they planted it; she dropped it; they built it; he dug it; she lost it; they hid it; they burnt it; she swept it; she dialled it.

  (b) To elicit: statements involving the use of *who*.

  > TEACHER: Who telephoned you yesterday?
  > ... A man.
  > He works in the bank.
  > PUPIL: The man who works in the bank.

  Substitute the following:
  A woman. She rescued him./Some children. They came yesterday./An assistant. She served me./A waiter. He served us./Some people. They live next door./A girl. She found my pencil-box./ A boy. He played a game with us./Some boys and girls. They came to our party./A policeman. He knows father./A lady. She came yesterday.

  (c) To elicit: statements involving the use of *that*.

  Conduct the exercise in the way shown in (b) above using the same substitutions. Point out that *that* can be used in the same way as *who*, but that *who* is more common.

  (d) To elicit: Who did (you meet yesterday).

  Point out that we can say *who* or *whom*, but that *who* is more common in spoken English.

  > TEACHER: I met him yesterday.
  > PUPIL: Who did you meet yesterday?

Substitute the following:
I telephoned them; I saw them; I found him; I heard her; I took them to the cinema; I remembered him; I rescued him; I served them; I thanked him; I expected her.

(e) To elicit: (He's the man) who (I met.)

Point out that we can say *who* or *whom*, but that *who* is more common in spoken English

> TEACHER: He's the man. I met him.
> PUPIL: He's the man who I met.

Substitute the following:
She's the girl. I asked her./They're the boys. I followed them/ They're the thieves. The police caught them./He's the boy. I saw him./She's the girl. I drew her./That's the boy. I rescued him./That's the lady. I thanked her./That's the assistant. I telephoned her.

(f) To elicit: (He's the man) that (I met).

Conduct the exercise in the way shown in (e) above using the same substitutions.

- **Unprepared Reading**

Marley Castle, page 46.

- **Activity**

Dictation
Dictate the following passage:

> "Díd you cléan the cár yoursélf, dád?"/ Sándy ásked./
> "Nó./Sómeone élse cléaned it fór me./I hád it cléaned," fáther ánswered./
> "Hów múch did it cóst, dád?"/
> "It cóst fórty pénce."/
> "It cán't have cóst só múch,"/Sándy sáid./ "Súrely it dídn't./That's móre than my pócket-móney."

- **Writing**

Workbook 3b, Lesson 106.

Lesson **106** Who, Who(m) and That

1

Who borrowed some
money?
The man who/that
is coming out of the
bank.

2

Who complained about
the food?
The woman who/that
is sitting at that
table.

3

Who wants to buy some
things at the sales?
The people who/that
are trying to get into
the shop.

4

Who rescued that cat?
The boy who/that is
climbing that tree.

5

Who rang the bell?
The girl who/that is
standing at the door.

6

Who won't let you play?
The boys who/that are
kicking that ball.

7

I served him
yesterday.
He's the man who(m)/
that I served
yesterday.

8

I drew her yesterday.

She's the girl who(m)/
that I drew yesterday.

9

I played with them
yesterday.
They're the children
who(m)/that I played
with yesterday.

Lesson 107 A lucky tramp

Tramp: Góod áfternóon, Mŕs.
            Háve you gót any óld clóthes?
Mother: Júst a mínute pléase.

Mother: Jím! There's a trámp at the dóor.
            He wánts some óld clóthes.
Father: You can gíve him my old jácket.

Mother: Hére you áre.
            You can have thís óld jácket.
Tramp: Thánk you, Mŕs.
            That's véry kínd of yóu.

Father: Whích jácket did you gíve him, Bétty?
Mother: The jácket which was ín the wárdrobe.
            The brówn óne.

Father: The brówn óne!
Mother: Yés. Whát's the mátter, Jím?
Father: You've gíven him my bést jácket!

Father: Thís is my óld jácket.
            Thís is the jácket
            that you shóuld have gíven him!

Three blind mice

Three blind mice,
Three blind mice,
See how they run,
See how they run.
They all ran after the farmer's wife,
Who cut off their tails with a carving-knife,
Did you ever see such a thing in your life,
As three blind mice?

Content and Basic Aims

PATTERNS AND STRUCTURAL WORDS	VOCABULARY		
Which (comic/comics) did you (read)? *This is/these are the (film(s)/horse(s)/tree(s)) which/that I (saw).*	*Nouns*		
	jacket	tramp	wardrobe

- **General Remarks**

Patterns involving the use of the relative pronouns *which* and *that* are introduced here in connection with things, animals and plants (singular and plural).

- **Aural/Oral Procedure**

(a) Listening (Books shut)
(b) Listening and Understanding (Books open; pictures only)
(c) Listening (Books shut)
(d) Listening and Chorus Repetition (Books shut)
(e) Listening and Group Repetition (Books shut)
(f) Reading Aloud: Chorus and Individual (Books open)

- **Graded Comprehension Questions**

(a) Yes/No Tag Answers: does/has/is/can/did/ was/should have.

TEACHER: Does the tramp want some new clothes?
PUPIL: No, he doesn't.
TEACHER: Does he want some old clothes?
PUPIL: Yes, he does. etc.

(b) Question Tags.

TEACHER: The tramp wants some old clothes.
PUPIL: The tramp wants some old clothes, doesn't he?
TEACHER: He doesn't want any new clothes.
PUPIL: He doesn't want any new clothes, does he? etc.

(c) Questions with Who: does/has/is/can/did/ should have.

TEACHER: Who wants some old clothes?
PUPIL: The tramp does. etc.

(d) Double Questions.

TEACHER: Does the tramp want some old clothes or some new clothes?
PUPIL: He doesn't want any new clothes. He wants some old clothes. etc.

(e) General Questions: What, Where, Why, Which.

TEACHER: What does the tramp want?
PUPIL: Some old clothes. etc.

(f) Asking questions in pairs: What, Where, Why and Which.

TEACHER: Ask me if the tramp wants some old clothes.
PUPIL: Does the tramp want some old clothes?
TEACHER: What . . .
PUPIL: What does the tramp want? etc.

- **Acting the Scene**

Invite three pupils to come to the front of the class to act the scene. Two jackets would be useful props.

- **Unprepared Reading**

Marley Castle, page 47.
New Word: *arrested.*

- **Activity**

Song: Three blind mice. See page 255 for music. Teach this song as a four-part round.

- **Writing**

Workbook 3b, Lesson 107.
Guided Composition. The correct answer reads: The tramp *who* came to our house yesterday afternoon asked mother for some old clothes. Mother asked father *and* he said, "You can give him my old jacket." Mother gave the tramp father's brown jacket which was in the wardrobe. The tramp was very pleased *and* left the house quickly. Later in the afternoon father looked for his new jacket, *but* he couldn't find it. He was cross with mother *because* she gave the tramp his best jacket.

78 Words

Lesson 108

- **Spelling Drill:** Books shut.

  Oral and Written
  caps; cups; maps; gossips; lumps; stripes;
  ropes; mumps; slopes; pipes; lamps; shapes.
  Remind the pupils that we form plurals by
  adding 's' to the singular of nouns; after p/pe
  's' is pronounced softly: [s].

- **Phonic Practice:** Sounds and Spellings: Books
  open.

  The letters ts [ts] j [dʒ] and ch [tʃ]
  Chorus and Group Repetition

- **Reading and Repetition Drill:** Books open.

  Chorus and Group Repetition
  Ask the pupils to repeat the captions in Lesson
  108.

- **Pattern Drill:** Books open or shut.

  (a) To elicit: Which (comic) did you (read)?

  TEACHER: I read that comic.
  PUPIL: Which comic did you read?

  Substitute the following:
  played that record; rode that horse; bought
  that dog; fed that elephant; climbed that tree;
  picked that apple; rescued that cat; ironed that
  shirt; repaired that shoe; dusted that table;
  broke that plant; peeled that potato; delivered
  that letter; swept that room; printed that
  negative; emptied that basket.

  (b) To elicit: Which (comics) did you (read)?

  TEACHER: I read those comics.
  PUPIL: Which comics did you read?

  Substitute the statements given under (a) above:
  use *plural* nouns throughout.

  (c) To elicit: This is the (film) which I (saw).

  TEACHER: This is the film. I saw it.
  PUPIL: This is the film which I saw.

  Substitute the following:
  This is the bag. I found it./This is the window.
  I broke it./This is the plate. I dried it./This is
  the flower. I picked it./This is the skate. I used
  it./This is the picture. I painted it./This is the
  animal. I fed it./This is the letter. I received it./
  This is the exercise-book. I corrected it./This
  is the piece. I practised it.

  (d) To elicit: This is the (film) that I (saw).

  Conduct the exercise in the way shown in
  (c) above using the same substitutions.
  Point out that *that* and *which* can be used
  in the same way.

  (e) To elicit: These are the (films) which I (saw).

  TEACHER: These are the films. I saw them.
  PUPIL: These are the films which I saw.

  Substitute the statements given under (c)
  above: use *plural* forms throughout.

  (f) To elicit: These are the (films) that I (saw).

  Conduct the drill in the way shown in (e)
  above substituting the same statements.

- **Unprepared Reading**

  Marley Castle, page 48.

- **Activity**

  It's time for a story: The Pound Note, page 267.
  New Word: *washing-machine*.

- **Writing**

  Workbook 3b, Lesson 108.

Lesson **108** **Which and That**

<u>h</u>ats <u>J</u>apan <u>ch</u>eer   <u>c</u>ats <u>j</u>ump <u>ch</u>imney   <u>p</u>ut<u>s</u> <u>j</u>ar <u>ch</u>ild

1

Which comic did you
read?
The comic which/that
is on the table.

2
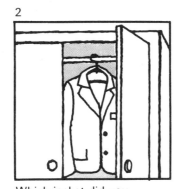
Which jacket did you
wear?
The jacket which/that
is in the wardrobe.

3

Which roller-skates did
you use?
The roller-skates which/
that are on the floor.

4

Which horse did you
ride?
The horse which/that
is in the field.

5

Which dog followed you
home?
The dog which/that
is in the garden.

6

Which elephants did you
feed?
The elephants which/that
are near that pool.

7

Which tree did you
climb?
The tree which/that
is in the garden.

8

Which apple did you
pick?
The apple which/that
I'm eating.

9

Which flowers did you
pick?
The flowers which/that
are in the vase.

Lesson **109**   Not good enough

Narrator: Míck is the náme of the trámp
who has fáther's néw jácket.
He's tálking to his fríend, Hárry.

Mick: Hów do you líke thís jácket, Hárry?
Harry: Véry níce, Míck.
Whó gáve it to you?
Mick: The lády who líves in thát hóuse.

Harry: Whích hóuse is thát?
Mick: The hóuse on the córner.
Harry: I'll gó and ásk for a jácket, tóo.

Harry: Good mórning, Mŕs.
Háve you gót any óld clóthes pléase?

Mother: You can háve this jácket.
Harry: Máy I sée it pléase?

Harry: Nó thánks, Mŕs.
It's tóo óld for mé.
Í want a jácket líke the óne
you gáve my fríend yésterday.

Content and Basic Aims

PATTERNS AND STRUCTURAL WORDS	VOCABULARY
Who . . .? The man/woman/people (coming out of the house). *(He's the boy I served yesterday).* *Which . . .? (I read the comic on the table).* *(This is/these are the comic(s) I read yesterday).*	*Expression*
	How do you like (my new jacket)?

- **General Remarks**

Statements involving the omission of the relative *(who, whom, that* and *which)* will be practised in this Unit; only transitive verbs will be used.

- **Aural/Oral Procedure**

(a) Listening (Books shut)
(b) Listening and Understanding (Books open; pictures only)
(c) Listening (Books shut)
(d) Listening and Chorus Repetition (Books shut)
(e) Listening and Group Repetition (Books shut)
(f) Reading Aloud: Chorus and Individual (Books open)

- **Graded Comprehension Questions**

(a) Yes/No Tag Answers: is/has/does/did/will/can/may.

TEACHER: Is Mick talking to mother?
PUPIL: No, he isn't.
TEACHER: Is he talking to his friend, Harry?
PUPIL: Yes, he is. etc.

(b) Question Tags.

TEACHER: Mick is talking to Harry.
PUPIL: Mick is talking to Harry, isn't he.
TEACHER: He isn't talking to mother.
PUPIL: He isn't talking to mother, is he? etc.

(c) Questions with Who: is/has/does/did/will/can/may.

TEACHER: Who's talking to Harry?
PUPIL: Mick is. etc.

(d) Double Questions.

TEACHER: Is Mick talking to mother or to Harry?
PUPIL: He isn't talking to mother. He's talking to Harry. etc.

(e) General Questions: Who, What, How, Where, Which, Why.

TEACHER: Who's Mick talking to?
PUPIL: Harry. etc.

(f) Asking questions in pairs: Who, What, How, Where, Which, Why.

TEACHER: Ask me if Mick is talking to Harry.
PUPIL: Is Mick talking to Harry.
TEACHER: Who . . .
PUPIL: Who is Mick talking to? etc.

- **Acting the Scene**

Invite three pupils to come to the front of the class to act the scene. Two jackets would be useful props.

- **Unprepared Reading**

Marley Castle, page 49.
New Word: *kissed.*

- **Activity**

Song: Three blind mice. See page 255 for music. Repeat this four-part round several times.

- **Writing**

Workbook 3b, Lesson 109.
Guided Composition: The correct answer reads: Yesterday Mick the tramp showed his friend, Harry, the jacket *which* Mrs Clark gave him. Harry liked it, *so* he decided to ask for one, too. Mick pointed to Mrs Clark's house *and* Harry went there. Mother gave him father's old jacket, *but* he didn't want it. "No thanks," he said. "It's too old for me. I want a jacket like the one you gave my friend yesterday."

68 Words

Lesson 110

- **Spelling Drill:** Books shut.

  Oral and Written.
  apples; bananas; bills; films; languages;
  measles; ideas; friends; cushions; porters; taxis.
  Remind the pupils that we form plurals by
  adding 's' to the singular of nouns; in most
  cases (except those indicated earlier) 's' is
  pronounced: [z].

- **Phonic Practice:** Sounds and Spellings: Books
  open.

  The letters sh [ʃ] ch [tʃ] and j [dʒ]
  Chorus and Group Repetition

- **Reading and Repetition Drill:** Books open.

  Chorus and Group Repetition
  Ask the pupils to repeat the captions.

- **Pattern Drill:** Books open or shut.

  (a) To elicit: Yes. The (man com)ing (out of the
      bank).

      TEACHER: Who spoke to you? The man
      who is coming out of the bank?
      PUPIL: Yes. The man coming out of the
      bank.

      Point out *who is/are* may be omitted.

  Substitute the following:
  the waiter who is serving food; the boy who is
  feeding the ducks; the children who are hiding
  behind that tree; the man who is digging in the
  garden; the people who are burning the rubbish;
  the lady who is complaining to the waiter;
  the boy who is pointing at the glider;
  children who are skating across the lake; the
  postman who is delivering letters; the men
  who are exploring the cave; the people who are
  waiting outside; the tramp who is knocking at
  the door.

  (b) To elicit: Yes. (He)'s the (boy) I (served)
      yesterday.

      TEACHER: Did you serve him yesterday?
      PUPIL: Yes. He's the boy I served
      yesterday.

      Point out that *who(m)* is usually omitted.

  Substitute: boy/girl/children *and:*
  visit her; ask him; call them; hear her; fight
  them; draw him; measure her; rescue him;
  thank her; meet them; catch them; telephone
  her.

  (c) To elicit: Yes. I (read the comic on the
      table).

      TEACHER: Which comic did you read? The
      one which is on the table?
      PUPIL: Yes. I read the comic on the
      table.

  Point out that *which is/are* is often omitted.

  Substitute:
  tree/climb/in the garden; horse/ride/in the
  field; elephants/feed/at the zoo; flowers/pick/in
  the garden; skates/use/on the floor; record/
  play/ on the shelf; jacket/wear/in the wardrobe;
  shirt/iron/on the shelf; dog/buy/in the window;
  bike/borrow/in the street; towels/wash/in the
  bathroom; cave/explore/under the mountain.

  (d) To elicit: That's the (jacket) I (wore)
      yesterday.

      TEACHER: That's the jacket. I wore it
      yesterday.
      PUPIL: That's the jacket I wore
      yesterday.

      Indicate how the two statements can be
      joined to omit *which* and *it*.

  Substitute:
  bag/found; window/broke; bike/borrowed;
  exercise-book/marked; plate/dried; shirt/
  washed; letter/delivered; horse/rode; elephant/
  fed; tree/climbed.

  (e) To elicit: Those are the (jackets) I (wore)
      yesterday.

      TEACHER: Those are the jackets. I wore
      them yesterday.
      PUPIL: Those are the jackets I wore
      yesterday.

      Indicate how the two statements can be
      joined to omit *which* and *them*.

  Substitute the expressions given under (d)
  above, using plural forms throughout.

- **Unprepared Reading**

  Marley Castle, page 50.
  New Words and Expressions: *shook our hands*
  (greeted), *proud, gold, smugglers, I thought so,
  worth, bar* (of gold).

- **Activity**

  A Guessing Game.
  A pupil is asked to leave the room. In his
  absence the teacher borrows a number of
  identical objects from a few members of class.
  He places them in obvious positions round the
  room. The pupil is recalled and he has to guess
  which object belongs to a particular pupil.

  TEACHER: Which pencil is (Bob)'s?
  PUPIL: The one on the table.
  TEACHER: No, it isn't.
  PUPIL: The one under the table.
  TEACHER: Yes, it is. Sit down A. Now you B.

- **Writing**

  Workbook 3b, Lesson 110.

Lesson 110 Who, Who(m), Which and That

wa**sh**   **ch**air   **j**ump   fi**sh**   **ch**ief   **j**am   pu**sh**   **ch**ur**ch**   **j**ug

1

Who borrowed some
money?
The man coming out of the
bank.

2

Who complained about
the food?
The woman sitting at that
table.

3

Who wants to buy some
things at the sales?
The people trying to get
into the shop.

4

I served him yesterday.
He's the man I served
yesterday.

5

I drew her yesterday.
She's the girl I drew
yesterday.

6

I played with them
yesterday.
They're the children I
played with yesterday.

7

Which comic did you read?
I read the comic on the
table.

8

Which tree did you climb?
I climbed the tree in the
garden.

9

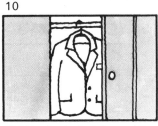

Which elephants did you
feed?
I fed the elephants near
that pool.

10

This is the jacket. I wore it
yesterday.
This is the jacket I wore
yesterday.

11

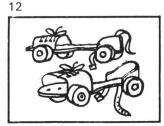

This is the horse. I rode it
yesterday.
This is the horse I rode
yesterday.

12

These are the skates. I used
them yesterday.
These are the skates I used
yesterday.

Lesson **111** People are so forgetful!

Narrator: Fáther trávelled to wórk by tráin.
This is the tráin he trávelled on.
He léft his umbrélla
in óne of the compártments.

Father: I léft my umbrélla on this tráin.
Porter: Is thís the tráin you trávelled on, sír?
Father: I'm súre it is.

Porter: Whích compártment did you léave
your umbrélla in, sír?
Father: I cán't remémber.

Father: I thínk I sat thére.
Porter: Hére's an umbrélla.
Is thís the óne you're lóoking for?
Father: Of cóurse not!
Thís is a lády's umbrélla.

Father: I thínk thís is the compártment
I trávelled in.
Porter: Hére's anóther umbrélla.
Ís it yóurs?
Father: Nó, it ísn't.

Father: Thís is the ríght compártment.
And hére's my umbrélla.
Porter: We were lóoking for óne umbrélla
and we fóund thrée!
Péople are só forgétful!

There was a crooked man

There was a crooked man who went a crooked mile,
He found a crooked sixpence upon a crooked stile,
He bought a crooked cat which caught a crooked mouse,
And they all lived together in a crooked little house.

Lesson 111

Content and Basic Aims

PATTERNS AND STRUCTURAL WORDS	VOCABULARY
(This is the boy/film) (about) whom/which (I told you). (This is the boy/film) whom/which (I told you) (about). (This is the boy/film) (I told you) (about).	*Nouns*
	compartment (in a train) hotel
	Adj.
	forgetful

● **General Remarks**

Statements involving the displacement of pre-positions and the use and omission of relative pronouns will be practised in this Unit.

● **Aural/Oral Procedure**

(a) Listening (Books shut)
(b) Listening and Understanding (Books open; pictures only)
(c) Listening (Books shut)
(d) Listening and Chorus Repetition (Books shut)
(e) Listening and Group Repetition (Books shut)
(f) Reading Aloud: Chorus and Individual (Books open)

● **Graded Comprehension Questions**

(a) Yes/No Tag Answers: did/is/can/does/were.

TEACHER: Did father travel to work by bus?
PUPIL: No, he didn't.
TEACHER: Did father travel to work by train?
PUPIL: Yes, he did. etc.

(b) Question Tags.

TEACHER: Father travelled to work by train.
PUPIL: Father travelled to work by train, didn't he?
TEACHER: He didn't travel to work by bus.
PUPIL: He didn't travel to work by bus, did he? etc.

(c) Questions with Who: did, is, can't, does.

TEACHER: Who travelled to work by train?
PUPIL: Father did. etc.

(d) Double Questions.

TEACHER: Did father travel to work by bus or by train?
PUPIL: He didn't travel to work by bus. He travelled to work by train. etc.

(e) General Questions: How and Where.

TEACHER: How did father travel to work?
PUPIL: By train. etc.

(f) Asking questions in pairs: How and Where.

TEACHER: Ask me if father travelled to work by train.
PUPIL: Did father travel to work by train?
TEACHER: How . . .
PUPIL: How did father travel to work? etc.

● **Acting the Scene**

Invite two pupils to come to the front of the class to act the scene. Three umbrellas would be useful props.

● **Unprepared Reading**

Marley Castle, page 51.

● **Activity**

Song: There was a crooked man. See page 255 for music. Teach the new song to the class.

● **Writing**

Workbook 3b, Lesson 111.
Guided Composition. The correct answer reads: Yesterday father left his umbrella in a railway-compartment *and* he looked for it with a porter. It wasn't easy to find *because* father couldn't remember the compartment he travelled in. They looked in some of the compartments *and* found three umbrellas. The last one they found was father's. "We were looking for one umbrella," the porter said, "and we found three. People are so forgetful."

65 Words

Lesson 112

- **Spelling Drill:** Books shut.

  Oral and Written
  boats/lemons; desks/rubbers; tricks/errands;
  gossips/gardens; corks/hammers.
  Remind the pupils once more of the way 's' is
  pronounced in plural nouns: [s] after k/ke, t/te
  and p/pe and [z] after most other letters.

- **Phonic Practice:** Sounds and Spellings: Books
  open.

  The letters ch [k] and tch [tʃ]
  Chorus and Group Repetition

- **Reading and Repetition Drill:** Books open.

  Chorus and Group Repetition
  Ask the pupils to repeat the sentences in Lesson
  112.

- **Pattern Drill:** Books open or shut.

  (a) To elicit: (This is the boy/film) about
  (whom/which) (I told you) about.

    TEACHER: This is the boy. I told you about
    him.
    PUPIL: This is the boy about whom I
    told you.

  Point out that statements of this kind are
  stilted.

  Substitute the following:

  This is the woman. I wrote to you about her./
  This is the film. I spoke to you about it./These
  are the girls. You read about them/This is the
  girl. You heard about her./ This is something.
  I must ask about it./This is something. I must
  decide about it./This is something. I mustn't
  talk about it./These are the boys. You know
  about them./This is something. You mustn't
  complain about it./This is something. You
  mustn't worry about it.

  (b) To elicit: (This is the boy/film) (whom/
  which) (I told you) about.

    TEACHER: This is the boy. I told you about
    him.
    PUPIL: This is the boy whom I told you
    about.

  Substitute the expressions given under (a)
  above.

  (c) To elicit: (This is the boy/film) (I told you)
  about.

    TEACHER: This is the boy. I told you about
    him.
    PUPIL: This is the boy I told you about.

  Point out that statements of this kind are
  extremely common. Substitute the expressions
  given under (a) above.

  (d) To elicit: (This is the girl to whom I wrote).

    TEACHER: This is the girl. I wrote to her.
    PUPIL: This is the girl to whom I wrote.

  Point out that statements of this kind are stilted.

  Substitute:
  This is the lake. I swam in it./This is the horse.
  I rode on it./This is the restaurant. I ate at it./
  These are the boys. They looked for them./
  This is the girl. I danced with her./This is the
  house. I moved into it./This is the boy. I
  borrowed some money from him./This is the
  play. I appeared in it./This is the piano. I
  practised on it./These are the children. I played
  with them./These are the records. I listened to
  them./This is the ship. I travelled on it./

  (e) To elicit: (This is the girl whom I wrote to).

    TEACHER: This is the girl. I wrote to her.
    PUPIL: This is the girl whom I wrote to.

  Substitute the expressions given under (d)
  above.

  (f) To elicit: (This is the girl I wrote to).

    TEACHER: This is the girl. I wrote to her.
    PUPIL: This is the girl I wrote to.

  Point out that statements of this kind are
  extremely common.
  Substitute the expressions given under (d) above.

  (g) To elicit: This is the (coat I took off).

    TEACHER: This is the coat. I took it off.
    PUPIL: This is the coat I took off.

  Substitute:
  tyre/pumped up; candle/blew out; shoes/tried
  on; tap/turned off; light/turned off; coat/put
  on; light/switched off; joke/laughed at; book/
  asked for; record/listened to.

- **Unprepared Reading**

  Marley Castle, page 52.
  New Word: *glass* (of a window).

- **Activity**

  Dictation
  Dictate the following passage:

  Mŕs Dúmpling hád a méal/at a réstaurant/and
  compláined about the fóod./"Whó sérved you,
  mádam?"/the mánager ásked./
      "The wáiter stánding néar that táble,"/shé
  sáid./"The fóod I áte was cóld/and there wásn't
  enóugh of it./I'm stíll húngry."

- **Writing**

  Workbook 3b, Lesson 110.

Lesson **112** Whom and Which

stomach   watch   chemist   catch   ache   kitchen

This is the boy. I told you about him.
This is the boy about whom I told you.
This is the boy whom I told you about.
This is the boy I told you about.

This is the film. I spoke to you about it.
This is the film about which I spoke to you.
This is the film which I spoke to you about.
This is the film I spoke to you about.

This is the girl. I wrote to her.
This is the girl to whom I wrote.
This is the girl whom I wrote to.
This is the girl I wrote to.

This is the hotel. We stayed at it.
This is the hotel at which we stayed.
This is the hotel which we stayed at.
This is the hotel we stayed at.

These are the shoes. I tried them on.
These are the shoes which I tried on.
These are the shoes I tried on.

Lesson 113 Still pretty good!

1st Old Man: Lóok at thóse bóys pláying fóotball.   1

2nd Old Man: Did yóu ever pláy fóotball, Dán?   2
1st Old Man: Óh, yés.
I úsed to pláy fóotball
a lóng tíme agó,
but I dón't pláy ány móre.

1st Old Man: I úsed to be céntre-fórward   3
when Í was a boy.
Did yóu use to pláy?
2nd Old Man: Yés, Í used to be góal-kéeper.

1st Old Man: Lóok!   4
The báll's cóming towárds us.
2nd Old Man: Píck it úp.

Sandy: Máy we háve our báll pléase?   5
1st Old Man: I'll kíck it to you, són.

2nd Old Man: Wéll dóne!   6
You're stíll prétty góod!
1st Old Man: But nót as góod as I úsed to bé.

Lesson **113**

Content and Basic Aims

PATTERNS AND STRUCTURAL WORDS	VOCABULARY	
	Nouns	*Expressions*
(I) used to be (a waiter/rich) a long time ago, but (I'm) not any more. *(I) used to (collect stamps) a long time ago, but I don't) any more.* *No, but I used to be.* *No, but I used to.* *What/Where did you use to . . .?*	centre-forward goal-keeper son (= boy)	pretty good Well done!
		Adv.
	Prep.	pretty (= rather)
	towards	

- **General Remarks**

The form *used to (be)* is practised here in patterns involving the use of *nouns, adjectives* and *verbs*.

- **Aural/Oral Procedure**

(a) Listening (Books shut)
(b) Listening and Understanding (Books open; pictures only)
(c) Listening (Books shut)
(d) Listening and Chorus Repetition (Books shut)
(e) Listening and Group Repetition (Books shut)
(f) Reading Aloud: Chorus and Individual (Books open)

- **Graded Comprehension Questions**

(a) Yes/No Tag Answers: are/did/does/is/will.

TEACHER: Are the boys playing basket-ball?
PUPIL: No, they aren't.
TEACHER: Are they playing football?
PUPIL: Yes, they are. etc.

(b) Question Tags.

TEACHER: The boys are playing football.
PUPIL: The boys are playing football, aren't they?
TEACHER: The boys aren't playing basket-ball.
PUPIL: The boys aren't playing basket-ball, are they? etc.

(c) Questions with Who: are, did, does, will, is.

TEACHER: Who's playing football?
PUPIL: The boys *are*. etc.

(d) Double Questions.

TEACHER: Are the boys playing basket ball, or football.
PUPIL: They aren't playing basket-ball. They're playing football. etc.

(e) General Questions: What and When.

TEACHER: What are the boys doing?
PUPIL: They're playing football. etc.

(f) Asking questions in pairs: What and When.

TEACHER: Ask me if the boys are playing football.
PUPIL: Are the boys playing football?
TEACHER: What . . .
PUPIL: What are the boys playing? etc.

- **Acting the Scene**

Invite three pupils to come to the front of the class to act the scene. A ball would be a useful prop.

- **Unprepared Reading**

Marley Castle, page 53.
New Words: *blinked, shoot*.

- **Activity**

Repeat: There was a crooked man. See page 255 for music.

- **Writing**

Workbook 3b, Lesson 113.
Guided Composition. The correct answer reads:
While Sandy and his friends were playing football in the park, two old men were watching them. They remembered the time when they used to play football, too. The first old man used to play centre-forward *and* the other used to be a goal-keeper. Just then, the ball came towards them *and* the first old man picked it up. *When* Sandy asked for it, he kicked it to him.
    "Well done!" his friend said. "You're still pretty good!"
    "But not as good as I used to be," the first old man said sadly.

93 Words

Lesson 114

- **Spelling Drill:** Books shut.

  Oral and Written
  potatoes; tomatoes; actresses; classes; glasses; dresses; boxes.
  Point out that after *o, s* and *x* we usually add -*es* to make a plural.

- **Phonic Practice:** Sounds and Spellings: Books open.

  The letters ck [k] ch [tʃ] and ch [k]
  Chorus and Group Repetition

- **Reading and Repetition Drill:** Books open.

  Chorus and Group Repetition
  Pictures 1–8 only.
  TEACHER: *Picture 1.*
  I used to be a waiter a long time ago, but I'm not any more. *All together!*
  I was a waiter a long time ago, but I'm not any more. *All together!*

  Practise these patterns with each of the items given. Indicate how *used to be* may be used in place of *was*.

- **Pattern Drill:** Books open.

  Pictures 1–8 only.

  (a) To elicit: Yes, I was (a waiter) a long time ago, but I'm not any more.

  TEACHER: *Picture 1.*
  Were you a waiter?
  PUPIL: Yes, I was a waiter a long time ago, but I'm not any more. etc.

  (b) To elicit: Yes, I used to be (a waiter) a long time ago, but I'm not any more.

  TEACHER: *Picture 1.*
  Did you use to be a waiter?
  PUPIL: Yes, I used to be a waiter a long time ago, but I'm not any more. etc.

  (c) To elicit: (He) used to be (a waiter).

  TEACHER: *Picture 1.*
  Tell me what you know about him.
  PUPIL: He used to be a waiter. etc.

  (d) To elicit: No, but I used to be.

  TEACHER: *Picture 1.*
  Are you a waiter?
  PUPIL: No, but I used to be. etc.

- **Reading and Repetition Drill**

  Pictures 9–17 only.
  Ask the pupils to repeat the following patterns:
  I used to collect stamps a long time ago, but I don't any more.

I collected stamps a long time ago, but I don't any more. etc.

- **Pattern Drill**

  (a) To elicit: Yes, I (collected stamps) a long time ago, but I don't any more.

  TEACHER: *Picture 9.*
  Did you ever collect stamps?
  PUPIL: Yes, I collected stamps a long time ago, but I don't any more. etc.

  (b) To elicit: Yes, I used to (collect stamps) a long time ago, but I don't any more.

  TEACHER: *Picture 9.*
  Did you use to collect stamps?
  PUPIL: Yes, I used to collect stamps a long time ago, but I don't any more. etc.

  (c) To elicit: (He) used to (collect stamps). Ask questions using *What* or *Where*.

  TEACHER: *Picture 9.*
  What did he use to do?
  PUPIL: He used to collect stamps. etc.

  (d) To elicit: No, but I used to.

  TEACHER: *Picture 9.*
  Do you collect stamps?
  PUPIL: No, but I used to. etc.

  (e) To elicit questions in pairs: What and Where. All pictures.

  TEACHER: *Picture 1.*
  Ask me if I used to be a waiter.
  PUPIL: Did you use to be a waiter?
  TEACHER: What . . .
  PUPIL: What did you use to be? etc.

- **Unprepared Reading**

  Marley Castle, page 54.

- **Activity**

  It's time for a story: The Family Photograph Album, page 268.
  New Words and Expressions: *album, turned over* (pages), *cot, shorts, team* (football).

- **Writing**

  Workbook 3b, Lesson 114.

Lesson **114** I used to be . . . /I used to . . .

<u>ba</u>ck <u>ch</u>eer <u>stoma</u><u>ch</u> kno<u>ck</u> <u>ch</u>air <u>ch</u>emist <u>th</u>i<u>ck</u> <u>ch</u>ild a<u>ch</u>e

I used to be . . ./I was . . ./a long time ago, but I'm not any more.

1

a waiter

2

an artist

3

a porter

4

a bank manager

5

rich

6

thin

7

lazy

8

pretty

I used to . . ./I . . ./a long time ago, but I don't any more.

9

collect stamps

10

live in Africa

11

grow my own tomatoes

12

sing very well

13

drive a car

14

repair my own shoes

15

work in the hat
department

16
appear on TV

17
develop and print my
own films

Lesson 115 Television Day: Captain Cook

TV Commentary:

The great explorer, Captain Cook, set out from England in 1768 in his ship, *Endeavour*. He wanted to explore the South Pacific. After he had sailed round the two islands of New Zealand, he travelled up the east coast of Australia. The Dutch explorer, Tasman, had discovered the west coast of Australia in the 17th century. He had also been to New Zealand, but he hadn't brought back much information. Tasman didn't discover that New Zealand was really two islands. He didn't know that Australia was an enormous continent. Captain Cook made maps of the coast-line of New Zealand and Australia. His great journey took nearly three years. The *Endeavour* returned to England on July 13th, 1771. Ninety-three men had sailed with Captain Cook and thirty-eight of them had died on the journey.

Content and Basic Aims

PATTERNS AND STRUCTURAL WORDS	VOCABULARY		
	Nouns		*Adj.*
(I asked Sandy for a penny, but he) had already (spent his pocket-money).	Australia	island	Dutch
After/When (they) had (had breakfast, they) went to school).	captain	New Zealand	enormous
(They went to school) after (they) had (had breakfast).	century	Pacific	
(We) had (finished breakfast) before (the postman arrived).	coast		
I hadn't (before), but I have now.	coast-line	*Verbs*	
	continent		
	information	discover set out (= begin a journey)	

● **General Remarks**

Patterns involving the use of the past perfect simple with *when, after* and *before* are introduced here.

● **Aural/Oral Procedure**

(a) Listening (Books shut)
(b) Intensive Reading (Books open)
  The passage should be played or read to the class in small units. During each pause, explain unfamiliar words. Rather than give direct explanations, try to elicit as much information as possible from the pupils.
(c) Listening (Books shut)
(d) Reading Aloud: Individual (Books open)

● **Graded Comprehension Questions**

(a) Yes/No Tag Answers: did/had/was.

  TEACHER: Did Captain Cook set out in 1868?
  PUPIL: No, he didn't.
  TEACHER: Did he set out in 1768?
  PUPIL: Yes, he did. etc.

(b) Question Tags.

  TEACHER: Captain Cook set out in 1768.
  PUPIL: Captain Cook set out in 1768, didn't he?
  TEACHER: He didn't set out in 1868.
  PUPIL: He didn't set out in 1868, did he? etc.

(c) Double Questions.

  TEACHER: Did Captain Cook set out in 1768, or in 1868?
  PUPIL: He didn't set out in 1868. He set out in 1768. etc.

(d) General Questions: Where, When, What, How.

  TEACHER: Where did Captain Cook set out from?
  PUPIL: England. etc.

(e) Asking questions in pairs: Where, When, What and How.

● **Oral Composition**

Write the following notes on the blackboard:
Captain Cook set out — England — 1768. *Endeavour.* Wanted to explore S. Pacific. Sailed round 2 islands, N.Z. and east coast, Aust.
Dutch explorer, Tasman—West coast Aust, 17th cent.
N.Z. too, but brought little information.
N.Z.: 2 islands; Aust.: a continent.
Cook—maps, coast-line.
Journey took 3 years.
Returned 1771.
93 men had sailed—38 had died.

Now ask one or two pupils to reconstruct the passage by referring to the notes.

● **Unprepared Reading**

Marley Castle, page 55.
New Expression: *all at once.*

● **Activity**

Repeat the following:
(a) There was a crooked man, Lesson 111.
(b) Three blind mice, Lesson 107.

● **Writing**

Workbook 3b, Lesson 115.
Guided Composition. The correct answer reads:
Captain Cook sailed from England to the South Pacific in his ship, *Endeavour,* in 1768. He sailed round the two islands of New Zealand *and* made maps of the coast-line. After he had done this, he explored the east coast of Australia. The Dutch explorer, Tasman, had been to Australia and New Zealand in the 17th century, *but* he hadn't brought back much information. Captain Cook returned to England on July 13th, 1771. He had been away for nearly three years.

81 Words

Lesson 116

- **Spelling Drill:** Books shut.

  Oral and Written
  sandwiches; torches; watches; churches;
  brushes; dishes; fishes.
  Point out that after *ch* and *sh* we always add
  -es to make a plural.

- **Phonic Practice:** Sounds and Spellings: Books
  open.

  The letters y [j] and j [dʒ]
  Chorus and Group Repetition

- **Reading and Repetition Drill:** Books open.

  Chorus and Group Repetition
  Ask the pupils to repeat the captions in Lesson
  116.

- **Pattern Drill:** Books open or shut.

  (a) To elicit: It wasn't necessary. (The fireman)
  had already (rescued it).

  > TEACHER: Why didn't you rescue the cat?
  > . . . The fireman.
  > PUPIL: It wasn't necessary. The fireman
  > had already rescued it.

  Substitute the following:
  close the window/mother; burn the rubbish/
  father; sweep the floor/mother; dig the hole/
  father; build the sandcastle/Sandy; serve the
  food/Sue; dial the number/Sandy; repair the
  bike/Billy; collect the parcel/mother; peel the
  oranges/father; iron the shirt/mother; mark the
  exercise-books/the teacher; empty the basket/
  Sue; dust the furniture/mother.

  (b) To elicit: When (they had had breakfast)
  they went to school.

  > TEACHER: First they had breakfast. Then
  > they went to school.
  > PUPIL: When they had had breakfast,
  > they went to school.

  Substitute in place of '. . . they had breakfast':
  cleaned their teeth; did their homework;
  combed their hair; had a wash; drank their
  milk; polished their shoes; had a bath; left
  home; listened to the news; helped mother;
  dried the dishes; saw the postman; read the
  newspaper; said goodbye to their parents.

  (c) To elicit: After (they had had breakfast)
  they went to school.

  > TEACHER: First they had breakfast. Then
  > they went to school.
  > PUPIL: After they had had breakfast,
  > they went to school.

  Substitute the expressions given under (b) above.

  (d) To elicit: They went to school after (they
  had had breakfast).

  > TEACHER: They went to school, but they
  > had breakfast first.
  > PUPIL: They went to school after they
  > had had breakfast.

  Substitute the expressions given under (b) above.

  (e) To elicit: No, I hadn't, but I have now.

  > TEACHER: So you've just sailed down the
  > river. Had you ever done that
  > before?
  > PUPIL: No, I hadn't, but I have now.

  Substitute:
  seen that film; played centre-forward; been to
  the sales; skated on ice; ironed your own
  pyjamas; looked after the baby; heard this
  piece of music; tasted French food; weighed
  yourself; noticed that building; met Mrs Hart;
  spoken to him.

- **Unprepared Reading**

  Marley Castle, page 56.

- **Activity**

  A Game: Find a Good Excuse
  Invite five children to come to the front of the
  class and ask each of them a question: e.g.:
  Why didn't you rescue the cat? Why didn't you
  clear the table? Why didn't you declare this
  watch at the customs? Why didn't you turn
  off the television? Why didn't you come to
  school yesterday? The pupils are given a few
  minutes to think up a suitable answer (which
  may be more than one sentence). (Note that
  it is not necessary for them to use the past
  perfect in their answers.) The pupils then state
  their 'excuses' aloud and the class decides by
  vote which excuse was the best.

- **Writing**

  Workbook 3b, Lesson 116.

Lesson 116 It had already happened

you jar   young jam   year jug   yet Japan

1

I asked Sandy for a penny, but he had already spent his pocket-money.

2

Father ran all the way to the station, but the train had already gone.

3

Why didn't you rescue the cat? It wasn't necessary. The fireman had already rescued it.

4

Why didn't you close the window? It wasn't necessary. Mother had already closed it.

5

When they had had breakfast they went to school.

6

They all went home after they had seen the play.

7

We had finished breakfast before the postman delivered the letters.

8

He had worked in a department-store before he became a waiter.

9

So you've just sailed down the river. Had you ever done that before? No, I hadn't, but I have now.

10

So you've just watched this programme. Had you ever watched it before? No, I hadn't, but I have now.

Lesson 117 Father used to be a Boy Scout

Narrator: The Clárks wént cámping
lást wéek-énd.
They pút up théir tént
in a fíeld.

Father: If yóu colléct some sticks, chíldren,
Í shall líght a fíre.

Sandy: Hére you áre, dád.
Sue: We've brought lóts of drý sticks.
Mother: Hére's a bóx of mátches, Jím.

Father: Í don't wánt any mátches!
Í used to be a Bóy Scóut.
Íf I rúb thése twó sticks togéther,
I can líght a fíre.

Sue: Whát's the mátter, dád?
Father: I've been rúbbing
thése twó sticks togéther
for a lóng tíme
but nóthing's háppened yét!

Mother: Í'll light it, Jím.
It's éasy to líght a fíre
with twó stícks—
if óne of the sticks is a mátch!

Sweetly sings the donkey

Sweetly sings the donkey at the break of day;
If you do not feed him this is what he'll say,
Hee Haw! Hee Haw! Hee Haw! Hee Haw! Hee Haw!

Content and Basic Aims

PATTERNS AND STRUCTURAL WORDS	VOCABULARY
If I (arrive home early) I shall (take you to the cinema).	*Nouns*
I shall (take you to the cinema) if I (arrive home early).	
If (he) (arrives home early) (he) will (take you to	Boy Scout
the cinema).	camping
(He) will (take you to the cinema) if (he)	tent
(arrives home early).	
If I'm (hungry) I'll (eat my dinner).	*Verb*
If he's (hungry) he'll (eat his dinner).	
	rub (together)

- **General Remarks**

Type 1 conditional sentences involving the use of *if* are introduced in this Unit.

- **Aural/Oral Procedure**

(a) Listening (Books shut)
(b) Listening and Understanding (Books open; pictures only)
(c) Listening (Books shut)
(d) Listening and Chorus Repetition (Books shut)
(e) Listening and Group Repetition (Books shut)
(f) Reading Aloud: Chorus and Individual (Books open)

- **Graded Comprehension Questions**

(a) Yes/No Tag Answers: did/will/have/does/ can/has/is.

TEACHER: Did the Clarks go sailing?
PUPIL: No, they didn't.
TEACHER: Did they go camping?
PUPIL: Yes, they did. etc.

(b) Question Tags.

TEACHER: The Clarks went camping.
PUPIL: The Clarks went camping, didn't they?
TEACHER: They didn't go sailing.
PUPIL: They didn't go sailing, did they?

(c) Questions with Who: did/will/have/does/ can/has.

TEACHER: Who went camping?
PUPIL: The Clarks did. etc.

(d) Double Questions.

TEACHER: Did the Clarks go sailing or camping?
PUPIL: They didn't go sailing. They went camping. etc.

(e) General Questions: When, Where, What, How.

TEACHER: When did the Clarks go camping?
PUPIL: Last week-end. etc.

(f) Asking questions in pairs: When, Where, What, How.

TEACHER: Ask me if the Clarks went camping.
PUPIL: Did the Clarks go camping?
TEACHER: When . . .
PUPIL: When did the Clarks go camping? etc.

- **Acting the Scene**

Invite four pupils to come to the front of the class to act the scene. Some twigs would be a useful prop.

- **Unprepared Reading**

Marley Castle, page 57.
New Word: *get away* (escape).

- **Activity**

Song: Sweetly sings the donkey. See page 255 for music.
Teach this song as a three-part round.

- **Writing**

Workbook 3b, Lesson 117.
Guided Composition. The correct answer reads: The Clarks went camping last week-end. *After* they had put up their tent, the children collected some sticks *because* father wanted to light a fire. He didn't want to use matches *because* he had once been a Boy Scout. He rubbed two sticks together instead, *but* he couldn't light the fire. Then mother said, "I'll light the fire, Jim. It's easy to light a fire with two sticks—if one of the sticks is a match!"

76 Words

Lesson 118

- **Spelling Drill:** Books shut.

  Oral and Written
  boats/sandwiches; books/boxes; cups/dresses; forks/tomatoes; mumps/fishes.
  Remind the pupils that we usually add -es to form the plural of words ending in *ch*, *x*, *sh*, *s* and *o*.

- **Phonic Practice:** Sounds and Spellings: Books open.

  The letters m [m] and n [n]
  Chorus and Group Repetition

- **Reading and Repetition Drill:** Books open.

  Chorus and Group Repetition
  Ask the pupils to repeat the captions in Lesson 118.

- **Pattern Drill:** Books open or shut.

  (a) To elicit: If I arrive home early, I shall (take you to the cinema).

    TEACHER: What will you do if you arrive home early? . . . take you to the cinema.
    PUPIL: If I arrive home early, I shall take you to the cinema.

  Substitute the following:
  work in the garden; play a game of football; cook the evening meal; dig a hole in the garden; listen to some records; repair my bicycle; help mother; practise the flute; mend the clock; paint a picture; write some letters; watch television; read a book; draw some pictures; clean the car.

  (b) To elicit: I shall (take you to the cinema) if I arrive home early.

    TEACHER: What will you do if you arrive home early? . . . take you to the cinema.
    PUPIL: I shall take you to the cinema if I arrive home early.

  Substitute the expressions given under (a) above.

  (c) To elicit: If father arrives home early, he will (take you to the cinema).

    TEACHER: What will father do if he arrives home early? . . . take you to the cinema.
    PUPIL: If father arrives home early, he will take you to the cinema.

  Substitute the expressions given under (a) above.

  (d) To elicit: Father will (take you to the cinema) if he arrives home early.

    TEACHER: What will father do if he arrives home early? . . . take you to the cinema.

    PUPIL: Father will take you to the cinema if he arrives home early.

  Substitute the expressions given under (a) above.

  (e) To elicit: If I'm (hungry), I shall (eat my dinner).

    TEACHER: Perhaps you're hungry. Don't you want to eat your dinner?
    PUPIL: If I'm hungry, I shall eat my dinner.

  Substitute the following:

  better/go to school; thirsty/drink some water; ready/go out; dirty/have a bath; cold/put on your coat; warm/take your coat off; ill/stay in bed; tired/go to bed; sleepy/have an early night.

  (f) To elicit: If he's (hungry), he'll (eat his dinner).

    TEACHER: Perhaps he's hungry. Doesn't he want to eat his dinner?
    PUPIL: If he's hungry, he'll eat his dinner.

  Substitute the expressions given under (e) above.

  Note that the patterns practised in (e) and (f) may be repeated to elicit *can* in place of *shall/will*.

- **Unprepared Reading**

  Marley Castle, page 58.
  New Words: *shot* (noun), *smashed, fired, loose, rolled.*

- **Activity**

  Dictation
  Dictate the following passage:

  Sándy and Í/úsed to stáy at hóme/on Sáturday áfternóons,/but nów we gó to the cínema./ Áfter we had had lúnch/lást Sáturday/we wént out togéther./The cínema we wént to/was álmost émpty./It was an óld fílm/and lóts of péople had álready séen it./But Sándy and Í/ hadn't séen it befóre/so we bóught two tíckets/ and wént in.

- **Writing**

  Workbook 3b, Lesson 118.

239

Lesson **118** If . . .

<u>m</u>ap <u>n</u>ew   <u>m</u>eet <u>n</u>eat   <u>m</u>eal <u>n</u>ail   <u>m</u>ake <u>n</u>ice

1

If I win a lot of money, I shall
buy a new car.

2

If I buy some sweets, I shan't give
you any.

3

If it's a nice day tomorrow, we
shall go to the seaside.

4

We shan't go to the seaside if it
isn't a nice day tomorrow.

5

If father arrives home early, he
will take us to the cinema.

6

Father won't take us to the cinema
if he doesn't arrive home early.

7

If you finish your homework
quickly, you can watch television.

8

You can't watch television if you
don't finish your homework quickly.

Lesson **119**   Who's silly? Boys or girls?

Narrator: It's the énd of térm.
Sándy and Súe are góing to a schóol párty.
Sándy sáys he's réady,
but Súe isn't réady yét.

Sandy: Húrry úp, Súe!
Áren't you réady yét?
Sue: Nó, I've gót to pút ón my párty dréss.
And I've gót to cómb my háir.

Sandy: Cóme on, Súe! Húrry úp!
Sue: Bé quíet, Sándy!
Whén I'm réady, I'll téll you.

Sue: Whích dréss shall I wéar, múm?
The réd one, or the blúe one?
Mother: The réd one, Súe.

Father: Whát's the mátter, Sándy?
Sandy: I'm wáiting for Súe.
I've been wáiting for hóurs!
Áren't gírls sílly!

Sue: I'm réady now.
Sandy: At lást!
Mother: Sándy! You háven't pút your shóes on yét.
Sue: Áren't bóys sílly!

241

Content and Basic Aims

PATTERNS AND STRUCTURAL WORDS

When I (come home from school) I shall (play a game of football).
I shall (play a game of football) when I (come home from school).
When (he) (comes home from school) (he) will (play a game of football).
(He) will (play a game of football) when (he) (comes home from school).
When I'm (hungry) I'll (eat my dinner).
When he's (hungry) he'll (eat his dinner).

- **General Remarks**

Patterns involving the use of the simple present after the temporal conjunction, *when,* are introduced in this Unit. Compare Type 1 conditional sentences in TU 59.

At the end of Lesson 120, the pupils should be set the Attainment Test which appears on the final pages of Workbook 3b. The teacher may set the 'Alternative or Supplementary Test' (see page 245) *instead of* or *in addition to* the Attainment Test in the Pupil's Workbook if he wishes to. For Mark Scales, see page 250.

- **Aural/Oral Procedure**

(a) Listening (Books shut)
(b) Listening and Understanding (Books open; pictures only)
(c) Listening (Books shut)
(d) Listening and Chorus Repetition (Books shut)
(e) Listening and Group Repetition (Books shut)
(f) Reading Aloud: Chorus and Individual (Books open)

- **Graded Comprehension Questions**

(a) Yes/No Tag Answers: is/are/does/has/will.

TEACHER: Is it the beginning of term?
PUPIL: No, it isn't.
TEACHER: Is it the end of term?
PUPIL: Yes, it is. etc.

(b) Question Tags.

TEACHER: It's the end of term.
PUPIL: It's the end of term, isn't it?
TEACHER: It isn't the beginning of term.
PUPIL: It isn't the beginning of term, is it? etc.

(c) Questions with Who: are/does/isn't/has/will.

TEACHER: Who is going to a party?
PUPIL: Sandy and Sue *are*. etc.

(d) Double Questions.

TEACHER: Is it the beginning or the end of term?

PUPIL: It isn't the beginning of term. It's the end of term. etc.

(e) General Questions: Why, What, Which, How long.

TEACHER: Why are Sandy and Sue going to a school party?
PUPIL: Because it's the end of term. etc.

(f) Asking questions in pairs: Why, What, Which, How long.

TEACHER: Ask me if they're going to a school party.
PUPIL: Are they going to a school party?
TEACHER: Why . . .
PUPIL: Why are they going to a school party? etc.

- **Acting the Scene**

Invite four pupils to come to the front of the class to act the scene. The Narrator's part, frame 1, should be omitted. The boy taking the part of Sandy should take off his shoes.

- **Unprepared Reading**

Marley Castle, page 59.
New Words: *body, dead, has stolen, sell.*

- **Activity**

Song: Sweetly sings the donkey. See page 255 for music.
Repeat this song as a three-part round.

- **Writing**

Workbook 3b, Lesson 119.
Guided Composition. The correct answer reads: Sandy and Sue were going to an end-of-term party at school. Sandy was in a hurry to leave, *but* Sue wasn't ready. *While* Sue was putting on her red dress, Sandy sat down and waited.

"I've been waiting for hours!" he told his father. "Aren't girls silly!"

At last Sue was ready to leave, *when* mother noticed that Sandy wasn't wearing his shoes. He wasn't ready yet!

"Aren't boys silly!" Sue said.

72 Words

Lesson 120

- **Spelling Drill:** Books shut.

  Oral and Written
  man/men; woman/women; child/children; tooth/teeth; foot/feet. Point out the irregular plurals.

- **Phonic Practice:** Sounds and Spellings: Books open.

  The letters m [m] and n [n]
  Chorus and Group Repetition

- **Reading and Repetition Drill:** Books open.

  Chorus and Group Repetition
  Ask the pupils to repeat the captions in Lesson 120.

- **Pattern Drill:** Books open or shut.

  (a) To elicit: When I come home from school, I shall (play a game of football).

  TEACHER: What will you do when you come home from school? . . . play a game of football.
  PUPIL: When I come home from school, I shall play a game of football.

  Substitute the following:
  work in the garden; play some records; cook the evening meal; dig a hole in the garden; listen to some records; repair my bicycle; help mother; practise the flute; mend the clock; paint a picture; write some letters; watch television; read a book; draw some pictures; clean the car.

  (b) To elicit: I shall (play a game of football) when I come home from school.

  TEACHER: What will you do when you come home from school? . . . play a game of football.
  PUPIL: I shall play a game of football when I come home from school.

  Substitute the expressions given under (a) above.

  (c) To elicit: When Sandy comes home from school, he will (play a game of football).

  TEACHER: What will Sandy do when he comes home from school? . . . play a game of football.
  PUPIL: When Sandy comes home from school, he will play a game of football.

  Substitute the expressions given under (a) above.

  (d) To elicit: Sandy will (play a game of football) when he comes home from school.

  TEACHER: What will Sandy do when he comes home from school? . . . play a game of football.

  PUPIL: Sandy will play a game of football when he comes home from school.

  Substitute the expressions given under (a) above.

  (e) To elicit: When I'm (hungry), I shall (eat my dinner).

  TEACHER: Perhaps you're hungry. Don't you want to eat your dinner?
  PUPIL: When I'm hungry, I shall eat my dinner.

  Substitute the following
  better/go to school; thirst/drink some water; ready/go out; dirty/have a bath; cold/put on your coat; warm/take your coat off; ill/stay in bed; tired/go to bed; sleepy/have an early night.

  (f) To elicit: When he's (hungry), he'll (eat his dinner).

  TEACHER: Perhaps he's hungry. Doesn't he want to eat his dinner?
  PUPIL: When he's hungry, he'll eat his dinner.

  Substitute the expressions given under (e) above.

  Note that the patterns practised in (e) and (f) may be repeated to elicit *can* in place of *shall/will.*

- **Unprepared Reading**

  Marley Castle, page 60.
  New Words and Expressions: *reward, long past* (your bedtime).

- **Activity**

  It's time for a story: Dreams, page 269.
  New Words and Expressions: *dreams, goal posts, rest* (relaxation), *grow up, footballer, team, own* (vb.), *conversation.*

- **Writing**

  Workbook 3b, Lesson 120.

Lesson **120** When . . .

1

When I earn enough money, I shall
buy a new car.

2

When I buy some sweets, I shan't
give you any.

3

When it's fine we shall go to the
seaside.

4

Sandy will go back to school when
he's better.

5

When father arrives home from work
he will take us to the cinema.

6

Mother will go to the grocer's when
she finishes the housework.

7

Come when you have time.

8

Come when you are ready.

Terminal Tests

General Remarks

The Attainment Test at the end of Workbook 3b may now be set. The test below may be given *instead of* or *in addition to* the test in the Workbook. Mark scales for the written tests appear on page 250.

Alternative or Supplementary Test

Guided Composition: Wrong number

Read the story, then answer the questions:

The telephone rang and Sue answered it. "May I speak to Mrs Potts please?" a man asked.

"I'm afraid you've got the wrong number," Sue said.

"I'm sorry," the man said.

A few minutes passed and the telephone rang again, so Sue answered it. It was the same man. He
5 had made a mistake again. Three minutes later the phone rang once more, but Sue didn't answer it this time. It rang and rang. Mother was in the kitchen and she heard the noise. "Why don't you answer the phone, Sue?" she called. "It's been ringing for three minutes."

"Oh, all right," Sue said. "I'm sure it's that man again." But she was wrong. It was father and he was rather cross!
10 "Is that you, Sue?" he cried. "Why doesn't anybody answer the phone? It's been ringing and ringing!"

Questions

Answer these questions in one paragraph. Do not use more than 80 words.
1 Did the telephone ring, or not? Who answered it? *(so)*
2 Was it a man or a woman? Who did he want to speak to? *(who)*
3 What did Sue say?
4 Did the man make the same mistake a few minutes later, or not?
5 Did the telephone ring once more, or not? Did Sue answer it at first, or not? *(When)*
6 Did she answer it, or not? Who told her to? *(because)*
7 Who was it? Was he pleased, or rather cross? Had he had to wait a long time, or not? *(and) (because)*

....

....

....

....

....

....

....

Multiple Choice Questions

Only one answer is right in each exercise. Put a circle round the correct letter: A, B, C or D.
1 The last time the telephone rang Sue
   A answered it at once.
   B let mother answer it.
   C let it ring.
   D said, "I'm sure it's father."
2 . . . has it been ringing? Three minutes.
   A Since when   B How long   C When   D Why
3 The man had made a mistake. He had . . . the wrong number.
   A wanted   B asked   C dialled   D rang

Language Questions

A. Look at this example. Then do the same.

> Sandy must return home by train. (would like to)
> *That's just what he would like to do.*
> *Sandy would like to return home by train.*

1 Mr Blake must wake up early. (must remember to)

. . . .

. . . .

2 Sandy must mend this clock. (will try to)

. . . .

. . . .

3 Mother must turn off the electricity. (forgot to)

. . . .

. . . .

B. Look at this example. Then do the same.

> The food tastes awful. (father thinks)
> *Guess what father thinks!*
> *He thinks the food tastes awful.*

1 He'll be able to skate soon. (Sandy has told me)

. . . .

. . . .

2 He'll lose his marbles. (Sandy is afraid of)

. . . .

. . . .

3 He must remain in bed. (Sandy is unhappy about)

. . . .

. . . .

C. Look at this example. Then do the same.

> I'm sure I'll miss the bus.
> *I'm sure to miss the bus.*

1 I'm certain I'll see you.

. . . .

2 I'm afraid I'll fall.

. . . .

3 I'm glad I'll meet him.

. . . .

D. Put in *may, can't, must, may have, can't have* or *must have*:

1 How much does it cost? It .... cost £5. I'm sure it does.

2 How much did it weigh? It .... weighed 2 kilos. I'm sure it did.

3 What does it measure? It .... measure 48 metres. Surely it doesn't!

4 How did he feel? He .... felt ill. I'm not sure.

5 What does it taste like? It .... taste bitter. I'm not sure.

6 How was he? He .... been ill. Surely he wasn't!

7 What shape is it? It .... be round. Surely it isn't.

8 What was he doing? He .... been reading. I'm not sure.

E. Look at these examples. Then do the same.

> Mrs Hart/correcting exercise-books/yesterday
>
> Mrs. Hart has been correcting exercise-books since yesterday.
>
> The baby/crying/three hours
>
> The baby has been crying for three hours.

1 The men/exploring the cave/two months

....

2 The tree/growing/1932

....

3 Sue/combing her hair/three minutes

....

4 Father/travelling abroad/he was a boy

....

5 Sue/skating/quite a while

....

F. Look at this example. Then do the same.

> Did you develop the film yourself?
>
> No, I didn't do it myself. I had it developed.

1 Did she wash the clothes herself?

....

2 Did he mend the clock himself?

....

3 Did you cut your hair yourself?

....

4 Did they paint the fence themselves?

....

G. Look at this example.

> Sue was drying the dishes. She dropped a plate and broke it.
>
> *When Sue was drying the dishes, she dropped a plate and broke it.*

Now join these sentences in the same way. Use *when, while,* or *just as.*

1 They were going to leave the house. Someone knocked at the door.

. . . .

2 The children were watching television. Mother was making tea.

. . . .

3 The children came home from school. Mother was ironing.

. . . .

4 Mother saw a nice hat. She was walking through the hat department.

. . . .

H. Look at these examples. Then do the same.

> Are you an artist?
>
> *No I used to be an artist, but I'm not any more.*
>
> Does he collect stamps?
>
> *No. He used to collect stamps, but he doesn't any more.*

1 Is he rich?

. . . .

2 Do you grow your own tomatoes?

. . . .

3 Does she work in the hat department?

. . . .

4 Are you a waiter?

. . . .

I. Look at this example. Then do the same.

> First they had breakfast. Then they went to school. (When)
>
> *When they had had breakfast, they went to school.*

1 First they cleaned their teeth. Then they went to school (When)

. . . .

2 First they did their homework. Then they went to school. (When)

. . . .

3 First they had a wash. Then they went to school. (After)

. . . .

248

Written Tests: Mark Scales

A hundred marks may be allotted to each of the written tests. Each test consists of three parts. Guided Composition, Multiple Choice Questions and Language Questions.

Workbook 3a

The allocation of marks for each part is as follows:

Guided Composition:	25 marks
Multiple Choice Questions:	10 marks
Language Questions:	65 marks
Total:	100 marks

The following scales are suggested:

Marks

Guided Composition

Two marks for each correct answer:	20
For keeping within limit and noting word total:	5

Multiple Choice Questions

1	Comprehension:	4
2	Structural Choice:	3
3	Lexical Choice:	3

Language Questions

A	One mark for each correct question:	3
B	One mark for each correct statement (8 statements):	8
C	One mark for each correct statement (8 statements):	8
D	One mark for each correct statement:	12
E	Two marks for each correct statement:	8
F	Two marks for each correct question:	10
G	One mark for each correct answer:	5
H	One mark for each correct answer:	5
I	One mark for each correct sentence (6 sentences):	6
Total:		100

Workbook 3a

Alternative or Supplementary Test

The allocation of marks for each part is as follows:

Guided Composition:	25 marks
Multiple Choice Questions:	10 marks
Language Questions:	65 marks
Total:	100 marks

The following scales are suggested:

Marks

Guided Composition

Two marks for each correct answer:	20
For keeping within limit and noting word total:	5

Multiple Choice Questions

1	Comprehension:	4
2	Structural Choice:	3
3	Structural/Lexical Choice:	3

Language Questions

A	One mark for each correct question:	3
B	Two marks for each correct statement (4 statements):	8
C	One mark for each correct statement (8 statements):	8

D	One mark for each correct statement:	12
E	Two marks for each correct statement:	8
F	Two marks for each correct statement:	10
G	One mark for each correct answer:	5
H	One mark for each correct statement:	5
I	One mark for each correct sentence (6 sentences);	6
Total:		100

Workbook 3b

The allocation of marks for each part is as follows:

Guided Composition:	26 marks
Multiple Choice Questions:	10 marks
Language Questions:	64 marks
Total:	100 marks

The following scales are suggested:

Marks

Guided Composition

Questions 1–3, three marks each:	9
Questions 4–8, two marks each:	10
For keeping within limit and noting word total:	7

Multiple Choice Questions

1	Comprehension:	4
2	Structural Choice:	3
3	Lexical Choice:	3

Language Questions

A	One mark for each correct statement:	6
B	One mark for each correct statement:	6
C	Two marks for each correct statement:	6
D	One mark for each correct insertion:	6
E	One mark for each correct insertion:	6
F	One mark for each correct insertion:	6
G	One mark for each correct insertion:	6
H	One mark for each correct insertion:	6
I	One mark for each correct insertion:	6
J	One mark for each correct statement:	6
K	One mark for each correct statement:	4
Total:		100

Workbook 3b

Alternative or Supplementary Test

The allocation of marks for each part is as follows:

Guided Composition:	26 marks
Multiple Choice Questions:	10 marks
Language Questions:	64 marks
Total:	100 marks

The following scales are suggested:

Guided Composition

Marks

Three marks for each correct answer:	21
For keeping within limit and noting word total:	5

Multiple Choice Questions

1	Comprehension:	4
2	Structural Choice:	3
3	Lexical Choice:	3

Language Questions

A One mark for each correct statement: 6
B One mark for each correct statement: 6
C One mark for each correct statement: 3
D Two marks for each correct insertion: 16
E Two marks for each correct statement: 10
F One mark for each correct statement (8 statements): 8
G Two marks for each correct statement: 8
H One mark for each correct statement: 4
I One mark for each correct statement: 3

Total: 100

Songs

● **There's a Hole in my Bucket**

(First introduced in Lesson 21.)

● **Sing This Grave and Simple Strain**

(First introduced in Lesson 33.)

● **The More We are Together**

(First introduced in Lesson 35.)

● **I Love Sixpence**

(First introduced in Lesson 41.)

- **Sally in Our Alley**

  (First introduced in Lesson 55.)

- **I Had a Little Nut-tree**

  (First introduced in Lesson 61.)

- **Oh, Dear! What Can the Matter Be?**

  (First introduced in Lesson 65.)

- **Some Folk Do**

(First introduced in Lesson 73.)

- **Sandy Macnab**

(First introduced in Lesson 83.)

- **Billy Boy**

(First introduced in Lesson 95.)

- **Three Blind Mice**

(First introduced in Lesson 107.)

- **There Was a Crooked Man**

(First introduced in Lesson 111.)

- **Sweetly Sings the Donkey**

(First introduced in Lesson 117.)

ACKNOWLEDGEMENTS

We are grateful to the following for permission to reproduce copyright material:

Campbell, Connelly & Co. Ltd for 'The more we are together'; J. Curwen & Sons Ltd for 'Some folk do' and 'Billy Boy'.

Stories

Words which have not been formally introduced in the course are printed in italics.

The Holidays

(See Lesson 6.)

Sandy and Sue had a good time during the summer holidays. They left home on August 15th. They stayed at an *hotel* near the sea. It was a lovely little hotel and the children enjoyed their holiday. The name of the hotel was 'Seaview'. It was in a beautiful *bay*. The name of the bay was 'Long Bay'.

Father, mother, Sandy and Sue went to the *beach* every day. They can all swim very well. Sue can dive, too, but Sandy can't dive. He always jumps into the water.

One day, Sue said to Sandy, "You mustn't jump into the water, Sandy. You must dive."

"I can't dive," Sandy said.

"Watch me," Sue said. "It's easy. Look. Like this." Sue dived into the water beautifully and Sandy watched her. "Now you do it, Sandy," Sue called.

Sandy put his arms over his head and dived. "Ouch!" he shouted.

"What's the matter?" Sue asked and she laughed.

"I hit my *tummy* on the water," Sandy said. "It's not funny."

"It was very funny," Sue said. "Do it again, Sandy."

Sandy went out of the water and dived again. "You're right, Sue," he said. "It's easy."

"Mum, dad!" Sue called. "Watch Sandy. He can dive now."

Mother and father watched Sandy. He dived into the water again. He dived very well. "That's very good." mother and father said. Then mother and father dived into the water, too.

Sandy went to the beach and got his *snorkel*. Mother, father and Sue didn't see him. Sandy put on his snorkel and went back into the water. Sandy can swim under water very well and he swam *towards* Sue. Then he dived under Sue and *pinched* her toes.

"Ouch!" Sue cried.

"What's the matter?" mother asked.

"There's a big fish under the water," Sue said. "It pinched my toes."

"Don't be silly, Sue," mother said. "There aren't any big fish here. Mother, father and Sue didn't see Sandy. Sandy dived under mother and pinched her toes, too. "Ouch!" mother cried.

"What's the matter, Betty?" father asked.

"Sue's right, Jim," mother said. "There's a big fish under the water. It pinched my toes, too."

"I'll have a look under the water," father said. Father can swim very well. He dived down and swam under the water. Of course, he saw Sandy. But Sandy didn't see his father. Sandy swam towards Sue. He wanted to pinch his sister again. Then father swam behind him and *grabbed* his foot. He pulled Sandy out of the water. Father laughed and Sandy laughed, too, "You're right, Betty," he said. "There is a big fish in the water. I've just caught it."

"Where is it?" Sue and mother asked.

"Here," father said and he *pointed* at Sandy.

"Sandy can swim like a fish and he can dive like a *seagull*," father said.

"Yes," Sue said, "and he can pinch like a *crab!*"

Sandy and Sue have gone back to school now, but they often remember their summer holidays. Don't you?

The Blakes Move In

(See Lesson 12.)

"Where have you been, children?" Mother asked.

"We've been next door, mum," Sue answered.

"Next door?" mother asked. "Where? To Mrs Gasbag's?"

"No, mum. To the *other* house," Sandy said.

"But that house is empty," mother said.

"No, it isn't, mum," Sue said. "Look out of the window. That's Mr Blake. And that's his wife. They've got three children: Alan, Wendy and Timmy."

"How do you know their names?" mother asked.

"We've already met them, mum." Sue answered.

Mother looked out of the window again. "Who are those two men?" she asked.

"They're workmen, mum," Sandy said. "Their names are Dick and Harry. They're very strong. They're carrying a piano."

Dick and Harry carried the piano into the house. They put it in the kitchen. Then they carried it to another room. Mrs Blake came in and looked at it. "My goodness!" she cried. "You've turned it upside-down!"

"Sorry, Mrs," Dick and Harry said.

"Bring that heavy table in now," Mrs Blake said. "It's going to rain. You can turn the piano over in a moment."

Dick and Harry went out to the van. The heavy table was in the street near the van. The two workmen carried it into the house. "Careful, Dick," Harry said. "Don't drop it on your toes." Suddenly, they heard a noise. *Bang! Crash!*

"What's that?" Harry asked.

"I don't know," Dick said. "Put the table down, Harry." They put the table down. Then Mrs Blake hurried downstairs.

"What's that noise?" she asked.

"We don't know, Mrs," Dick said.

"Have you brought the bathroom mirror in

yet?" Mrs Blake asked.

"Yes," Harry said.

"When did you bring it in?" Mrs Blake asked.

"We brought it in a moment ago, Mrs," Harry said.

"Where did you put it?" Mrs Blake asked.

"On the floor, Mrs," Harry said.

"Which floor?" Mrs Blake asked.

"This floor, Mrs," Harry said.

Dick looked on the floor.

"Eh! Harry!" he cried. "Harry! The mirror! Look! You're standing on it."

"Oh! Oh! My beautiful mirror," Mrs Blake cried.

"Sorry, Mrs," Harry said.

"You broke it with your big feet," Mrs Blake said. "You're a careless man!"

"Sorry, Mrs," Harry said.

"I'll pick up the pieces," Dick said. He picked up the pieces. "Ouch!" he cried.

"What's the matter, Dick?" Harry asked.

"Look!" Dick cried. "I've just cut my finger. It's *bleeding*."

"Oh! Oh!" Mrs Blake cried. "Now there's *blood* on my nice clean *carpet*. Get out of the house, both of you!"

The two workmen ran out of the house. "We can bring in some chairs," they said.

Just then, Mr Blake arrived. He was in a hurry.

"Where have you been, dear?" Mrs Blake asked.

"I've been in the living-room," Mr Blake said. "Have you seen my new hat, dear?"

"No, I haven't seen your new hat," Mrs Blake said. "Where did you put it?"

"I put it in the living-room. It was there a moment ago, but it isn't there now. It's a very good hat. It cost a lot of money."

"Well I haven't seen it," Mrs Blake said. She was cross. Then Dick and Harry came in. They had some chairs.

"Put those chairs down and go into the living-room," Mrs Blake said. "Turn the piano over. It's upside-down."

Dick and Harry went into the living-room. They are very strong men and they turned the piano over quickly.

"What's that, Harry?" Dick asked.

"I don't know," Harry said. "It was under the piano."

Then Mr Blake came into the room. "Oh! Oh! Oh!" he cried. "It's my hat. My lovely new hat. Look at it now!"

Father Meets the Blakes

(See Lesson 18.)

Father was in the garden with the children. He cut the *grass* and the children helped him. "Have you met our new neighbours yet, dad?" Sandy asked.

"No, I haven't, Sandy," father said.

"Their name is Blake," Sue said. "They have three children. There are two boys. Their names are Alan and Timmy. There is one girl. Her name is Wendy."

Then Mr Blake went into his garden and the children noticed him. "Look, dad," Sandy said. "There's Mr Blake."

Mr Blake looked over the fence and smiled at father and the children. "Good afternoon," he said.

Father smiled at Mr Blake. "Good afternoon," he answered.

"My name's George Blake," Mr Blake said.

"My name's Jim Clark," father said.

Mr Blake looked at father's garden. "You have a lovely garden," he said. Then he looked at his own garden. "Look at my garden," he said. "It isn't a garden at all. I must work very hard and I'm not a good *gardener*." Poor Mr Blake! His garden was full of *weeds*. "Excuse me, Mr Clark," he said. "May I call you Jim?"

"Of course, you may," father said. "Can I call you George?"

"Certainly," Mr Blake said. "We are neighbours now. It's so good to have neighbours."

"Yes," father said.

Mr Blake watched father. Father cut the grass and the children helped him. "Jim," he called.

"Yes," father answered and he stopped work again.

"I haven't got many *garden tools*. May I *borrow* you *spade* and your *garden fork* please?"

"Of course, you may," father said. "I'll get them for you." Father got the spade and fork for Mr Blake and gave them to him.

Just then, Mrs Blake came into the garden. "Good afternoon," she said to father. "My name's Marion Blake."

"I'm Jim Clark," father said and smiled. "Please call me Jim."

"And you must call me Marion," Mrs Blake said. "It's so nice to have neighbours. This house has been empty for a long time. We must do a lot of work. May I borrow your ladder please?"

"Of course," father said. "I'll get it for you." Father got the ladder. "Here you are, Marion," he said.

The ladder was very heavy. "Please let me help you," father said and he carried the ladder into Mrs Blake's house. Then he went into Mr Blake's garden.

"This is hard work, Jim," Mr Blake said "I'm a very bad gardener."

"Please let me help you," father said.

"Thank you very much, Jim," Mr Blake said. "Perhaps you can *dig* the garden for me."

"All right, George," father said.

Mother was in the kitchen. She looked out of the window, but father wasn't in the garden. So she called Sandy, "Sandy," she said. "Tell your father to bring the ladder into the kitchen please. I want him to fix this shelf."

"He can't, mum," Sandy said. "Mrs Blake has borrowed our ladder."

"It doesn't matter," mother said. "I'll come into the garden and help your father." Mother went into the garden, but, of course, father wasn't there.

Just then, Mrs Blake looked over the fence. "Hullo, Betty," she said. "May I borrow some flour and some sugar please?"

"Of course, Marion," mother said. "I'll get some for you." Mother went to the kitchen and got some flour and some sugar. "Have you seen Jim?" she asked Mrs Blake.

Mrs Blake laughed. "We've borrowed your spade, your garden fork, your ladder, some flour and some sugar. And we've borrowed your *husband*, too. He's in our garden. He's helping George. It's so nice to have neighbours!"

The Wrong Car

(See Lesson 24.)

Yesterday father saw Mr Blake. He told him about his car.

"Betty tried to unlock the door of this car," father said, "but she couldn't. Do you know why? It was the wrong car. It wasn't our car. It didn't belong to us. Then a stranger ran up to us and said, 'What are you doing to my car?'"

Mr Blake laughed. "That happened to me, too," he answered. "Let me tell you the story."

"Please tell me the story," father said.

"Well," Mr Blake began. "One day last year I went shopping with my wife. Marion always buys lots of things at the shops. She bought a dress and then she said to me, 'Would you carry this dress for me, George?' and she gave it to me. She bought a big hat and then she said to me, 'Could you carry this hat for me please, George?' and she gave it to me. She bought a blouse and then she said to me, 'Could you carry this blouse for me please, George?' She bought lots of things and I carried them. I had lots of parcels. My hands were full. I couldn't see, so I wasn't able to walk properly. 'Please show me the way, Marion,' I said. 'I can't see.' Marion showed me the way and we went back to the car together. Marion stopped in front of a small red car.

'This car is ours,' she said.

'I'll open the door, dear,' I said. I put my hand in my pocket and found my key. I took the key out of my pocket and put it in the lock. Then I tried to unlock the door of the car. "That's funny," I said to Marion.

'What's funny, dear?' she asked.

'The key fits into the lock,' I said, 'but it won't turn.' I tried to turn the key, but I couldn't. I wasn't able to turn it at all. I tried very hard and suddenly, the key broke. I was very cross. I said some very bad things. I dropped all the parcels.

'Be careful,' Marion said. 'Be careful of my new clothes.'

'I don't care about your new clothes,' I said. 'I can't get into my car. I've broken my key.' I

was terribly terribly cross. So I broke the window of the car and opened the door. 'Put the parcels in the back seat,' I said. 'Now get into the car please.'

Just then a man ran up to us. He was very cross, too. 'I saw you,' he shouted. 'I saw you. You broke the window of my car.'

'This is my car,' I said. 'My key broke in the lock and I broke the window.'

'It isn't your car!' the man shouted. 'You're a thief!' 'It's my car. Police! Police!' he called.

A policeman heard him and came to the car. 'Now, now,' the policeman said. 'What's happening here?'

'This man and this woman are thieves,' the man cried. 'They're taking my car.'

'Is this your car?' the policeman asked the man.

'Yes,' the man said and he showed the policeman some papers.

'Mm,' the policeman said. Then he looked at me and I looked at him.

'I'm sorry,' I said. 'I've made a mistake. My car is exactly like this one. I had a lot of parcels in my hands and I couldn't see properly.'

'Mm,' the policeman said. 'I often hear this story. Will you come to the police station with me?'

We went to the station and at last the police *believed* me. I paid a lot of money to the other man. Then my wife and I walked home and I carried all those parcels."

"Why?" father asked. "Couldn't you find your car?"

"Yes," Mr Blake said. "We were able to find our car, but of course, we didn't have a key!"

"That's a funny story," father said and he laughed and laughed.

At the Circus

(See Lesson 30.)

Last week father took the children to the circus. They saw lots of things, but they liked the clown best. The clown played many clever tricks. The clown appeared with the weight-lifter. The clown's name was Boris. The weight-lifter's name was Marvo.

Marvo was a very strong man. There was a heavy weight on the *ground*, but Marvo was strong enough to lift it. The weight was easy for him to lift.

Then Boris appeared. He looked very funny. He wore a funny hat and he had a big red nose. His shoes were very big.

"His shoes are like boats," Sandy said.

Poor Boris! He couldn't walk easily because his shoes were so big. He walked like this: *flip, flop,* flip, flop. And he often *fell over*. Suddenly Boris saw Marvo, the weight-lifter, and laughed. Then he tried to lift Marvo's big weight. He tried and tried, but it was too difficult for him to lift it. He wasn't able to lift it at all. Marvo watched Boris, then he pushed him away and lifted up the weight. Boris fell over and hurt his head.

Then Boris found his own 'weight'. It wasn't a *real* weight. It was just a bar and two balloons. Boris *pretended that* his weight was very heavy. He tried to lift it and he pretended that he couldn't. Marvo watched him. Then Boris picked up the weight with one hand and held it above his head. He showed it to Marvo. Marvo was very *surprised*. Suddenly, Boris hit Marvo on the head with one of the balloons. Of course, this didn't hurt Marvo at all, but he pretended that the clown hurt him.

Marvo ran after Boris. Boris tried to run, but he couldn't. He wasn't able to run because his shoes were so big. Marvo caught Boris and took the weight. Then he burst the balloons and broke the bar with his hands. Boris watched this, then he took out his *handkerchief* and cried. Marvo *felt sorry* for Boris. He went near him and suddenly Boris gave him a hard kick in the leg. Marvo pretended that he couldn't walk. His leg hurt, so it was difficult for him to walk. He was very, very cross. He caught Boris again and he took off one of Boris's shoes. Then he put Boris over his knees and *spanked* him with the shoe. Boris cried like a baby: *Boo hoo!* Boo hoo! He took out his handkerchief again and cried and cried.

Marvo didn't pay any attention to Boris. He went back to his weight and lifted it up. What did Boris do? Well, he went away and came back with a *bucket*. He stood behind Marvo and Marvo couldn't see him. Suddenly, Boris put the bucket over Marvo's head. Marvo dropped the weight and shouted. He ran here and there, but he couldn't see at all. He wasn't able to see because the bucket was over his eyes. Boris picked up a small weight and hit the bucket very hard. Marvo tried to pull the bucket off, but he wasn't able to. He looked very funny with the bucket on his head. Boris laughed and laughed and the children *clapped*. Sandy and Sue enjoyed the programme very much. Have you ever been to a circus? Didn't you enjoy it, too?

The Dancing Competition

(See Lesson 36.)

It was a very *important* day yesterday. Sue *entered a dancing competition*. There were lots of girls in the competition. Mother, father and Sandy went to see the competition. *"Good luck, Sue!"* they said.

Sue wore a pretty white dress and lovely *silver* shoes. She wore a number on her back. Her number was 16. There were twenty girls in the competition. They danced together and six *judges* watched them. Then the dancing ended and the judges talked about the dancers.

"I think numbers 6, 16, 7 and 8 were very good indeed," a judge said. "They were the best."

"I *agree*," another judge said. "Numbers 2, 4, 9 and 12 were very bad indeed. They were the worst."

The *judges* agreed about the best dancers and the worst dancers, but they couldn't agree about the *winners*. They talked and talked.

"Number 7 was better than number 8," one of the judges said.

"I don't agree," another judge said. "Number 7 is a taller girl than number 8. She dances very well, but she is not as good as number 8."

"Who was that girl on the left?" one of the judges said. "She danced very well."

"That was number 6," another judge said.

"Number 16 was the quickest and neatest of them all," another judge said.

"I don't agree. She's a good dancer, but she's not the quickest and the neatest."

"I don't agree," another judge said. "She was very good indeed."

The judges talked and talked. At last they appeared and all the people waited to hear them. The girls stood behind the judges. They looked very pretty. They all wore white dresses and silver shoes. Which girl was the prettiest? That's a very hard question. They were all so pretty.

Sue could see her mother and father and Sandy. Sue smiled at them and mother, father and Sandy smiled at Sue.

"Will she win, Jim?" mother asked father.

"I don't know, Betty," father said. "She danced very well. She danced better than numbers 2 and 9."

"Numbers 2 and 9!" mother cried. "They didn't dance well at all. They were awful. Their dancing was very poor."

"Quiet please," the judges called.

"Sh!" father said. "They're going to call the winners. They always give the third prize first, then the second and then the first."

One of the judges stood up. "It was very difficult for us to judge this competition," he said. "All the girls danced so well. They are all very good dancers indeed. The third prize went to number 8. Number 8 came third."

The people *clapped* and number 8 went to the judges. She *shook hands* with them and she got £2 and a *certificate*.

'The next prize went to number 6," the judge said. "Number 6 came second."

Number 6 went to the judges and shook hands. She got a prize of £5 and a certificate.

"And the first prize . . ." the judge went on.

"Oh!" mother said.

"The first prize," the judge said, "went to number 16!"

Mother and father and Sandy clapped and clapped.

"Hurray!" Sandy shouted. "Good old Sue!"

Sue went to the judges and they gave her a *silver cup* and a prize of £10. Sue was very happy.

"Congratulations," mother, father and Sandy

said.

"It's the happiest day of my life," Sue said.

"Let's see the cup," Sandy said. "What are you going to do with it?"

"I'm going to put it on a shelf in my room," Sue said.

"But first I'm going to fill it with *champagne*," father said, "and we can all drink from it. We're all very *proud* of you Sue."

Mr Blake's Car

(See Lesson 42.)

Mr Blake's car is very old indeed. It's a very old car, so it isn't very reliable. Of course, Mr Blake doesn't *think* so. He loves his car. "My car is the smallest car in the world. But it's the most reliable and the most well-behaved car I've ever seen," he always says. "Of course, it's less expensive than a big car. Still, it's as good as a big car."

Last week, Mr Blake took his family out. Mr and Mrs Blake sat in the front of the car and the children sat in the back.

"We can have a picnic today," Mr Blake said. "But first we must go to the *garage*." Mr Blake drove to the garage.

"Have you got enough *petrol?*" the man at the garage asked.

"No," Mr Blake answered. "Will you fill the car please?"

"You haven't got enough *air* in your tyres," the man said. "You need some more. Shall I blow them up for you?"

"Yes, please," Mr Blake said, so the man blew up the tyres.

"Do you need any *oil?*" the man said.

Mr Blake looked at the oil in the engine. "No," he said. "I've got plenty of oil. There's enough oil in the engine." Mr Blake paid the man and drove away.

"Where shall we go, dear?" Mrs Blake asked.

"I don't know," Mr Blake said.

"Let's go to the seaside," the children said.

"All right," Mr Blake said, "but it's rather cold at this time of the year. Still, we can spend the day at the seaside."

It was rather cold, but the Blakes had a lovely day. They played games on the *beach*. They ate their sandwiches on the beach, too. They were very hungry.

"Let's see," Alan said. "Who can eat the most sandwiches? Let's have a *competition*."

Alan, Wendy and Timmy had a competition. Alan had seven sandwiches, but Wendy won. She had seven and a half.

"Oh, I can't eat any more," Alan said.

Later they all got into the car and Mr Blake started the engine. The car went very well, but suddenly it stopped. They were *a long way from* home. "What's the matter, dear?" Mrs Blake asked.

"I don't know," Mr Blake said. "I'll have a look at the engine." He got out of the car and had a look.

"Can you see anything?" the children asked.

"No," Mr Blake said. "I can't understand it."

"The most reliable car in the world," Alan said and laughed.

Mr Blake tried to start the engine. He turned the key, but he couldn't start it. "Perhaps there's too little petrol," he wife said.

"No, there isn't," Mr Blake said. "We filled it this morning. Get out and push. We can all push," he said.

All the family got out and Mr Blake sat in front. The family pushed. The car was very small so it was easy for them to push it. They pushed and pushed, but it didn't start.

"What shall we do?" Mrs Blake said. "It's rather late."

Just then, a big truck stopped near them. "Do you want any help?" the driver asked.

"Yes, please," Mr Blake said. "My engine won't start."

"I'll pull your car," the truck driver said. He got out of his truck. "Oh dear," he said. "I can't find a *rope* or a *chain*."

"What shall we do now?" Mrs Blake said.

"Don't worry," the truck driver said.

There were two workmen in the truck and the driver called them. "You can help us too," he said to the Blakes. "We're going to lift your car on to the back of the truck. We'll carry you home."

It was easy to lift the little car. The Blakes sat in their own car and the driver took them home.

"Thank you very much." Mr Blake said.

"It's all right," the driver said.

"You see," Mr Blake said later. "Our car *broke down*, but it's still the most reliable car in the world. It took us to the seaside and it brought us home, too."

Gramophone Records

(See Lesson 48.)

Last month father bought a new record-player. Now he wants to buy lots of new gramophone records. He goes to the record shop very often. Father likes *classical* music very much, so he buys lots of classical records. He went to the record shop yesterday. He saw some very nice records there.

"I haven't got these two records," he said to an assistant.

"They're both very good records," the assistant answered.

"Are they the same quality?" father asked.

"No, they are different in quality," the assistant said. "The record on the left is better than the record on the right. Of course, the record on the left is more expensive than the one on the right."

"I like records very much," father said, "but they're very expensive. May I have one of those please?"

"Which of the two do you want, sir?" the assistant asked.

"The cheaper one," father said.

The assistant smiled politely. She put the record in a bag. Father paid some money and left the shop. He went home quickly because he wanted to play his record. At home, father played the record on his new record-player. He called Betty.

"Come and listen to this new record dear," he said. "It's very beautiful music."

Mother listened to the new record. "Yes, dear," she said. "It's lovely music."

Just then the children came in.

"You must listen to this new record," father said.

"It's very nice," Sue said. "We like classical music, but we like *pop*, too."

"Ugh!" father said. "Don't talk to me about pop!"

The children enjoyed the music very much. Then Sandy said, "I want to buy a record, too, but I haven't got any money. Have you got any money, Sue?"

"I've got no money," Sue said.

"Neither have I," mother said. "Don't look at me, Sandy."

"I've got none either," father said. "I've just bought this new record."

"Never mind," Sandy said. "Let's go out and play, Sue."

Sandy and Sue went out to play. Then mother spoke to father. "You can give Sandy some extra pocket-money, Jim. He likes good music. He wants to buy a record."

"Perhaps you're right," father said. Then he called Sandy and Sue. "Haven't you got any money?" he asked them.

"No, we're broke," they said.

"Well," father said. "I'm going to give you both a little present. You can go out and buy a good gramophone record."

Father gave Sandy and Sue some money and they went to the record shop. They didn't look at the classical records!

"Father's got plenty of classical records," Sue said, "but he hasn't got any pop records."

"He doesn't like pop," Sandy said.

"But we do," Sue said.

Sandy and Sue listened to two new pop records. "How much are these?" they asked the assistant.

"They're different in price," the assistant said. "The larger one is more expensive."

"May we have the cheaper one please?" Sue said.

The children bought the record and ran home quickly. Sandy played the record on the new record-player.

"Come and listen to our new record, dad," Sandy said.

"I can here it from here," father said. "It's a terrible noise! Is it music?"

"Of course, it is," Sue said. "It's pop music."

"It sounds awful," father said. "I gave you some extra pocket-money because I wanted you to buy a good record.

"Oh, dad!" Sue cried. "Sometimes you're so *old-fashioned!*"

Mother and Sue Go Shopping

(See Lesson 54.)

Yesterday, mother and Sue went shopping together. "You need some new clothes, Sue," mother said. "You haven't got many dresses and you need a new pair of shoes. We can go shopping together."

"Oh thank you, mum!" Sue said. "I'm going to enjoy that."

"I shall buy some nice clothes for you," mother said.

Sue looked cross. "Mum," she said, "you always *choose* my clothes. I want to choose my own clothes."

"Well, you can help me, Sue," mother said. "I always let you choose your own clothes."

"No, you don't," Sue said. "You always choose them for me. You say: 'This suits you. That doesn't suit you. You can't wear this.' I'm a big girl now. I'm twelve years old. I can choose my own clothes."

"We'll see," mother said. "Now *get ready* please."

Mother and Sue went to the shops. They looked at the lovely window display in a big shop.

"Look at that lovely blouse, mum," Sue said. "How much is it? It's £1·50 pence."

"Yes, it's a lovely blouse," mother said, "but it's not for you. It doesn't suit you. It's all right for me, but it's not for a girl like you."

Sue didn't say anything. She looked cross. Then they both went into the shop. First they bought a pair of shoes. They went to the *shoe department*.

"A pair of shoes for the young lady please," mother said.

"What size?" the assistant asked.

"Size 30," mother said.

The assistant brought a few pairs of shoes and mother let Sue choose a pair. "I like this pair," Sue said. "They're lovely red shoes and they're a nice shape."

"They're a nice price, too," mother said. "They cost £3·75 pence. They're too expensive for me. I can't afford £3·75. You must choose a cheaper pair."

Sue found a cheaper pair. They cost £2·14 pence. Then mother and Sue went to the dress department.

"I want a dress for this young lady, please," mother said.

"What size?" the assistant asked.

"I don't know," mother said.

"Then we must measure you," the assistant said to Sue. The assistant measured Sue and said. "You're quite a tall girl. You need a big dress."

Mother let Sue choose her own dress. Sue chose a lovely green and white dress. She tried it on and looked in the mirror. "Does it suit me?" she asked her mother.

"Yes," mother said. "It's the right length and it looks nice."

"I like it very much, mum," Sue said. "May I have it please?"

"Of course," mother said. "It isn't too expensive."

"You see!" Sue smiled. "I can choose my own clothes."

Mother smiled too. "Now you need a blouse," she said.

Sue wanted the blouse in the window and mother said no.

"It doesn't suit you," mother said.

Sue *insisted* and mother insisted and they had a big *argument*.

Then mother said "All right" and she bought the blouse.

It really didn't suit Sue at all. "That blouse is for a woman of 35, not for a girl of 12," mother said.

"I don't care," Sue said. "I'm going to wear it."

Mother and Sue went home with the new things. "Thank you very much, mum," Sue said. "I want to show dad all these new things."

Mother didn't say anything. She looked at Sue and said at last, "I like your dress and I like your shoes, but I don't like that blouse!"

Sue showed her new clothes to father. Father liked the dress and shoes, but he didn't like the blouse either. "It really doesn't suit you, Sue," he said. "It looks funny."

Sue looked in the mirror. "You're right, dad," she said. "It looks very funny and I can't wear it."

"What can we do with it, Betty?" father asked.

"Well," mother said. "I like it and it's almost my size."

"Try it on," father said.

Mother tried it on and it fitted her.

"It suits you very well," Sue and father said.

Mother laughed. "I didn't choose any clothes for you, Sue," she said, "but you *chose* a blouse for me!"

Timmy

(See Lesson 60.)

Mrs Blake's little boy often says funny things. Don't you remember? A few weeks ago, he said to his father: "Ours is the nicest garden in the neighbourhood. Nobody's grass is longer than ours." Well, yesterday at tea-time, Timmy was very, very hungry. He ate and ate and ate and he couldn't stop.

"Would you like a *boiled* egg?" his mother asked.

"Yes, please. I'd love one," Timmy said.

"Would you like some bread and butter?"

"Yes, please. I'd love some," Timmy said.

"I'm very hungry."

"So am I," his sister, Wendy, said, "but I'm not as hungry as Timmy is."

Everyone finished tea, but Timmy didn't finish. "My goodness, young man," his father said, "you'll burst. Aren't you *full* yet?"

"No, I haven't started yet," Timmy said.

"Well, I can't eat any more," Mr Blake said.

"Neither can I," Wendy said.

"And I don't want any more," Alan said.

"Neither do I," Mrs Blake said.

"Mum," Timmy said. "Would you cut another slice of bread for me please?"

"Another slice of bread?" his mother said. "There's none on the table." His mother looked for some bread, but she couldn't find any. "I'm sorry," she said. "There's none left, Timmy. You mustn't eat any more. You'll burst. Aren't you full yet?"

"No," Timmy said. "I haven't started yet."

Wendy laughed. "You'll get fat," she said. "There's a boy at school. His name's Billy Briggs. He's terribly fat. You'll be like him. He's the fattest boy in the school."

"I won't be like him," Timmy said. He was angry.

"Yes, you will."

"No, I won't."

"Don't shout," Mrs Blake said. "Timmy's hungry, so he can eat some more. He hasn't had enough yet. There's no bread in the house, so you can have some biscuits, Timmy," his mother said. And she went out of the room and *fetched* some biscuits. She brought a plate full of biscuits. "You can have one or two biscuits," his mother said and she went out of the room. Then she came back. What did she see? The plate was empty! "My goodness!" she cried. "Timmy has eaten all the biscuits! Timmy, you'll burst. You'll be sick!"

"I don't want any more food, mum," Timmy said. "I don't feel very well."

"He doesn't look very well, either," Wendy said. "Look at him. He looks ill."

"What's the matter Timmy?" Mrs Blake said. "Do you feel sick?"

"No, mum. Something terrible's happened."

"What?" Mrs Blake asked. "What's happened, Timmy?"

"He's going to be sick and it serves him right, the greedy boy," Wendy said.

"Quiet, Wendy," Mrs Blake said.

"I'm not going to be sick," Timmy said.

"What's the matter with you then?"

"Nothing," Wendy said. "Nothing's the matter with him."

"Quiet, Wendy," Mrs Blake said.

Everything was quiet. Then Timmy got up. He had his hand on his *tummy*. "Mum," he said softly. "I've eaten too much and I've burst. I've really burst."

Mother looked at Timmy and laughed. Then Timmy's *pants* fell down and everybody laughed.

"He really has burst," Wendy said. "Look, his

pants have fallen down."

"Don't be silly," Mrs Blake said. "You can't really burst."

"What's happened to me then?" Timmy asked.

Mrs Blake looked at Timmy's pants. "You've eaten too much, Timmy," she said, "and the *elastic* on your pants has broken!"

New Roller-skates

(See Lesson 66.)

Sandy and Sue sat in the living-room and watched television. They watched it for a long time. "What are you doing, children?" mother asked. "Haven't you got anything to do?"

"No, mum," Sue said. "We've done our homework and now we've got nothing to do."

"Play with something," mother said.

"We've got nothing to play with," Sandy said.

"Nothing to play with!" mother cried. "There are so many toys in your rooms! What about your new roller-skates?"

"We can't skate," Sandy said.

"Well," mother answered, "you must learn to skate. You can't sit here and watch television all evening."

"Come on, Sandy," Sue said. "Let's go out into the street. We can try to skate."

Sandy and Sue are learning to skate. They can't skate very well and they always fall down. They'd both like to skate very much. Sandy put on his roller-skates and walked carefully.

"I'd love to skate, Sue," he said.

"I'd love to skate, too," Sue said. She put on her roller-skates and walked very carefully. "I'm ready," Sue said. "I'll try to skate to you and you can try to skate to me."

"All right," Sandy said.

"Whoops!" Sue cried. "I can't stand up."

"Whoops!" Sandy cried. "Neither can I!"

Suddenly, there was a loud *crash!* Sandy and Sue fell down.

"Did you hurt yourself, Sandy?" Sue asked.

"No," Sandy said.

"Neither did I," Sue answered.

They both sat on the ground and laughed. Suddenly, Sue looked up. "Oh, look!" she cried. "Here comes Alan Blake."

Alan Blake has a new bike. He can ride it very well, but he likes to show off. "Look at me," Alan said. "Look, *no hands!*" Alan waved both his hands at them. He rode very well and he didn't fall.

"That's dangerous," Sandy said.

"No, it isn't. It's easy," Alan Blake said. Then he looked at Sandy and Sue. "What are you two doing?" he asked. "Why are you sitting on the ground?"

"We're learning to skate," Sue said. "We fell down."

"Ha! Ha!" Alan laughed. "Can't you skate? I can skate. It's easy to skate. Anyone can skate.

Lend me your skates, Sue." Alan got off his bike and Sue gave him her skates. Alan put them on and Sue watched him. Now, of course, Alan can't skate. He has never skated in his life. He is showing off. Sue knows this and she's smiling. Alan stood up carefully. "It's easy to skate," he said. "Remember to go like this."

"That's just what we want to do," Sandy said.

Suddenly, there was a loud crash and Alan fell down.

"Whoops!" he cried. "I'm falling."

Sandy and Sue laughed. "Don't show off," they said.

"It's easy to skate, isn't it?" Sue said.

"I'm sorry," Alan smiled. "I can't skate, really, but I can ride a bike. I really can ride very well."

"I've got a good idea," Sandy said. "You can ride your bike, and we can wear our skates and you can pull us."

The children *tied* the end of Sue's skipping-rope to Alan's bike. Alan got on his bike and rode. Sue held the other end of the rope. Then it was Sandy's turn.

"It's good fun," Sandy cried. "We'll learn to skate soon."

At the Park

(See Lesson 72.)

Last week, Sandy, Sue and Alan went to the park. It's very nice at the park and the children like to play games there. There was an old *keeper* at the park for many years. He was a very kind old man. He loved children and he often played games, too. But the kind old keeper died last year. There's a young man there now. He's a nasty fellow.

"Where's the old keeper?" Sue asked.

"Didn't you know?" Sandy said. "He died last year. There's a new keeper here now."

"I'm very sorry to hear that," Sue said.

"I'm sure that we can still play games on the grass," Sandy said. "We always play games on the grass."

The children ran on to the grass. "Throw the ball to me," Sandy cried. "Remember to throw it high up."

Just then, they heard a loud cry. "Hey! What are you doing?" It was the new keeper. He was very angry. "What are you children doing?" he called. "Look at this sign. It says, KEEP OFF THE GRASS. Can't you read?"

"But we always play on the grass," Sandy said.

"I don't care," the new keeper said. "You're not allowed to play on the grass any more."

Sandy, Sue and Alan went off the grass. They were sorry to stop their game. The new keeper smiled.

"Look," Sue whispered. "He's pleased that we must get off the grass."

Now there's a big lake in the middle of the

park, so the children went to it. "I've remembered to bring some bread with me," Sue said, "so we can feed the ducks." The children began to feed the ducks. But suddenly the new keeper appeared. They were all surprised to see him.

"Look at that sign," he shouted. "DO NOT FEED THE DUCKS. You're not allowed to feed the ducks. Can't you read?"

"But we always feed the ducks," Sue said.

"I don't care," the keeper said. "You're not allowed to feed the ducks any more."

Poor Sandy! Poor Sue! Poor Alan!

"What can we do now?" Sue said. "Let's sit on that seat." The children went to the seat. "Oh dear!" Sue said. "I don't think that we can sit here. Look at that sign. It says, WET PAINT."

"No," Alan said. "I don't want green stripes on my trousers."

"Neither do I," Sandy said.

"And I don't want green stripes on my skirt, either," Sue said.

"Well, what can we do?" Alan asked.

"I know!" Sandy cried. "We can stand beside the lake and watch the ducks."

The children went to the lake. On the way there, they saw the keeper. The keeper spoke to a lady in a car.

"You can't park here," he said. "It says, NO PARKING, so you mustn't park here. You're not allowed to."

The poor lady was sorry to leave. "There are always cars here," Sandy said. "The old keeper let anyone park here." The children stood beside the lake. Then they saw some people in a boat. The new keeper saw the people, too.

"You can't sail on the lake," the new keeper cried. "It says, NO BOATS. Can't you read?"

"But we always sail on the lake," the people answered.

"I don't care," the new keeper said. "You're not allowed to." The new keeper was very cross. He shouted and waved his arms. Then, suddenly, he fell into the lake. The people in the boat laughed. "It serves you right," they said. And Sandy, Sue, and Alan laughed, too. "You can't swim here," a man in the boat said. "Look at that sign. It says, NO SWIMMING. Can't you read?"

The Pot of Stew

(Lesson 78.)

Last Saturday mother didn't feel very well, so father called the doctor.

"Well, Mrs Clark," the doctor said. "You've got a temperature and you mustn't get up. You must stay in bed for three days."

"Three days!" mother cried. "I can't stay in bed during the week-end. Who'll *look after* the family?"

"I'm afraid they'll have to look after *themselves*," the doctor said. He gave mother some medicine and left the house.

Then father came into the room. "Well, dear?" he asked. "How are you?"

"The doctor says I've got a temperature," mother said. "He thinks I've caught a bad cold and he says I must stay in bed."

"Of course," father said.

"But I can't stay in bed," mother said. "Who'll look after you all? I must get up. I'll have to *do the shopping.*"

"You certainly won't get up!" father cried. "You're not allowed to get up. You must stay in bed. Sue, Sandy and I shall look after you."

Father went downstairs and spoke to Sue. Then they both went shopping. They bought lots of things. They bought meat, fruit and vegetables. "I hope you can cook," father said to Sue.

"I'm learning at school," Sue said. "I can't cook very well yet."

"Well," father laughed, "we've both got to cook this week-end."

They arrived home and father went up to see mother.

"Jim," mother said. "I'm going to get up. I must go to the shops to buy some fruit, some meat and some vegetables."

"You needn't worry," father said. "We've already bought the food for the week-end. Now Sue, Sandy and I shall *prepare* the lunch. Come on, Sandy. Come on, Sue," father called.

"Dad," Sandy said. "I'm afraid I can't help you in the kitchen."

"Why, Sandy?"

"Because I've got to write two hundred *lines.*"

"Two hundred lines!" father cried. "What do you have to write?"

"I have to write: 'I mustn't talk during the lesson'."

Sandy sat down. He wrote "I mustn't talk during the lesson" again and again and again and again.

Father and Sue went into the kitchen. "We can make a nice *stew*," father said. "Cut up some onions and some potatoes, Sue, and I'll prepare the meat."

Sue peeled the potatoes and cut them into small pieces. Then she peeled the onions. Suddenly father looked at her. "Why are you crying?" he asked.

"Guess!" Sue laughed. "It's these onions!"

Father laughed. "You mustn't cry, Sue," he said.

They put the meat, the potatoes, the onions and some carrots into a pot. It was a tremendous amount of food. Then they cooked the food for a long time. Father looked into the pot.

"What's it like?" he asked.

"I'll taste it," Sue said.

"Oh!" she cried. "It doesn't taste very nice."

"What's the matter with it?"

"We've forgotten to put any *salt* in it."

"Now where's the salt?" father said. He looked round the kitchen and found a big jar. Suddenly, Sue saw him.

"Oh, dad!" she cried. "You mustn't put that

into the stew. That isn't salt! It's sugar! Here's the salt."

Then Sandy came into the kitchen. "I mustn't talk during the lesson. I mustn't talk during the lesson," he said. "Is dinner ready, yet, Sue?"

"Yes, and please don't talk now. We're busy," Sue said.

Father and Sue prepared a *tray* of food for mother and took it to her room.

"Mm," she said. "It's *delicious*. You must give me the *recipe*."

"We didn't use a recipe," father said. "We just put some meat and vegetables in a pot and cooked them together."

"We're glad you like it, mum," Sue said.

"What are you going to cook for tonight and tomorrow?" mother asked.

"We don't have to cook anything at all," father said. "We've cooked enough food for a week! We're going to eat stew all today, tomorrow, and every day during the week!"

"Oh!" Sandy cried. "Please get well soon, mum!"

Just One of Those Days!

(Lesson 84.)

Last Monday was a holiday. Father didn't have to go to work and the children didn't have to go to school. Mother got up early, but father and the children got up very late.

"You're all very lazy today," mother said. "How are you going to spend the day today? Well, children?"

"We don't know," Sue answered.

"Why don't you do your homework, Sue?" mother asked.

"I should do my homework," Sue said, "but I don't feel like it. It's a holiday."

"What about you, Sandy?" mother asked. "Why don't you finish that book? You're reading it, aren't you?"

"Yes, mum. I should finish it, but I don't feel like it."

"You are lazy today," mother said.

Then father came into the room. "How are you going to spend the day, Jim?" mother asked.

"I don't know," father said.

"Will you repair the fence please?"

"Oh," father complained. "I should repair it, but I don't feel like it."

"Isn't our breakfast ready yet?" Sandy asked.

"No, it isn't," mother answered.

"You ought to have got it ready," Sandy said.

"Sandy!" father said. "You shouldn't talk like that to your mother."

Mother got very cross. "It's a holiday for you," she said, "but it isn't a holiday for me. You don't have to go to school or to work but I have to cook breakfast, lunch and dinner. I have to iron the clothes, too."

"I'm sorry, mum," Sandy said.

"We're all *bad-tempered* this morning," father said. "We can all go out."

"That's a good idea," mother said.

"Hurrah!" the children shouted.

"But I want to have a bath first," father said.

"And I want to iron some clothes," mother said.

Mother stayed in the kitchen and ironed some clothes. The children played in the garden. Half an hour later father went out into the garden, too. "We're ready now," he called. "Let's all get into the car."

The family got into the car and father drove into the country.

An hour later, mother said, "Jim, I think I forgot to turn off the electricity. I ironed some clothes and I should have turned off the electricity, but I forgot."

"My goodness!" father cried. "We must go back at once. Father turned back. He was very bad-tempered. He complained all the way home. "You should have turned off the electricity!" he said. "Perhaps the house is burning."

Father drove very fast and soon the family arrived home. They opened the front door quickly and mother rushed into the kitchen.

"Well?" father asked.

"It's all right," mother said. "I turned it off."

"I'm glad," father said.

Then Sandy went into the bathroom. "Mum!" he called. "The bathroom's full of water."

"Oh!" father cried. "I had a bath. I should have turned the tap off, but I forgot."

There was water everywhere. They all worked very hard and cleaned up the *mess*.

"It's been a very bad day," mother said. "We've all been bad-tempered and so many nasty things have happened today."

"Life's like that sometimes," father said. "Everything is fine and suddenly, everything is very bad and we all feel unhappy. It was just one of those days!"

Father and Sandy Go Fishing

(Lesson 90.)

Last Sunday, father and Sandy got up very early.

"Where are you going, Jim?" mother asked.

"Sandy and I are going fishing," father said.

Father woke Sandy up. Then he went into the kitchen and made some sandwiches. Sandy came into the kitchen, too. "What must we take with us, dad?" he asked.

"We've got to take our *fishing-lines*, a basket and some sandwiches," father said.

"We needn't take a basket," Sandy said and smiled. "We won't catch any fish."

"Yes, we will," father said.

Father and Sandy left home. Father had to drive to the seaside. They arrived at the seaside and both went on to the *pier*. "We can fish from the end of the pier," father said. They both put some *bait* on their *hooks*. Then they threw their lines into the sea.

"The fish are biting, dad," Sandy said. He pulled in his line quickly.

"Did you catch anything?" father asked.

"No," Sandy said. "I needn't have pulled my line in. I pulled it in for nothing."

"No, you didn't, Sandy," father laughed. "The fish have eaten your bait. You've got to put some more bait on your hook." Sandy had to pull the line in and had to put more bait on his hook. "You mustn't feed the fish, Sandy," father laughed. "You must catch them!"

"The fish are hungry and so am I," Sandy said. "May I have a sandwich please, dad?"

"Of course," father said. "I'll have one, too." Sandy and father ate two sandwiches each. Suddenly, father pulled his line. "There's a fish on the end of it," he cried. "I can feel it."

"Pull it in, dad," Sandy cried.

"I must be careful," father said. He pulled the line in carefully and Sandy looked into the water. He could see a *silver* fish on the end of the line. Then father pulled it up.

"Look at it, dad," Sandy laughed. "It's very small. It's a baby."

"You're right, Sandy," father said. "We mustn't keep this fish. It's too small." Father threw the fish back into the sea.

Suddenly, Sandy felt his line. It was very heavy. "There's a big fish on the end of my line!" Sandy shouted. He pulled it in quickly. Father looked into the water. He could see a big silver fish.

"Sandy!" he cried. "You've caught a big one! Be very careful!"

Sandy was very *excited*. He pulled in the line suddenly.

"Oh!" father cried. "You shouldn't have pulled the line like that. You should have pulled it in slowly!"

Poor Sandy! He lost the fish. "It was very big," he said. "I'll tell mum, but she won't believe me. That fish was thirty centimetres long."

"You oughtn't to have pulled the line like that, Sandy," father said. "But never mind."

The day passed, but father and Sandy didn't catch any more fish. "We must go home now," father said.

"What will mum say?" Sandy asked.

"She'll laugh," father said. "We're not very good fishermen."

At the end of the pier they saw a real fisherman. He had a big sign. It said "Nice *Fresh Fish*".

"We can buy some fish, Sandy," father said. He bought lots of nice fresh fish. Then they went home.

Mother looked into their basket. "My goodness!" she cried. "Did you catch all those fish?"

Father looked at Sandy and Sandy looked at father. They both laughed. "That's our secret, isn't it, Sandy?" father said. They both laughed again and mother didn't know why!

The Remarkable Rooster

(Lesson 96.)

Mr Blake's garden looks very nice now. He has been working very hard for a long time. He has been working in his garden since last September. Mr Blake has planted trees and flowers. He has planted vegetables, too. He has mended the old fence. Of course, he hasn't finished yet. He's been working in the garden for a long time and he's still working hard. In one corner of the garden Mr Blake has built a *hen-run*. He has five *hens* and they *lay* lots of eggs. Last week Mr Blake arrived home with a *rooster*. The rooster looks very fine indeed. Alan, Wendy and Timmy call him 'Doodle'. Do you know why? They call him 'Doodle' because he *crows* every morning. Every morning everyone in the neighbourhood hears Doodle. *"Cock-a-doodle-doo!* Cock-a-doodle-doo!" Doodle has been waking Sandy and Sue up every morning. But they don't mind.

Timmy likes Doodle very much. He goes into the hen-run every day. Last Sunday he ran into the house and called his father. "Dad!" he cried. "Come to the hen-run quickly!"

"What's the matter, Timmy?" Mr Blake asked.

"It's something very strange," Timmy said. "Doodle's *laid an egg*."

"Laid an egg!" Mr Blake cried.

"Don't be silly, Timmy. Roosters don't lay eggs!"

"But he has laid an egg. Come and see," Timmy said.

Mr Blake went to the hen-run. Doodle was sitting in the hen-run and Mr Blake picked him up. There was an egg under the rooster.

"See," Timmy said. "Doodle's sitting on an egg. He's laid it."

"This is very strange," Mr Blake said. He looked at the rooster again. "He can't be a hen. Surely he isn't a hen!"

The next day Timmy called his father again. "Dad!" Timmy said. "Doodle's laid another egg."

"Don't be silly!" Mr Blake said.

"Come and see," Timmy said.

Mr Blake went to the hen-run. He found an egg under the rooster again. "I can't understand it. Perhaps Doodle's really a hen. He may be a hen. I'm not sure."

The next day Doodle laid another egg. "This is very strange indeed," Mr Blake said. "This rooster's been laying eggs since Sunday."

Soon the neighbours heard about this *remarkable* rooster. "Is it true?" they asked. "It can't be true! It must be a mistake! Rooster's don't lay eggs."

Mr Spencer is a *vet*. He lives near the Blakes. He heard about the remarkable rooster, too, so he came to Mr Blake's house to see Doodle. "I've heard about Doodle," Mr Spencer said. "May I see him please?" Mr Spencer had a look at Doodle and laughed. "He's a rooster, Mr Blake," he said, "and he isn't laying eggs."

"But he is," Mr Blake said. "He's been laying eggs every day this week."

"No," Mr Spencer said. "Someone's playing a trick on you. Who collects the eggs from the hen-run every morning?"

"Timmy," Mr Blake said. Then he called Timmy.

"Timmy," Mr Spencer said, "tell me about these eggs."

Timmy laughed and laughed. "I played a trick on dad," he said. "I've been putting an egg under Doodle every day this week."

Mr Spencer laughed and so did Mr Blake. The neighbours heard the story and they laughed, too. "Perhaps he'll lay a *golden* egg one day," Timmy said.

The Ghost Story

(Lesson 102.)

"Your father and I are going out this evening, Sue," mother said. "We shan't come home late. We'll be home at 10 o'clock."

"That's all right, mum," Sue said. "Sandy and I will be all right alone. We'll do our homework and then we'll read and go to bed."

"It's Saturday night," father said. "So you can stay up a little later."

"All right, dad," Sue said.

Mother and father said goodbye to the children. Sandy and Sue did their homework. They finished it at 8.0 o'clock.

"What shall we do now, Sue?" Sandy asked.

"We can read," Sue said. "I'm going to read an *exciting ghost story.*"

"Please read it to me, Sue," Sandy said.

The children sat down in the living-room and Sue got her book of Ghost Stories. Sue began to read a story. The name of the story was 'The Ghost Returns'. Sandy listened quietly. It was very quiet in the living-room and it was very dark outside.

" 'Then,' Sue read, 'the clock *struck 12.0*. It was midnight. James Cooper was alone, in the *haunted* house. He was waiting for the ghost. The ghost should have come at midnight. It's after midnight, Jim thought. I haven't see a ghost yet. I don't believe in ghosts. I think I'll go to bed. Just as Jim was going upstairs, he heard a sound. It was a knock at the door. Jim stopped and listened. Then he heard the sound again. Jim went downstairs and opened the door. There was no one there. It can't have been a ghost, Jim laughed. It must have been the wind. He shut the door and went upstairs. Then he heard the knock again. This is silly, Jim said. It must be a cat. He looked up and saw something at the top of the stairs. It was white. It didn't move. Then Jim heard the knock again . . .' "

"Oh, stop it, Sue," Sandy cried. "Please don't read any more."

"Don't be silly, Sandy," Sue said. "It's only a story."

Suddenly, the children heard a knock at the front door. It wasn't very loud. "Listen, Sue!" Sandy whispered.

"I didn't hear anything," Sue answered. "It must have been the wind."

Then there was another knock. It was louder this time.

"Did you hear it, Sue?" Sandy asked. "What shall we do?"

The children went to the door quietly and listened. "I'm not going to open the door," Sandy whispered. "It might be a ghost."

"It can't be, Sandy," Sue said. "Don't be silly."

Then there was another knock. It was louder!

"Who is it?" Sue called.

"Open the door please, Sue," a voice said. "It's me." ·

"It's mum and dad," Sue said and she unlocked the door.

"We forgot our key," father said. "We didn't knock loudly because we didn't want to disturb you. It's ten o'clock. I was sure you must both be in bed."

Sandy and Sue gave their parents an extra big *kiss.*

"What's the matter, children?" mother said. "You both look *frightened.*"

"We were frightened, but we aren't now," Sue said. "We were reading an exciting ghost story."

"It was too exciting for me," Sandy said. "I don't want to hear another ghost story for a long time!"

The Pound Note

(See Lesson 108.)

Yesterday morning there was a knock at the door. Sue opened the door. "Who was it, Sue?" mother called.

"The postman who delivers our letters," Sue answered. "There's a parcel for you, mum, and there are letters for Sandy and me."

The letters were from grandmother and grandfather. Guess what they sent to Sandy and Sue. One pound each!

"That's a lot of money," mother said. "What are you going to do with it, Sue?"

"I'm going to put it in my money-box," Sue said.

"Don't be silly," Sandy said. "You can't put paper money in a money-box."

"Oh yes, I can," Sue said. "I'm going to fold it and put it in the money-box. I don't want to spend it."

"What are you going to do with your money, Sandy?" mother asked.

"I'm going to spend it," Sandy said. "May I spend it, mum?"

"Yes, you may, Sandy," mother answered. "But put your money in a safe place now. Don't lose it."

"No, I shan't lose it, mum," Sandy said.

On the way to school Sandy passed a toy shop. "Look at that glider," he said to Sue.

"Which glider?" Sue asked.

"The one which is near that electric train. I'm going to buy it," Sandy said.

"How much is it?" Sue asked.

"I don't know," Sandy said. "There's no price on it."

"Go in and ask, Sandy," Sue said.

Sandy went in and asked the price. It was 85 pence. Then he went into the street. "It's 85 pence," he said to Sue.

"Who did you ask?" Sue said.

"The man who is in the shop," Sandy answered.

"Are you going to buy that glider?" Sue asked.

"Yes," Sandy said. "I haven't got my pound with me. It's at home."

"Where did you put your pound?" Sue asked.

"In the pocket of my grey trousers. I changed my trousers this morning."

"That's not a safe place," Sue said.

"Of course, it is," Sandy said. "My grey trousers are at home and there's a pound in one of the pockets."

"Well, my pound is in my money-box," Sue said.

Sandy was very excited. He thought about the glider all day at school. In the afternoon he hurried home. Mother was very busy. She was washing clothes.

"Mum," Sandy said. "I'm going to buy a glider which I saw in a shop. Where are my grey trousers?"

"Which grey trousers?" mother asked.

"The grey trousers which I was wearing yesterday," Sandy said.

"They're very dirty," mother said. "I'm going to have them cleaned."

"Yes," Sandy said, "but where are they?"

"They're in your room, I think," mother said.

Sandy looked in his room, but he couldn't find them. He looked everywhere. He looked in his wardrobe. He looked under the chair and under the bed, but he couldn't find his grey trousers anywhere. "I can't find them," he complained.

"I'm sorry, Sandy," mother said. "I made a mistake. I'm washing the clothes. I put your grey trousers in the *washing-machine* a moment ago."

"In the washing-machine!" Sandy cried. He looked very sorry. "Did you take anything out of the pockets, mum?"

"No, Sandy. Was there anything in the pockets?"

"Yes, mum. The pound which grandma and grandpa sent me. It's in the pocket!"

"Oh, dear," mother said. "Your trousers are in the washing-machine now. You should have put your money in a safe place not in one of your pockets!"

Poor Sandy! He nearly cried. He was terribly sorry. He wasn't careful and he lost his pound

note and now he couldn't buy his glider.

The Family Photograph Album

(See Lesson 114.)

Last Saturday, mother, father and the children looked at the family photograph *album*. Sandy and Sue love to look at all the old photos in the album. They love to hear mother and father tell them about the photos and about the people in them.

"Look at this photograph of grandma," Sue said. She pointed at an old, yellow photograph. "She looks very nice, doesn't she, mum? But her clothes are rather strange."

"Women used to wear very long skirts in those days," mother said.

"I like grandma's large hat," Sue said.

"Look," mother said. "There's a photograph of the house I lived in when I was a girl."

"You lived there for ten years, didn't you, mum?" Sue said.

"What's happened to it now?" Sandy asked.

"I don't know," mother said. "Perhaps it's still there. It was a very nice house with large rooms. There was a big garden at the back and I used to play there with my friends years ago."

Sandy *turned over* a few pages of the album and saw a big ship.

"I like this big ship," Sandy said.

"Daddy and I had a holiday in South America years ago," mother said. "That's the *ship* we travelled on. Grandmother took that photo. Look at it carefully. You can see your father and me. We are standing at the side of the ship. We are waving."

"I can see you," Sue said.

"You weren't born then," mother said. "Look! Here's the first photograph of Sue. She was a lovely baby, but she used to cry a lot."

"Lovely baby," Sandy laughed, "— she still is!"

"You be quiet, Sandy Clark," Sue said. "Look at your photograph. You used to be an ugly baby."

"Now, now, children," mother said. "You mustn't quarrel. Sandy used to smile a lot when he was a baby. Look! There he is in his *cot*. He's smiling. And this is a photograph of the two of you. You are both smiling. You are both saying 'cheese' at the camera."

Sue turned over a few pages of the album. Then she saw a photograph of some boys. They were wearing shirts and *shorts*.

"What's this photo, dad?" Sue asked.

"That's a school photo," father said. "That's the football *team* I played in. Can you find me?"

The children looked at the photo carefully. "Is that you, dad?" Sandy asked.

"Of course, not!" father laughed. "Don't you know your own father? That's me there!" He pointed at a little boy in shorts. "I was in the team. I used to play very well. I used to be centre-forward."

"But you can't play now," Sue said.

"Of course I can," father said.

"Let's have a game," Sandy said.

Sandy and father went into the garden and Sandy kicked the ball to father. "You can be centre-forward, dad," Sandy said. "And I'll be goal-keeper."

"Ready, Sandy?" father called and he ran towards the ball.

He kicked it very hard, but the ball didn't go towards Sandy. It went towards the kitchen window. There was a loud *crash* and the window broke. "My goodness!" mother called from the kitchen. "You used to play football, Jim, but you can't play any more!"

Dreams!

(See Lesson 120.)

When Sandy was having tea yesterday, Alan knocked at the door. Mother answered it. "Can Sandy come out and play please, Mrs Clark?" Alan asked.

"He hasn't finished his tea yet," mother said. "When he finishes his tea, he can come out and play."

Sandy was in the dining-room. He heard Alan at the door. "I'm coming, Alan," he called. "When I drink my milk, I'll come outside."

"Bring your football, Sandy," Alan said.

Sandy drank his milk quickly and went into the garden. "What shall we play, Alan?" Sandy asked.

"Let's play football," Alan said.

"All right," Sandy said. "I'll be centre-forward and you can be goal-keeper."

"All right," Alan said. "I'll stand between these two trees and I'll try and catch the ball when you kick it. These two trees will be the *goal posts.*"

The boys played for a long time. Sandy kicked the ball to Alan again and again, but Alan caught it every time.

"Whew!" Sandy cried. "I'm tired."

"You didn't get a goal," Alan said. "If you're tired, we can have a little *rest.*"

"All right," Sandy said.

The boys sat down on the grass. "You're a very good goal-keeper, Alan," Sandy said.

"I'm going to be a goal-keeper when I *grow up,*" Alan said. "When I grow up, I'll be famous. I'll earn a lot of money and I'll be rich. What are you going to be when you grow up, Sandy?"

"I don't know," Sandy said.

"You won't be a *footballer,* because you can't play very well," Alan said.

Sandy got cross. "Don't show off, Alan," he said. "When I grow up I'll be more famous than you. I'll be an astronaut."

"Don't be silly," Alan said.

"You'll see," Sandy said. "And if I'm an astronaut, I'll fly to the planets! When I'm famous, my name will be in all the newspapers."

"But I'll be more famous than you," Alan said. "Thousands and thousands of people will come and see me. I'll be goal-keeper in the England *team.* And I'll be rich too. I'll buy a big house and a fast car."

"I'll be richer than you," Sandy said. "If I'm an astronaut, I'll have my own rocket. I'll live on the moon."

"Don't be silly!" Alan said. "When you're an astronaut, you won't have your own rocket. Rockets cost a lot of money."

"Well, I'll have a rocket," Sandy said. "You'll see."

"If you have a rocket," Alan said. "I'll have ten aeroplanes."

"If you have ten aeroplanes," Sandy said. "I'll *own* the moon. The moon will be mine. If you want to visit me, or to play football on the moon, perhaps I'll let you come in my rocket."

"Then I'll own the earth," Alan said. "If you want to visit me, perhaps I'll let you. I don't know."

Sue was listening to this *conversation.* "What a silly conversation," she said. "Alan Blake will own the earth when he grows up and Sandy Clark will own the moon. Ha! Ha! You boys are silly."

"We were only talking," Sandy said.

"When I grow up," Sue said, "I'll be an actress. I'll be rich and famous. I shall have my own sweet shop, too, and I'll eat all the sweets in it."

"Sweets!" Alan said. "That's a good idea. Let's buy some sweets. Have you got any money?"

The children looked in their pockets, but they didn't have any money. "All these dreams," Sue said, "and we haven't got enough money for a few sweets!"

Vocabulary Index

Note that only words introduced in the course itself are included. Vocabulary items from other sources (songs, stories, etc.) are not listed. References are to Teaching Units, not Lessons or pages.

Countable Nouns, Place-names, etc.

weed(s) 17
weight 15
weight-lifter 15

width 23
window-display 25

wing (plane) 13
workman 4

zero 53
zoo 39

Uncountable Nouns

arithmetic 38

camping 59
candy-floss 16
centigrade 27

flying 13
furniture 4

grass 17

history 12

ice 34
information 58

knowledge 13

lather 20
leather 47
litter 39

marmalade 30
mass-production 18

maths 12
mink 25

oil (petroleum) 28

paint 34
pence 25
power 13

rubbish 11

salt 45
sand 32
sea 28
space (interstellar) 53

thirst 50
toast 30

window-shopping 25

Adjectives

absent 12
absent-minded 30
allowed 34
angry 21
Arabic 38

better 16
bottom 13
brave 15
bright 23

certain 34
clear (without obstacles)
  22

dark 43
deep 17
different 23
difficult 13
Dutch 58

enormous 58
enough 20

excited 51
exciting 53
expensive 7
extra 22

fair (just) 19
favourite 12
foreign 24
forgetful 56
free (costing nothing) 25
front 52

general 13
good 16
great 13
greedy 19
grown-up 16

important 28

last (the) 16
least 19
left (cp. right) 18

less 19
low (not high) 14

mashed (potato) 26
mass-produced 18
Mexican 24
modern 18
more 19
most 19
musical 14

necessary 39

other 11

pleased 34
plenty (of) 20
polite 9
poor 15
prehistoric 43

real 23
reliable 18

rich 15
right (cp. wrong) 27
Roman 38
round 47

safe 8
salty 45
same 18
simple 38
special 45
square 27
sure 34
surprised 34

tiny 48
tremendous 33
true 47

wide 23
wonderful 21
worse 16
worst 16
wrong 11

Regular Verbs

add 38
afford 25
appear 15

bang 36
believe 35
borrow 31

clear (the table) 11
close 9
collect 24
comb 29
compare 16
complain 38
continue 28

correct 11
crawl 10
cross 9
cry (weep) 10

decide 43
declare 32
deliver 11
develop (a film) 52
dial 35
die 33
disappear 43
discover 58
disturb 10
dive 2

dress 22
drill (bore) 28
drop 6
dust 40
dry 32

earn 22
empty 40
expect 41
explore 43

fit 11

guess 27

hope 33

imagine 48
iron 42

join 48

lift 14
lock 35
look for 28
love 30

mark (correct) 40
measure 27
mend 11

mind look after) 11
miss (fail to attend) 12

name 28

peel 37
plant 17
point at 49
practise 9
praise 33

press 36
print (a film) 52
promise 35

quarrel 29

receive 19
repair 40
rescue 43

return 32
rub (together) 59

sail 9
serve (food) 26
shop 7
skate 31
switch off 11
switch on 9

thank 38
tidy 40

unlock 11

water 41
whisper 22
wish 3
worry 31

Irregular Verbs

be able to 10
be unable to 12
become 15
begin with 45
build 18
burn 9

cost 25

dig 17

fall 29
feed 34

get (become) 33
give up (surrender) 37
grow 17

hear of 43
hide 28

learn 13
lend 20
lie (rest) 13
lose 28

set out (start a journey)
58
show off 31
sweep 11

take off (rise) 13

win 15

Adverbs

abroad 32
accidentally 43
A.D. 48
almost 26
alone 43
away 27

B.C. 48
because of 43
bottom 16

certainly 32
cheerfully 22

else 52
enough 14
exactly 11

fairly 16
further 22

hardly 26

indeed 16

poor (quality) 16
pretty (rather) 52
properly 12

quite (less than good) 16

rather 16

slowly 15
so 15
surely 47

too 13
top 16

Prepositions

about 27
above 15

against 27
among 49

till 34
towards 57

without 13

Idioms and Colloquial Expressions

a long time 39
a machine runs (on oil)
28
all the time 29
any more (any longer) 29
as usual 31

bang your head into
something 50
Brr! 2

Copycat! 29

degrees centigrade 27
Don't tell tales! 29

each other 23

far away 28

for instance 23
for nothing (to no pur-
pose) 41
give us a rise 21
go home 7
go on strike 20

Ha! Ha! 31
He came top/bottom 16
Here comes (Alan) 31
Here we are 11
How do you like (my
new jacket)? 55
I don't feel like it. (I'm
not in the mood for)
40
I see (I understand) 32

I'm broke 20
I'm full 39
in here 6
in some way 28
in the end 33
in there 33
it didn't work 21
It serves you right! 29

join hands 48

keep off (the grass) 34
kilometres away 27

Let me see (allow me to
look) 3
make up your mind 46
Mm? (What?) 30

(Mrs) Who? 35

Not too bad 16

of all time 33
on a diet 40
on the left 18
on the right 18

pretty good 57

Really? (Is that so?) 41
Right you are! 17

Say 'cheese' (smile) 52
See! (I told you so) 29
Service with a smile 41
Show off 31